Developing Presentation Skills
A Guide for Effective Instruction

Kathleen Schmalz
College of Mount Saint Vincent

Arlene Moliterno
College of Mount Saint Vincent

Allyn and Bacon
Boston   London   Toronto   Sydney   Tokyo   Singapore

Copy Editor: Maria Jerinic

Typographic Services: Edward A. Schmalz

Copyright © 2001 by Allyn & Bacon
A Pearson Education Company
160 Gould Street
Needham Heights, Massachusetts 02494-2130

Internet: www.abacon.com

ISBN 0-205-31959-9

Printed in the United States of America

10 9 8 7 6 5 4 3 2 1   03 02 01 00

Table of Contents

Preface

Experienced educators understand the very complex nature of student learning. Brooks and Brooks (1999) observed that teachers develop classroom practices and negotiate curriculum in an effort to enhance student learning, but it is virtually impossible to control what students learn. Even when teachers structure lessons and curriculum to promote learning for all students, each student still constructs his/her own unique meaning to the lesson. Teachers have some control over what they plan to teach, but have far less control over what students learn.

Constuctivist learning theory suggests that learners are active participants who pursue areas of knowledge based on their interests and a need to know. Given the nature of the learner, the teacher is viewed as a facilitator who structures the learning environment so that the student can actively construct knowledge.

Grennon, Brooks and Brooks (1993) identify five central tenets of constructivism that are useful in understanding productive teacher behavior in the classroom. The five tenets are:

- Constructivist teachers seek to understand their students.
- Constructivist teachers plan lessons to challenge students' understanding so that new knowledge is constructed.
- Constructivist teachers understand that the curriculum must be relevant to students.
- Constructivist teachers plan instruction holistically and relate details to the larger picture.
- Constructivist teachers assess student learning in the context of daily classroom experiences.

Developing Presentation Skills: A Guide for Effective Instruction offers a constructivist approach to instruction with an emphasis on the process that occurs within the classroom setting. Within the framework of the Instructional Plan Format (See page 2), Part I of this text directs teachers to take on the important tasks of planning instruction, presenting lessons and assessing learning. It also prompts teachers to better understand learners, challenge students' understanding, and make learning relevant.

Part II of this text is a collection of essays written by educational professionals from different academic disciplines. These essays are designed to provide the reader with a variety of pedagogical tools and assignment ideas for instructional presentations. The essays enhance the readers understanding and demonstrate the practical application of strategies for instruction and presentation.

Dr. Edward A. Schmalz discusses the issue of speech anxiety. Since teachers are often called upon to speak before a wide variety of audiences, speech anxiety can be a concern. He offers the classroom teacher some practical strategies to cope with this problem.

Dr. Margaret Egan, S.C. describes how to use graphic organizers to enhance teaching and support student learning in the college classroom. Although her focus is on the adult learner, the graphic organizer is a simple tool that teachers at all grade levels will want to use regularly within their instructional presentations.

Dr. Kathleen Schmalz discusses the importance of active learning within the classroom setting. She describes how writing assignments can be used effectively to engage students and enhance learning within specific disciplines and subject areas.

Dr. Barbara Smith's section also addresses the issue of student writing. Seeing the classroom as a community of learners, she provides some practical approaches to motivating reluctant student writers. Additionally, she describes thesis-based writing processes and assignments for interdisciplinary use. She presents writing as a tool for better understanding of course content, and holds that writing and thinking (both messy processes) are happily connected: writing clarifies thinking and clearer thought yields improved writing.

In consideration of student writing, Stephen Feyl addresses the issue of student research writing and reports. Feyl, a librarian, shares his expertise and experience in helping students approach library research assignments. He offers practical suggestions for structuring students' assignments and facilitating the research process. Classroom teachers will find his descriptions of how to use electronic databases and resources especially useful.

In an era when schools are expected to address more than academic subjects, the curriculum increasingly includes values' education, ethics and character education. To this end, Dr. Kathleen Schmalz writes about teaching as an ethical profession. In her essay, she describes professional ethics for classroom teachers and addresses teaching ethics to students. Dr. Edward Zukowski's essay further elaborates on these issues by describing how teachers can foster ethical thought within the classroom setting. He describes some general strategies and specific techniques that can be used by teachers to engage students in discussion of moral and ethical concerns.

According to Robin Fogarty (1999), effective learning within the classroom occurs naturally and with purpose. Such learning is characterized by the creativity of the teacher who must "design learning that empowers the learner to make meaning through the mindful manipulation of input." (p.78) We believe that *Developing Presentation Skills: A Guide for Effective Instruction* is a text that can assist teachers in designing creative, interactive and student-centered learning experiences within the classroom.

References

Fogarty, R. (1999). Architects of the intellect. Educational Leadership, 57, (3), 76-78.

Grennon Brooks, J. & Brooks, M.G. (1993). In search of understanding: The case for constructivist classrooms. Alexandria, VA: ASCD.

Brooks, M.G. & Grennon Brooks, J. (1999). The courage to be constructivist. Educational Leadership, 57, (3), 18-24.

About the Authors

Margaret Egan, S.C., Ed.D. is Professor and Chairperson of the Teacher Education Department at the College of Mount Saint Vincent, Riverdale, New York. After an extensive career in K-12 Education, she has had wide experience in teaching graduate and undergraduate level education courses. Egan is the author of numerous articles relating to effective teaching strategies in the classroom.

Steven Feyl, MLS is the Electronic Services/Periodicals Librarian at the College of Mount Saint Vincent, Riverdale, NY. Besides working at the college level, he has experience working in the New York Public Library System.

Arlene A. Moliterno, Ph.D. is Associate Professor in the Department of Teacher Education at the College of Mount Saint Vincent in Riverdale, New York. She is the author of numerous articles on topics relating to classroom instruction and the application of technology in educational settings. Among the courses she teaches are those that deal with instructional technology, methods of teaching reading, methods of teaching secondary education, foundations of education, and early childhood education. She supervises student teachers at the elementary and secondary level.

Edward A. Schmalz, Ed.D. is an adjunct instructor in the College of Education and Human Services at Seton Hall University in South Orange, NJ. He received his Ed.D. degree from Seton Hall University and teaches administration and supervision courses in the New Jersey State Police Graduate Studies Program.

Kathleen Schmalz, Ed.D., RN, CHES, is Associate Professor in the Department of Health Education and Addiction Studies at the College of Mount Saint Vincent in Riverdale, New York. She is active on the Writing- to-Learn Committee and successfully implements Writing Across the Curriculum (WAC) techniques and strategies into her own classrooms. She is the author of more than fifteen publications on current health issues and is an Associate Editor for *Health Promotion Practice: A Journal of Health Promotion/Health Education Applications, Policy and Professional Issues*. Among the courses she teaches are those that deal with multicultural issues, human sexuality, methods of teaching health education and supervised practice teaching.

Barbara Smith Ph.D. is currently the Director of Writing at the College of Mount Saint Vincent in Riverdale, New York, where she chairs the Writing-to-Learn Committee, edits the *Writing-to-Learn Newsletter*, teaches all levels of writing courses, and has worked to extend the College's writing minor to include students from various disciplines. She is the author of *The Women of Ben Jonson's Poetry, Female Representations in the Nondramatic Verse* (Scolar: 1995), a study of poetic rhetoric and gender, and co-editor with Alice Robertson of Teaching in the Twenty-First Century: Adapting Writing Pedagogies to the College Curriculum, (Falmer Press for Garland Press: 1999).

Edward J. Zukowski Jr., Ph.D. is an Associate Professor and Chair of Religious Studies at the College of Mount Saint Vincent in Riverdale, NY. He holds a doctorate in theological ethics from Fordham University. His published works include, The "*Good Conscience*" of Nazi Doctors in the 1994 Annual of the Society of Christian Elders.

Acknowledgments

No book is ever written through the effort of just one or two people. The ideas and concepts presented in this text, have developed over time through teaching experiences, discussions, observations and interviews. We would like to express our gratitude to the following individuals who significantly contributed to this book.

Special thanks to all of the following:

Dr. Maria Jerinic, who gave up all of her free time and sleep to edit this text. Her comments, guidance and suggestions, provided valuable feedback for the numerous drafts of our manuscript. Her expertise, kindness and friendship are greatly appreciated.

Dr. Rita Brause, a true mentor who spent endless hours making sense of an earlier version and whose comments helped provide a clear focus for this project.

Dr. Rosemarie Pace, whose expertise and insight challenged us to think critically about important issues and concepts.

Dr. Edward A. Schmalz, who worked tirelessly to edit and prepare the final version of our manuscript. Without his patience and diligence, the task could not have been achieved.

Our colleagues and friends, including, Dr. Barbara Shimmel, Dr. Barbara Smith, Sr. Margaret Egan, Robert Coleman and Dr. Maxine Weiss, who gave us the support we needed to complete our project. Their interaction and generosity contributed to this book which was grounded in classroom experiences and practices.

We would also like to thank Steven Dragin, Bridget Keane and Traci Mueller at Allyn & Bacon, for their assistance and guidance in moving this text from manuscript to publication.

And, of course, to our families and friends, who supported us during the holidays, the summers and the weekends, when our time was devoted to the development of the manuscript.

PART I
Section I: PREPARING THE INSTRUCTIONAL PLAN

INTRODUCTION

In this section, you will learn how to prepare the written plan for instruction. You will discover the rationale for writing the instructional plan and how each section contributes to the success of the presentation. We begin with an overview of the instructional plan and then discuss each component in detail.

THE NEED FOR A WRITTEN PLAN

Central to developing presentation skills is learning how to develop a written plan to communicate ideas. A written plan helps organize and focus the presentation. The written plan is called the instructional plan. It may also be referred to as a lesson plan. The terms can be used interchangeably. In this text, we will refer to the written plan as the instructional plan. Elements of the instructional plan are applicable to many other types of presentations.

Experts do not always agree on the form and structure for a written instructional plan. However, most experts concur that a written plan is mandatory. General guidelines to follow when writing plans for instructional presentations include the following:

- Analyze your target audience
- Determine the instructional objectives that you expect to achieve
- Locate suitable instructional materials
- Determine specific content to be covered
- Identify appropriate instructional strategies
- Prepare a written plan using an outline format
- Make provisions for special learners who may be in the group
- Determine appropriate follow up activities to extend the learning experience
- Provide a copy of the plan for review by supervisors or mentors
- Conduct a self-evaluation to further enhance and refine your presentation skills

THE INSTRUCTIONAL PLAN FORMAT

This text suggests the following outline for written instructional plans. You will note that the prescribed format assists the novice teacher by requiring that he/she consider all aspects of the teaching/learning situation. (See Appendix A for samples of instructional plans that address specific subject areas and grade levels.)

In completing the written plan, the teacher must give consideration to the subject matter to be learned and the special characteristics of the audience. What the learner already knows is an important consideration, since new content must be linked to previous learning experiences. The suggested format contains twelve sections to be completed. Some sections require only one or two words to adequately describe. The procedure is really the heart of the instructional plan. The procedure outlines the introduction, body and summary of the presentation. As you review the written plan format, keep in mind that you may find it easier to complete some sections of the plan first.

Sometimes an idea for instruction begins with a textbook chapter, a student worksheet or a film clip. The teacher must then decide how the particular material fits into the written plan format. Thus, an instructional plan may develop around the materials. An instructional plan may also develop around a particular instructional activity. For example, a teacher may want his/her students to participate in an organized panel discussion. The teacher would then use the instructional plan format that follows to build a lesson geared towards preparing his/her students for this discussion. Examine the following Instructional Plan Format and notice the twelve areas to be addressed. When you use this Instructional Plan Format, the authors suggest that you copy this format into your word processing program to use as a template. Be sure that your template includes numbers and labels for each section.

The Instructional Plan Format

1   **Name of teacher:**

2   **Subject/Topic:**

3   **Analyze the Target Audience:**   *(Grade level/ Age/ Characteristics of Group or Audience)*

4   **Behavioral Objective:**   *(What the learner will be able to do as a result of this lesson/presentation.)*

5   **Addressing Learning Standards:**   *(A listing of Learning Standards that will be addressed.)*

6   **Prior Knowledge:**   *(What the learner already knows about the topic).*

7   **Rationale for Lesson:**   *(Reason for teaching this topic; value of knowledge/skill)*

8   **Materials:**   *(A list of all materials needed for the presentation. Any published materials must be referenced according to American Psychological Association [APA] style.)*

9   **Procedures:**

       Motivational Activity: *(An introduction to get the learner interested in the topic.)*

       Developmental Activity: *(An instructional procedure that presents and teaches the topic)*

       Summary Activity: *(An activity that reviews the topic and ascertains that the objective is attained.)*

10   **Procedural Adaptation:**   *(Identify special learners in the group and describe how you plan to meet their special needs)*

11   **Determining Appropriate Follow-up Activities/Homework:**   *(Suggest two assignments to further enhance learning. Assignments may be review, preparation, application or long range.)*

12   **Evaluation:**

       Teacher performance: *(Do a self-assessment in terms of objective, content and method. Identify two strengths and two weaknesses.)*

OVERVIEW OF THE INSTRUCTIONAL PLAN

Let's examine the Instructional Plan Format in greater detail. Items 2 and 3 require that you, as the classroom teacher, think about the Topic for presentation and the **Target Audience**. Item 4 specifies the Behavioral Objective. The **Behavioral Objective** indicates what the learner will be able to do as a result of being exposed to this presentation. Thus you must clearly state what you expect your students to accomplish as a result of this presentation.

Item 5 requires that you identify **Learning Standards** that are addressed in the lesson. The current emphasis on Learning Standards mandates that educators be ever mindful of the prescribed educational goals for learning.

Item 6 asks you to think about the learners' **Prior Knowledge**. New learning must be connected to ideas and concepts that we already understand. By considering the learners' prior knowledge, you will be successful in your presentation of new materials and ideas and enhance the process of student learning.

Item 7 of the format requires that you think about a **Rationale** for the presentation or lesson. Why are you presenting this topic? Why is this content important to know? What value does this information have for the audience? What is its relevance? If you cannot generate a reasonable rationale for conveying this information to your audience, then you might question, "Why am I doing this presentation?" Successful instruction occurs when the content is meaningful and valuable to the learner.

Item 8 of the format requires you to list all the **Materials** needed for the presentation. Material lists will help you to facilitate your preparation on the day of the presentation. For example, if you need markers and newsprint for a group activity, your failure to bring this material on the day of presentation will impede the success of your lesson.

Item 9 of the format, **Procedures**, is really the heart of the presentation. The **Motivational Activity** introduces the topic to the audience. It is usually short in duration, stimulates learner interest and activates **Prior Knowledge**. The **Developmental Activity** is the instructional procedure that actually allows you to convey the content to be learned. The **Summary Activity** helps you to bring closure to the presentation. Please keep in mind that the Summary Activity should be consistent with the Behavioral Objective.

Item 10, the **Procedural Adaptation**, asks you to think about special learners who may be in the classroom. Perhaps there are some hearing impaired participants in the group. Will you provide someone to sign to them? If you are showing a film, will you employ "closed caption?" A successful presentation will insure that all learners in your target audience are accommodated appropriately.

Item 11 requires that you determine appropriate **Follow-up Activities/Homework**. When a student participates in a learning activity, s/he benefits from assignments which require that s/he practices the skills or reviews the content that you covered in your lesson. The instructional plan format asks you to think about various types of activities that might extend the learning experience and help reenforce the lesson over a period of time.

Lastly, item 12 asks that you **Evaluate** the presentation so that you are able to reflect upon the teaching/learning experience. This reflection enables you to refine your skills for future presentations so that your students are able to benefit fully from your presentation.

ANALYZING THE TARGET AUDIENCE

The first step in preparing your presentation is to determine the nature and characteristics of your audience. Is your class made up of a group of young adolescents in middle school? Perhaps your audience is comprised of high school students or of adult-learners. Maybe you are speaking to a group of parents attending "Back to School Night." You may have an audience of one, of seventy-five, or one as large as two hundred. Regardless of the size of the class however, your first step is to identify who they are, what do they already know and what do they need to know.

Who are these learners?

Are they eager to learn? Are they motivated?

How long can you expect them to sit quietly and pay attention?

Do they prefer to work independently or in groups?

Why are they in this class? Is this a required course of study? Is this an elective class?

What do the learners already know?

What are their ability levels in terms of reading and writing skills?

What do they already know about this topic?

What did they learn about last week? Last month? Last year?

What do the learners need to know?
        What is the topic of this presentation?
        Why is this important knowledge?
        Why is this an important skill to acquire?

Analyzing the audience is rarely a simple task. If you are a classroom teacher, you will spend the first few weeks of the term learning about students' strengths and abilities. Asking questions and listening to your students during class discussions will help you to develop an understanding of your students and their prior knowledge. You will then be able to build future instruction upon what students already know.

Do not be afraid to extend your scope beyond traditional classroom materials. Discovering students' interests outside of the classroom can provide valuable insight into their learning processes and assist you in presenting instructional information. What are the ages of your students? What activities are they involved in after school? What topics seem to elicit the most interest in class? For example, are your students interested in the environment? Use this interest as a lead-in for a geography lesson. Do they participate in sports? Use sports scores and statistics to generate an interest in math. Grounding curriculum topics in the students' real-life concerns promotes interest, and encourages the students to engage with the material.

If you are teaching young children, listen carefully to the way they present their responses to your questions. The level of sophistication your students show in analyzing and synthesizing information may surprise you. Conversely, their level of cognitive comprehension may fall below your expectations. You want to challenge the learners to proceed to higher levels of information processing by allowing each answer to generate new questions and new answers.

If you are a student teacher, you may have to ask the cooperating teacher for some guidance. Student textbooks, course syllabi and curriculum guides provide additional data to help meet the needs of your target audience within the classroom. Once you ascertain who the students are, what they already know and what they need to learn, you can plan your instruction accordingly. Don't forget, however, to observe body language and visual cues which can be at least as valuable as verbal information when adapting your instructional style. Assess whether the group would be comfortable with a formal or informal style. Expand your sources and learn all you can to engage your audience.

Worksheet: Analyze the Target Audience
Directions: Ask yourself the following questions. Record your answers on a separate sheet of paper.
- How do you describe the learners in terms of age, sex and grade level?
- How long can you expect the class to sit quietly and pay attention?
- Do the students prefer to work independently or with others? Explain.
- What do the learners already know about this topic?
- What other topics are related to this lesson?
- What did students learn previously to enhance their understanding of this topic?
- How would describe the students' ability in terms of reading and writing skills?
- What do the students need to learn?
- Why is this knowledge or skill important to learn?
- How will this knowledge or skill be helpful for future learning?

BEHAVIORAL OBJECTIVES

Whether your students are a group of first graders using manipulatives to master basic arithmetic, MBA candidates engaging in role play to understand ethical practices in a multicultural workplace, or advanced beginners in tennis whose serve could use some improvement, behavioral objectives are an essential part of your teaching plan. Teachers want their strategy to be engaging and stimulating, but the lesson is incomplete unless you make your learners aware of the intended outcome.

This intended outcome is the <u>behavioral objective</u> of the instructional plan, workshop, or presentation. Some educators have moved away from the behaviorists' view of specifying a behavioral objective. However, the recent emphasis on learning standards represents a return to identifying learning outcomes. The authors suggest that the teacher identify the intended learning outcome in the form of a behavioral objective. This approach assists the classroom teacher in being mindful of the purpose of instruction. It also allows the teacher to observe or measure student learning within the context of the instructional presentation.

Determining Behavioral Objectives

When planning a lesson or presentation, you must first decide what you would like students to be able to do at the end of the presentation. This outcome is written in the form of a behavioral objective. Again, the behavioral objective is a statement that describes what the learner will be able to do as a result of his/her exposure to the lesson or presentation.

There are three basic types of behavioral objectives: cognitive, affective, and psychomotor. Each of the three examples cited above is targeted to one of the three types. The arithmetic lesson invokes the cognitive domain, the multicultural workshop addresses the affective domain, and the tennis lesson the psychomotor domain.

Cognitive Objectives

Of the three basic domains (cognitive, affective and psychomotor), the one that is given the most attention in the literature is the cognitive. Cognitive objectives are related to rational or intellectual thinking. The model used most often to classify cognitive objectives is the taxonomy developed by Benjamin Bloom (1984). Bloom's taxonomy reflects different levels of thinking from the least complex to the most complex.

The six levels of Bloom's taxonomy are: <u>knowledge</u>, <u>comprehension</u>, <u>application</u>, <u>analysis</u>, <u>synthesis</u>, and <u>evaluation</u>. Each level is represented by certain illustrative verbs which you, the teacher, should use to formulate an appropriate behavioral objective:

- Knowledge: The key concepts are <u>remembering and recalling</u>. The information gleaned at this level forms the basis for all further conceptual thought. The verbs used in the development of behavioral objectives include: *choose, complete, define, describe, identify, indicate, label, list, locate, match, name, recall, select, state.*
- Comprehension: The key concept is <u>understanding</u> the information beyond the level of mere recall. The verbs include: *classify, convert, defend, derive, describe, estimate, expand, explain, express, extrapolate, generalize, infer, interpolate, paraphrase, predict, recognize, summarize, translate.*
- Application: The key concept is <u>applying</u> the information to new situations. The verbs include: *apply, compute, construct, demonstrate, differentiate, discover, discuss, modify, operate, participate, perform, plan, predict, prepare, relate, show, use.*
- Analysis: The key concept is <u>converting into components</u>; that is drawing conclusions from the information and determining evidence. The verbs include: *analyze, debate, deduce, design, diagram, differentiate, discriminate, identify, generalize, illustrate, infer, organize, relate, select.*
- Synthesis: The key concept is <u>making predictions</u>. At this level, the learner brings parts together to form a whole. The verbs include: *arrange, categorize, combine, compile, compose, construct, create, design, develop, devise, generate, organize, plan, produce, relate, reconstruct, reorganize, summarize, synthesize, write.*
- Evaluation: The key concepts are <u>offering opinions</u> and <u>value judging</u>. The verbs include: *appraise, compare, conclude, contrast, criticize, decide, evaluate, interpret, justify, relate, summarize, support.*

For example, if you are an elementary school teacher who plans to present a history lesson on the American Revolutionary War, your Instructional Plan may contain the following cognitive behavioral objective: At the end of this presentation, the students will be able to "identify" and "describe" three important facts about the Boston Tea Party. (See Appendix A for more examples of cognitive behavioral objectives.)

A driving force behind education reform has been the tenet that traditional teaching has neglected the higher order critical thinking skills. While there is no doubt that critical thinking is essential to success in the real world of employment as well as in the academic environment, it is equally vital not to neglect the building blocks of higher cognitive skills. Burns and Gentry (1998), for example, argue that the basis of learning is the stimulation of curiosity. In order for you to effect this stimulation, your students must first become aware of what they do not know. This is the stage of enlightenment. Second, they must be motivated to close the knowledge gap. Curiosity will provide your students with this motivation. However, if the gap is too large, your students may become frustrated and overwhelmed. Instead of experiencing the stimulating effects of their peaked curiosity, they may experience a sense of learned helplessness. In other words, they may become paralyzed and unable to process the information you are trying to convey to them.

Affective Objectives

Eliciting curiosity falls under the heading of motivation or responding. This process is part of the affective domain which is as important as the cognitive domain in a learner-centered classroom. The following taxonomy, developed by Krathwohl, Bloom, and Masia (1964), provides a vocabulary which will help you to create an affective behavioral objective for your instructional plan. This affective taxonomy contains five levels: receiving, responding, valuing, organizing, and internalizing:

- Receiving: The key concept is attending, being aware of the affective stimulus and developing a willingness to receive it favorably. The verbs used in developing behavioral objectives include: *ask, attend, choose, discriminate, find, identify, listen.*
- Responding: The key concept is taking an interest in the stimulus and perceiving it favorably. Verbs include: *answer, perform, read, write.*
- Valuing: The key concepts are showing belief and developing commitment. Verbs include: *argue, commit, report, work.*
- Organizing: The key concept is systematizing values into dominant and supporting values.
- Internalizing: The key concept is demonstrating consistency of beliefs and behavior. Verbs include: *act, display, influence, practice, propose, revise, verify.*

For example, if you are preparing a lesson for your high school students which will examine the debate surrounding the issue of gun-control in the state of New York, you may create the following affective behavioral objective: At the end of this presentation, students will be able to "argue" confidently their opinions on gun control.

Note that this behavioral objective draws upon the level of valuing. In this lesson, you, as the teacher, wish to encourage students to express their informed opinions. Students will benefit from this lesson because they will learn that they are capable of forming intelligent opinions, worthy of respect, and they will come to understand that they have a right and are able to participate in civic debates. (Note that it is possible to teach the same content - the debate surrounding gun control in New York - with a cognitive behavioral objective which draws upon the level of evaluation as specified by Bloom's Taxonomy. At the end of this presentation, students will be able to write a critical evaluation of a journal article providing the pros and cons of gun control in the state of New York.)

In the classroom environment, the affective domain is important in developing a positive attitude toward learning in general, and toward the specific content area, but it is also the most difficult to evaluate. For example, if you wish to teach your ninth-grade students the hazards of smoking, you will able to evaluate the cognitive objective: By the end of your presentation, do they know the ingredients of a cigarette and the physical and psychological effects of smoking on them? It will be more difficult, however, for you to evaluate whether you have changed the students' attitudes towards, or feelings about smoking. (See Appendix A for Instructional Plans with examples of Affective Behavioral Objectives.)

<u>Psychomotor Objectives</u>

Behavioral objectives in the psychomotor domain involve the use of the body's muscular system. Harrow (1977) developed a taxonomy that involves four levels: <u>movement</u>, <u>manipulating</u>, <u>communicating</u>, and <u>creating</u>.

- Movement: The key concept is <u>coordination</u>. Verbs for developing behavioral objectives include: *adjust, carry, clean, locate, obtain, walk.*
- Manipulation: The key concept is <u>fine coordination</u>. Verbs include: *assemble, build, calibrate, connect, thread.*
- Communicating: The key concept is <u>communication</u> of ideas and feelings. Verbs include: *ask, analyze, describe, draw, explain, write.*
- Creating: The key concept is <u>coordination of all skills</u> in all domains. Verbs include: *create, design, invent.*

While you may assume that psychomotor behavioral objectives are used primarily in physical education classes, an instructional plan which asks that the students develop their communication skills also requires a psychomotor behavioral objective. For example, in the above-described instructional plan on the issues surrounding gun-control in the state of New York, you might create the following psychomotor behavioral objective: By the end of the presentation, students should be able to listen to their classmates' opinions on gun-control and then "describe" these opinions. (See Appendix A for an Instructional Plan with examples of psychomotor behavioral objectives.)

<u>Planning Behavioral Objectives</u>

As an illustration of a behavioral objective, consider the authors' objective for the reader of this text:

> *After reading Part I of this text, the reader will be able to prepare a written instructional plan, demonstrate the lesson, evaluate the presentation and plan for future instructional presentations.*

The terms "prepare," "demonstrate," "evaluate," and "plan" are illustrative verbs found in the cognitive domain of Blooms taxonomy. Consequently, this is a cognitive behavioral objective.

The behavioral objective must be well planned to provide guidelines for learning and to assist you, the teacher, in monitoring learner progress. Keep in mind that there are a variety of formats that you can use when you are writing behavioral objectives. The predominate belief is that regardless of format, the objective should delineate specific, observable learner behavior as we have done in the above example. However, not all sources agree. For example, Nuthall (1999) believes that the hierarchy of question types delineated by Bloom's hierarchy does not chart a hierarchy of cognitive processes, suggesting that only evidence from the students themselves can provide a guide to the cognitive processes involved. From this perspective, behavioral objectives may be modified as the teacher observes the processes used by the students as they master the course material.

<u>Cognitive Questioning</u>

The way that teachers structure questions plays a critical role in eliciting higher order thinking skills. Asking questions is a core component of teaching. The problem is that while research shows that teachers spend most of their instructional time asking questions, 70% to 80% of these questions only ask for factual recall (Savage, 1998). Additional research has shown that 80% to 90% of what students learn through factual questioning is forgotten! In order to elicit a higher order thinking, and in order to encourage better retention of material, you should formulate questions which demand that the students exercise their critical thinking abilities. Students should be able to do more than memorize, or parrot back your points. They should also be able to synthesize the information in order to arrive at their own formulations. For example, if you are teaching a lesson on William Faulkner's "A Rose for Emily" to high school sophomores, you want your students to be able to do more than repeat back to you the date of the story's publication, the important dates in Faulkner's life and your analysis of the significance of the rose. Instead, you might like your students to provide their own interpretations which they can support with textual examples. What do they think the rose in the title symbolizes? How can they support this analysis? Which passages in this short story support their reading of the title?

Many teachers, even experienced teachers, lack confidence in their ability to structure questions that will engage students in active dialogue. In response to this problem, courses and seminars have been developed to address "the teacher's role in discourse." These programs draw on Bloom's taxonomy as a framework (Ostergard, 1997; Savage, 1998).

Mathematics teachers, in particular, may find asking the right questions especially tricky. Traditionally, mathematics has been taught as a rigid discipline in which there was only one right answer to every question. In fact, Ostergard (1997) notes that <u>all</u> participants at a summer mathematics institute and graduate course reported that "learning how to ask questions is difficult." (p. 50)

Savage (1998) teaches courses designed to help teachers become savvy questioners. In workshops during the first two sessions, participants review Bloom's taxonomy and how the thinking skills described can be put into practice by way of problem solving, decision making, and conceptualizing. The focus is on creating an environment that will encourage higher level thinking skills and maximize verbal interaction. Following these sessions, the teachers identify the types of questions that will promote critical thinking. Savage outlines 11 questions that promote higher order thinking:

- What are your reasons for saying that?
- Why do you agree (or disagree) on that point?
- How do you define the term you just used?
- What do you mean by that expression?
- Is what you are saying consistent with what you said previously?
- Could you clarify that remark?
- When you said that, what was implied by your remarks?
- What follows from what you just said?
- Is it possible you and s/he are contradicting each other?
- Are you sure you are not contradicting yourself?
- What alternatives are there to such a formulation?

If these questions sound too sophisticated for younger children, it may simply be just a matter of revising the language rather than making the reasoning less complex. The earlier children learn to think critically, the more adept and the more confident they will become with their own critical thinking skills. Follow the example of one participant in the mathematics institute course:

> Before this semester I thought my students (elementary) were too young to answer a synthesis question. I assumed my knowledge and comprehension questions were their limit.... I started asking higher-level questions of my students, and lo and behold, they had great answers! (Ostergard, 1997, p. 50)

Synthesizing Learning

One way of looking at the three basic domains (cognitive, affective and psychomotor) is to compare them to Howard Gardner's theory of multiple intelligences (MI). Behavioral objectives can be designed to address any or several of the seven intelligences: verbal/linguistic, visual/ spatial, bodily/kinesthetic, interpersonal/social, logical/ mathematical, and musical/rhythmic.

Stuart (1997) describes one innovative fifth-grade teacher who wanted to ensure that her students developed their higher order reasoning skills. To this aim, she simply taught her students Bloom's taxonomy. Interestingly, although the theory sometimes evokes yawns in basic education courses, the fifth graders found it a valuable framework for focusing on the different levels of thinking.

No doubt the secret is in the presentation. This fifth-grade teacher posted Bloom's taxonomy as a chart that breaks down the levels of thinking into categories. The students reviewed the chart and discussed the verbs. The students were engaged in a learning contract in conjunction with the chart, in which they carried out projects that enabled them to use all levels of thinking. For example, in a unit on Native Americans, a group of students became interested in Native American medicine and decided to research the subject. Other students researched Native American art, dance, and tribal structure. The learning contract for each project contained behavioral objectives that encompassed MI theory as well as Bloom's taxonomy.

The teacher's success as reported by Stuart (1997) lies in the fact that once the student's have become familiar with Bloom's taxonomy, they realize when they are working at a lower level of thinking and push themselves to attempt a higher level--even in the absence of a learning contract or specific behavioral objectives.

Busching and Slesinger (1995) believe that the key to motivating students to use critical thinking skills is the use of authentic questions. The authors describe a project in which the students learned about the Holocaust by immersing themselves in the lives of the people. Instructional materials ranged from European and world
maps, to World War II novels, the <u>Diary of Anne Frank</u>, Picasso's <u>Guernica</u>, informational videos, and exploring family connections to World War II. The synthesis of learning included investigations of racism and hatred in the communities of the children today. The teachers delved into their own consciousness and identified several real questions:

- How can we study war in a way that leads to a commitment to peace?
- How can a Holocaust study avoid stimulating hatred for Germans or contempt for Jews?
- How can students find a personal connection to historical events?
- Will the unit lead to caring about injustice in our own world?

A behavioral objective might be: After this presentation, the students will be able to describe parallels between anti-Semitism in Nazi Germany and hate crimes in our own society.

Busching and Slesinger (1995) are skeptical about the use of a hierarchical scheme, such as Bloom's taxonomy, that values higher order questions over factual ones. They feel that perhaps <u>continuum</u> may be a better term than <u>hierarchy</u>. The students in their unit were hungry for facts, concurring with the perspective that curiosity results from a manageable knowledge gap: the students need basic knowledge if they are to formulate questions that will stimulate critical thinking (Burns & Gentry, 1998).

In the psychomotor domain, the teacher must go beyond cognitive knowledge. In learning new movement patterns, for example, students may appear to accept the changes on a cognitive level, but fail to incorporate them consistently in performance. Langley (1993), a physical education teacher, developed a strategy for refining the skills of his tennis students. This is an excellent model for designing behavioral objectives in the psychomotor domain:

- Have students identify and describe in writing a single aspect of their performance that requires improvement.
- Discuss with each student individually the degree of change that can be accomplished within limitations imposed by time/resources/facility.
- Create a supportive and motivational learning environment.
- Model the spatial pattern of each student, followed by the prescriptive model. Then have the student practice the pattern to mastery.
- Model the temporal aspects of the pattern in conjunction with the proper spatial pattern. Direct the students' attention to key aspects of timing and have them practice until mastery.
- Use simple outcome goals during the final phase of practice to enhance students' perceptions of success. Remain available until you assess that a student has developed the confidence to work independently.

With some adaptation, Langley's (1993) model can be applied across disciplines and domains. The most critical point is to create a supportive and motivational learning environment.

ADDRESSING LEARNING STANDARDS: (A listing of Learning Standards that will be addressed.)

The current emphasis on learning standards requires that classroom teachers focus instruction to meet specific goals. Learning standards are a way of specifying what students should know and what they should be able to do as a result of K-12 education in the United States. The concept of learning standards has been around in some form or another for quite some time. Sometimes standards are referred to as competencies, benchmarks, frameworks or essential skills. Standards and assessments are designed to hold teachers and school administrators accountable for student learning. In this section, we will examine the standards movement to learn why teachers are expected to consider learning standards when planning classroom instruction.

In 1983, the National Commission on Excellence in Education issued a report entitled, A Nation at Risk. The highly critical report indicated that the nation that had become complacent about the state of education in its public schools. The report strongly denounced the quality of education, citing the way in which American schools had fallen behind other nations, especially in the areas of mathematics and science. The report called for broad reform and the result was a strong movement toward educational change.

According to Louis (1998) the goal of school reform became a nationwide effort to provide an effective education for all students. Three basic concerns appeared consistently in discussions of school reform:

- The need to respond to an increasingly diverse population.
- The need for accountability in education.
- Concern over whether our current educational system is preparing students with the skills needed to compete in the global marketplace.

Early efforts at school reform were inconsistent and ineffective in addressing these issues. The "first wave" of reform in the wake of A Nation at Risk called for more rigorous standards for course requirements and minimum graduation requirements. The "second wave" of reform focused on decentralization and site-based management of schools (Louis, 1998).

Since education is not granted as a specific power to the federal government under the United States Constitution, in most educational domains the individual states take precedence in decision-making. Therefore, nationwide reform is a complex issue. Educational policymaking takes place at the state level in a multi-tiered and essentially decentralized system. The federal agencies attempt to influence state decision-making by granting funds to those who comply with federal guidelines. Basically there are four levels of governance for educational institutions: the federal government, the state government, the local municipal government, and the school administration. The boundaries and responsibilities for authority and decision making are complex and far from clearly defined (Louis, 1998).

This latest mandate for systemic education reform was unique in that it originated at the national level. McGee Banks (1997) traces the development of the standards movement that officially began in 1989 when President Bush held an education summit for the nation's governors. She notes that as a result of the summit, a number of proposals were made to fix our nation's schools, including returning to basics, developing a national curriculum, and using standardized tests to assess student knowledge. President Clinton, then Governor of Arkansas attended the 1989 summit. After becoming president, Clinton officially made education his "top priority," spearheading the most aggressive education initiative in the nation's history since mandatory public schooling. In 1994, the U.S. Congress passed Goals 2000 as part of the Goals 2000: Educate America Act. Goals 2000 stressed readiness for school, high school completion, student achievement and citizenship, world class standards in math and science, adult literacy and life-long learning, safe and drug free schools, teacher education and professional development, and parental participation (Morrison, 2000).

Broadly defined, systemic, nationwide school reform entails higher mandatory standards linked to new curricula and effective methods for assessing students' achievement of the standards (Louis, 1998). More specifically defined, it means that school districts that perform well will be rewarded while those that do not meet the prescribed standards risk losing some or all of their federal assistance (Broder, 1999).

In January 1999, Education Week published the results of, "Quality Counts," a comprehensive report on how well states are doing in their effort to hold schools and teachers accountable for student learning. Most states were still in the fledgling stage. Texas and North Carolina came closest to having a complete accountability system. New York fared poorly on this measure, ranking 30th, at least in part due to the lack of explicit consequences for schools that fail to make the grade. However, New York State earned a decent 10th place for its efforts to raise standards for teachers. Concerning standards for students, New York came in first in the nation for holding students to rigorous academic standards and assessments (Bronner, 1999).

The quest for high standards in New York State education hails back to the creation of the Board of Regents in 1784. Then at the turn of the 20th century, Governor Theodore Roosevelt proposed the creation of a department that would make education in the state of New York, "unified for the sake of greater efficiency, economy, and harmony" (New York State Education Department, 1998). Today the New York Board of Regents and its State Education Department oversee education from pre-kindergarten through graduate school. Similar boards and departments of education exist in other states as well.

Even before President Clinton announced his landmark policy, the New York State Board of Regents issued A New Compact for Learning (1991), a document that defined a vision and rationale for systemic education reform.

A New Compact for Learning was based on six fundamental principles:
1   All children can learn.
2.   Focus on results.
3.   Aim for mastery.
4.   Provide the means.
5.   Provide authority with accountability.
6.   Reward success and remedy failure.

A New Compact for Learning established a commitment to helping all students achieve. It established a commitment to "the core values of our democratic society," namely, effective citizenship and equitable educational opportunities. The strategic objectives of the Compact reflect John Dewey's ideal that education is a means to social reform.

Under A New Compact for Learning, the responsibilities of the State of New York are clearly defined. These include:
* Specifying standards of knowledge and skills for elementary, middle, and secondary education;
* Establishing standards of achievement for the content standards;
* Assisting local schools and school districts in the planning, development, and implementation of programs and practices to ensure that all students achieve the standards;
* Determining through a statewide assessment program if the standards are being met;
* Informing local schools and school districts about effective strategies related to curriculum, instruction, and assessment.

Therefore, as evident in this document, New York State defined its role as the leader of the reform movement. New York State accepted the responsibility to collaborate with all adult stakeholders - teachers, administrators, school boards, parents, and community members - to transform the education system statewide. Other states also adopted similar policies concerning their role in the reform movement.

Although reform takes place at all levels, teachers are most intimately involved with raising levels of student academic achievement. If students are to meet the new standards with confidence, teachers have to be up to the challenge. In all states teachers are expected to meet the new standards in professional preparation and beyond, through ongoing professional development (Emihovich, 1997). The focus across all curriculum areas is on <u>authentic knowledge</u> and <u>authentic assessment</u>. Authentic knowledge refers to knowledge that will serve students in the real world outside the classroom. These include reading, writing and problem solving tasks similar to those found in the workplace. Authentic assessments are appropriate measures for assessing authentic knowledge. An extensive discussion of authentic assessment can be found in Part I, Section III of this text. Therefore, teachers at all levels are expected to translate their own expertise into innovative, effective classroom practices.

<u>STANDARDS AND ASSESSMENT</u>

At this point you may be wondering "What are these learning standards like?" And probably more importantly, "How does a teacher know when he or she is meeting established learning standards?"

What are the learning standards like?

Learning standards have been compiled at the national, state and local levels for all subject areas and grade levels. When learning standards are clearly delineated, educators have clear-cut guidelines to expand the parameters of their discipline to meet new demands for excellence. When learning standards are used constructively, they facilitate consistency in curriculum content. Learning standards do not dictate conformity. Learning standards are expected to improve the level of student performance by providing goals or benchmarks to be reached. Much however depends upon how the learning standards are written.

Mathematics was the first academic area to establish a base of learning standards. Student performance on mathematics and science tests has long been a concern of parents and educators. The National Council of Teachers of Mathematics (NCTM) published <u>Curriculum and Evaluation Standards for School Mathematics</u> in 1989, followed by the new <u>Assessment Standards for School Mathematics</u> and <u>Professional Standards for Teaching Mathematics.</u> These documents comprise a model for learning standards that was emulated by other academic disciplines.

Learning standards currently exist for all subject areas including, English, language arts, science, social studies, foreign languages, health, physical education, technology and vocational subjects. There are also standards for evaluating programs, teachers, and others involved in the educational process. In addition to the continued publication of new standards' documents, there are continuous revisions of previously published standards.

Researchers at the Mid-continent Regional Educational Laboratory (McREL) (1997) indicate that two significant problems concerning learning standards are the existence of multiple documents and varying definitions of standards within each document. Most subject areas have multiple documents that address the standards in their domain. McREL notes that the National Council of Teachers of Mathematics' publication, <u>Curriculum and Evaluation Standards for School Mathematics</u> (1989), is considered the "official" description of what students should know and be able to do in mathematics. However, each of the following documents also list specific national learning standards for mathematics:

<u>Benchmarks of Science Literacy</u> (1993) by Project 2061 of the American Association for the Achievement of Science (AAAS)

<u>Framework for the 1994 National Assessment of Educational Progress Mathematics Assessment</u> (1992), by the National Assessment of Educational Progress (NAEP)

<u>Performance Standards: English Language Arts, Mathematics, Science, Applied Learning. Volume I, Elementary School.</u> (1997a) by the National Center on Education and the Economy.

<u>Performance Standards: English Language Arts, Mathematics, Science, Applied Learning. Volume 2, Middle School.</u> (1997b) by the National Center on Education and the Economy.

<u>Performance Standards: English Language Arts, Mathematics, Science, Applied Learning. Volume 3, High School.</u> (1997c) by the National Center on Education and the Economy.

<u>Group 5 Mathematics Guide</u> (1993) by the International Baccalaureate Organization.

<u>Middle Years Programme: Mathematics</u> (1995e) by the International Baccalaureate Organization (page 1).

To compound the problem of multiple documents, each state and local educational agency has adopted learning standards as well. The existence of multiple documents creates confusion for the classroom teacher. Questions for the teacher become, "Which documents do I use?" and "What standards do I address?"

The answer is, "It depends...." The best suggestion for new classroom teachers is to consult their immediate supervisor or principal for copies of the learning standards used in their school. Most likely the learning standards for your subject and grade level, as prescribed by your state department of education, are the most appropriate documents to consult. However this is not always the case, since most school districts have created their own curricula that align with state learning standards.

Once you have determined which set of standards to address within your classroom place the list in a prominent place. Some teachers post the standards on a bulletin board. Most importantly, share the standards with your students and their parents. Standards indicate your expectations and goals for your class. When students (and parents) know what they are expected to achieve, they have a goal to reach. When expectations are vague and unspecified, academic work lacks focus and purpose.

As you examine the learning standards documents, you will notice that some learning standards are written broadly allowing for individual interpretation. Others are much more specific and indicate specific student and teacher behaviors to be achieved. To illustrate a broadly stated objective, consider the following standard from the IRA/NCTE Standards for the English Language Arts. This standard is proposed by the joined national organizations of the International Reading Association (IRA) and The National Council of Teachers of English (NCTE). The standard proposes that:

> Students read a wide range of literature from many periods in many genres to build an understanding of the many dimensions (e.g. philosophical, ethical, aesthetic) of human experience.

In response to this learning standard, the classroom teacher is required to insure that the reading curriculum is broad based and that the students read many different types of texts and materials. A teacher thus has the flexibility of what books the children will read as well and how many. The teacher is also free to select the types of assignments that students will complete in response to these readings. For example, students may write book reports, research papers, and response journals. Students could also build dioramas, paint murals, compose music, or write a play. All these activities are appropriate responses to literature and provide opportunities to demonstrate understanding of the text material.

The spirit and intent of this standard is preserved but spelled out very differently in the New York State Core Curriculum Guide for English Language Arts (Pre-K through 12) which suggests:

> All students should read 25 books, write 1,000 words a month and have daily opportunities to practice and reinforce speaking and listening skills

In response to this learning standard, New York State classroom teachers must insure that students read 25 books over the course of the academic school year. In addition, the teacher must carefully plan and construct class assignments to insure sufficient and appropriate writing experiences. The New York State Core Curriculum Guide also contains suggested reading lists for students at all levels from Pre-K through high school. Thus, you will notice that some learning standards are broadly written and provide teachers with flexibility on what and how to teach. Other learning standards are more prescriptive with little flexibility. Therefore learning standards are capable of restricting a teacher's choice of daily learning activities.

Teachers are often asked to consider learning standards when writing daily instructional plans. Principals and other administrators often ask teachers to list specific learning standards within their plan books. School officials may drop in and inquire which specific learning standards are being addressed. Therefore, as a practical matter, listing learning standards within the instructional plan is a helpful strategy that keeps both students and teachers focused on the goals of instruction.

The Mid-continent Regional Educational Laboratory (McRel) in Aurora, Colorado has attempted to survey and consolidate the many national and state level initiatives to identify learning standards for grades K-12. Kendall and Marzano (1997) indicate that more than 116 national and state level documents were consulted for this project and the result is a comprehensive learning standards database that is available online at http://www.mcrel.org/standards. Sample instructional plans in this text list learning standards from the McRel database.

Appendix C of this text contains a listing of professional subject-area organizations that publish national learning standards for elementary and secondary students. Teachers are encouraged to consult these online sources to research appropriate learning standards. Information concerning learning standards is also available from individual state and local educational agencies.

You may want to ask yourself the following question:
How can I help my students meet the prescribed learning standards?

There are two ways to insure that your students meet the prescribed learning standards for your subject area and grade level. The first is to create a productive learning environment on a daily basis. The second is to assess student learning on a regular basis. In this section, we will discuss each of these strategies.

Another question to ask yourself is:
How does a productive learning environment help students achieve high standards of learning?

When teachers create productive learning environments, students are actively engaged in meaningful learning experiences throughout the day. Students are interested in learning and become successful participants in the process. Cooney (1994) observed that a stimulating classroom environment is characterized by the following: active student participation, cooperative learning, journal writing and ongoing discourse. In addition, Cooney observed that the teacher's role is to choose worthwhile and engaging tasks, orchestrate classroom discourse, and encourage critical thinking and problem solving.

Let us examine how the standards align with a stimulating classroom setting by using the language arts curriculum as an example. The IRA/NCTE Standards for the English Language Arts includes the following:

- Students read a wide range of print and non-print texts to build an understanding of texts, of themselves, and of the cultures of the United States and the world; to acquire new information; to respond to the needs and demands of society, and the workplace; and for the personal fulfillment. Among these texts are fiction and nonfiction, classic and contemporary works.
- Students will read a wide range of literature from many periods in many genres to building an understanding of the many dimensions (e.g. philosophical, ethical, aesthetic) of human experience.

Mastery of literacy skills is essential for success in virtually all areas of life. In particular, reading selections of all types foster a lifelong appreciation for language. Teachers can stimulate interest and exploration by using all types of reading materials in the classroom. Teachers should encourage students to take home books and share them with family and friends. Engaging parents and helping them to structure shared reading activities at home are also good ideas.

In a productive learning environment, teachers read aloud to young children. Listening to stories improves children's language skills and motivates them to read on their own. It promotes attention to the context in which language appears, increases vocabulary, promotes critical thinking, and allows children to respond and share their responses with others. Teachers should use one-to-one reading activities, pairing students with teacher, peers, or older students. Teachers should also arrange the class into small, cooperative reading groups where children can take turns reading and share ideas and responses.

A variety of follow-up activities can be used to augment a storytelling session (Saban, 1994). For older students, the same strategies can be used following reading assignments. In fact, the following strategies can be applied to other areas that involve reading, such as science and social studies. Augment assignments with:

- Discussion
- Creating artwork derived from the material
- Writing a poem based on the material
- Writing prose that expands on the content or characters
- Writing a journal as if one were a character in a story or event
- Constructing a play that involves the class as a whole
- Turning the material into a musical
- Creating a dance based on the material

Thus, the creation of a productive learning environment as described above serves to engage the student actively. Active engagement in the learning process is key to learning and helping student meet higher standards.

How do assessments help students achieve higher standards?

In addition to creating a productive learning environment, teachers must also assess students on a regular basis to insure that the learning standards are met. This means that teachers must never lose sight of what they expect students to achieve over the course of the academic year. When planning units of instruction and daily instructional plans, teachers must ask themselves, "How will my instruction help students meet the learning standards?" (You will note that the instructional plan format requires you to list appropriate learning standards.)

While teachers are encouraged to devise in-class assessments of student learning, state and local educational agencies have also identified testing procedures that are aligned with the learning standards. The purposes of assessment vary, depending upon who is doing the assessment and why.

The NCTM Assessment Standards discusses four broad categories of purposes that serve the needs of different stakeholders. Assessments are designed for:

- Monitoring students' progress
- Making instructional decisions
- Evaluating students' achievement
- Evaluating programs (Joyner, 1995)

Given the broad range of assessment needs, teachers can expect to administer all types of assessments within classroom settings. Generally, assessments fall into two categories: structured and unstructured. The most structured form of assessment is the standardized test. State educational agencies seem to favor standardized testing as a means of evaluation. Unstructured assessments can take the form of portfolios or performance based testing. (For a more comprehensive discussion of student assessment see Appendix C in this text).

Standardized tests have been soundly criticized for their emphasis on rote memorization, failure to provide an accurate picture of students' knowledge, disassociation from real life experience, and failure to encompass higher order thinking skills (Lee, 1992). The new Standards-based tests attempt to address these problems. Even critics of the new tests concede that they provide a much more accurate reflection of what students can do and cannot do than the traditional multiple choice tests (Saslow, 1999).

In Spring 1999, New York State administered its first standards based assessments to determine student progress toward meeting its new learning standards. In spite of the high marks New York State received for its standards, 51.9% of fourth graders who took the first Language Arts test fell short of the required standards (Saslow, 1999). The New York test was a pilot exam, and some confusion exists about how to interpret the scores. Optimists view the new test as a wake-up call - a starting point from which to identify curriculum strengths and weaknesses, and to improve on (or eliminate) existing programs.

Varied assessments or combinations of assessments are considered essential to give all students the opportunity to demonstrate what they know and understand. Assessments are expected to assist educators in measuring students learning, and enable teachers to devise the most effective strategies to help all students meet the new, challenging standards. Therefore, state educational agencies are feverishly working to develop authentic assessments that are aligned with standards.

Concerns about Learning Standards

According to Schmoker and Marzano (1999), clear, intelligible standards aligned with appropriate assessments are expected to enhance learning for all students. However, the authors do have some concerns about the standards movement, including the nature and length of state and professional standards documents and their unintended consequences.

Richard Wolk (1998) observes that the standards are written in language that is "absurd" and that the quantity is such that it would take a ten hour teaching day to cover the material suggested by the standards. Schmoker and Marzano (1999) indicate that efforts to include many suggestions concerning what is important has resulted in too many poorly written standards that are impossible to realistically teach to and adequately assess. They suggest that the overabundance of standards have served to frustrate teachers rather than provide a common focus and clarity.

Other researchers are also doubtful that learning standards are capable of accomplishing all that is promised. Cherry A. McGee Banks (1997) observes that the standards provide a false sense of security by suggesting that we have found a way to fix the problems in our schools. First, Banks finds it problematic that politicians, commentators, and political appointees were involved in constructing learning standards. Secondly, learning standards focus on how schooling relates to the world of work, potentially marginalizing subject areas such as art, music and foreign language. Third, initial drafts of some content standards (for example, history) have neglected to include significant groups such as women and people of color. In the case of the history standards, the standards have been reviewed, revised and expanded to be more inclusive, hence adding to the problem of an overabundance of standards.

Kenneth S. Goodman (1994) observed early on that the standards movement involves two erroneous assumptions. The first assumption is that up until now there has been no concern about the quality of education. The second assumption is that a lack of concern for quality has produced a crisis in public education. He concludes that neither is the case.

Goodman (1994) is also very concerned that the standards focus primarily on outcomes and ignore the learner. He observes that "Instead of starting with where the learner is, the standards start and end with where the learner must go, as determined by a national committee."(p.39) Goodman is concerned that the standards will attempt to make students more alike and ignore cultural differences and life experiences. He suggests that "For those who start out farthest from the standard, in language, culture, economic means, or willingness to conform, turning standards into single yardsticks can be devastating for their school experience." (p. 40)

As we approach the twenty-first century, raising academic standards is the challenge for teachers in every classroom. Despite the critics, the evolving form and content of learning standards continues to impact teaching and learning in the classroom. The trend to identify acceptable levels of academic performance for all students appears to grow stronger every day. One thing seems certain, learning standards that are aligned with assessments of student learning will continue to drive the school curriculum for many years to come.

Worksheet: Determine Appropriate Learning Standards

Directions: Ask yourself the following questions. Record your answers on a separate sheet of paper.

- Have I identified the learning standards that my students are expected to achieve?
- Are my students aware of the learning standards? How do I insure their awareness on a daily basis?
- Do I consider the learning standards when preparing daily instructional plans?
- Does the classroom environment support student efforts in achieving higher standards?
- How will the learning standards be assessed? How will the students be held accountable? (State mandated testing? Retention?)
- How will teachers be held accountable? Explain.

Suggested Activities:

- Search the Internet for your State Educational Agency. Locate the learning standards for each of the following subject areas:

   Mathematics
   Science
   English/Language Arts
   Social Studies
   Foreign Languages
   Health
   Physical Education
   Technology
   Vocational Education

- Visit the McREL website http://www.mcrel.org to learn more about learning standards.
- Search the Internet for your State Educational Agency. Locate the learning assessments for each of the following grade levels:

   Primary grades (grades K-2)
   Intermediate (grades 3-5)
   Middle School (grades 6-8)
   High School (grades 9-12)

PRIOR KNOWLEDGE: (What the learner already knows about the topic.)

In this section of the instructional plan, teachers are asked to think about what students already know about the topic or instructional content. Meaningful learning experiences require that new knowledge connect to what students already know. Therefore, teachers must consider students' prior knowledge when planning instructional presentations.

Some examples of connecting new learning to prior knowledge include:

- If the new topic for the lesson is word endings, students should already be familiar with many shorter root words. They should be able to read and write these words with little difficulty.
- If the topic of the lesson is subtraction of negative numbers, students must have a prior understanding about the concept of positive and negative numbers.
- If the new topic for the lesson is the culture of England and its relationship to other European countries, students must have an understanding of geographical location of Europe as well as knowledge of the countries that comprise the continent.

- If the new topic for the lesson is on patterns of sexual response, students must have a basic knowledge of the male and female human anatomy.

As the teacher thinks about students' prior knowledge and what is needed to understand new topics, the teacher will discover how to make learning relevant.

RATIONALE FOR LESSON: (Reason for teaching this topic; value of knowledge/skill.)

When planning instructional presentations, the teacher will want to consider why it is important for students to learn the topic and content of the lesson. Sometimes the rationale for instruction can be simple. For example, you want students to develop literacy skills or to develop computational skills in mathematics. At other times, the reason for learning a particular topic or skill is specified by others. For example, the reason for learning particular content may be to achieve a passing score on a standardized test.

Generally speaking, all instructional presentations should have a clear and reasonable rationale. The following list provides several rationales for instruction:

- to review or expand knowledge
- to understand abstract concepts
- to make informed decisions
- to develop an appreciation for…
- to change students' behavior
- to acquire skills
- to practice a skill

It's a good idea to communicate the instructional rationale to the students. This will enable the students to understand why they need to learn the new material and hopefully, this will make the content more meaningful to them.

MATERIALS: (A list of all materials needed for the presentation. Any published materials must be referenced according to American Psychological Association [APA] style.)

The selection of instructional materials will depend upon the subject matter and sophistication of the students. All types of materials are suitable for preparing instructional presentations. We encourage teachers to consult numerous resources to find creative and stimulating materials for instruction. In the following discussion we provide some guidelines to assist the teacher in finding suitable materials for instruction.

Locating Suitable Instructional Materials

Classroom teachers usually have a wealth of resources to use for instruction. Sometimes the plethora of materials requires that teachers make choices concerning which materials to use. Let us examine some types of materials that are commonly available.

Most teachers have access to commercial textbooks and workbooks that are appropriate for instructional purposes. Colleagues or supervisors may also offer suggestions and ideas for instruction. Libraries and bookstores have a wide variety of materials available for use in planning instruction. Teacher resource centers often contain samples of textbooks for all subject areas. Teacher editions of published textbooks include a copy of the student textbook and many suggestions for instruction. You can find many creative and interesting teaching strategies as well as the correct answers to all questions in the teacher editions. Student workbooks, which contain suitable worksheets for classroom use, may be also available. For instructional purposes, you can photocopy these pages for use in your lesson/presentation (if you buy the book).

Other instructional materials that you may want to include in an instructional presentation are: charts, diagrams, pictures, maps, globes, musical instruments, games, science and math instruments, magazines, periodicals, journals, flannel boards, puppets, films, filmstrips, audio-tapes, transparencies, and computer programs. You are encouraged to investigate appropriate media for instruction. Remember that visuals enhance learning by providing multiple sensory experiences for the learner.

Catalogues from booksellers, software sellers, and video dealers can be unexpected sources of valuable materials. Go beyond the advertiser's designated label. The "Grades 7-9" designation may hide material that is very well-suited to motivate upper primary students. Often media that is not designated as instructional can be well adapted to instructional needs. For example, clips from <u>Star Wars</u> or other popular media can enhance a discussion of the book, <u>The Fiction in Science Fiction.</u>

One of your best sources for material is your home computer. In addition to <u>Amazon.com,</u> which has an exhaustive array of books on virtually any topic, simply selecting a search engine and typing in key words can come up with sources you would never find anywhere but on the World Wide Web. Individuals sometimes post their favorite articles, or bits of their thesis. Private and government organizations post documents that provide extensive information often complete with a list of references. Searching the Web for sources is only limited by imagination.

Novice teachers will find that consulting published materials facilitates the planning process. Once you gain some experience you will want to compose your own worksheets and visuals. Be sure to cite the published source or reference that you use. Accurate citations in your instructional plans enable you to go back and find an original source. It also allows others to refer to the source. When citing published sources be sure to use the American Psychological Association (APA) formats. APA format is required in the field of psychology and education. APA also includes guidelines for citing references derived from electronic sources. (See Appendix B for guidelines in using the APA format.)

Worksheet: Determine Instructional Content

Directions: Ask yourself the following questions. Record your answers on a separate sheet of paper.

- Did I check the prescribed school district curriculum for this subject area?
    Is this topic appropriate for the grade level that I am teaching?
- Did I consult the appropriate learning standards?
    Does the lesson help the students meet the prescribed learning standards for the subject area and grade level?
- Did I review the students' textbook and workbooks?
    Are student resources helpful for instruction?
    Do the resources provide a framework for guided practice?
    Do the resources provide opportunities for independent practice?
- Did I examine the teacher's manual?
    Does it offer any ideas for instruction?
    Are there any activities suggested that can be used for classroom presentations?
    Are there any ideas on how to motivate students?
    Are there any suggestions on how to modify instruction for special learners?
    Are there any activities suggested that can be used for follow up or homework?
- Did I check out other resources such as the school library or teacher resource center?
    Are there materials available for classroom use related to my topic?
    How do I gain access to these materials?
- Are there any films or videos related to this topic?
    Where are these films located?
    How long are the films?
    Are they appropriate for this topic?
    Are there short clips that could be used to enhance the presentation?
- Did I check out computer resources?
    Are there computer software applications related to this topic?
    Are the programs suitable for independent student research?
    Can the programs be used during class to enhance the instructional presentation?
    Are there any web sites related to this topic?
    Are these sites useful for preparing the instructional plan?
    Are these sites suitable for student research on the topic?

Worksheet: Evaluate Instructional Materials
Directions: Ask yourself the following questions. Record your answers on a separate sheet of paper.

- Are the materials interesting and well written?
    - Do the materials stimulate student interest? Explain.
    - Are the materials appropriate for the students' grade level?
    - Are reading materials suitable for the students' reading ability?
    - Are the materials easy to follow and understand?
    - Is the format attractive and easy to follow?
    - Are the directions clear?
- Do students have adequate knowledge to relate to the materials?
    - Do students have experience working with this type of material?
    - Will students need special instructions?
    - Does the written text explore the content in adequate depth?
- Are the illustrations appealing and helpful in understanding the content?
    - Are illustrations realistic and accurate?
    - Are they cartoon-like?
    - Do the illustrations clarify the content?
- Is the content accurate and current?
    - Are important concepts represented to insure accuracy?
    - When wee the materials published?
    - Are all ethnic groups and women adequately represented?
- Did I examine the teacher's manual?
    - Does the teacher's manual provide suggestions to motivate students?
    - Are there numerous literacy activities to extend the student's learning?
    - Are there ideas on how to adapt instruction to meet the needs of special learners?

PROCEDURES:

In the classroom, instructional plan procedures typically include three distinct sections, a motivational activity, a developmental activity and a summary activity. Usually, instructional time is allocated for each of these activities. For a presentation, instructional time may be extended or shortened, however, organizing your plan in a similar manner will be helpful.

The Motivational Activity

The motivational activity is often very brief and used to introduce the topic to the group. The purpose of the motivational activity is to stimulate interest and activate prior knowledge. If learners are not interested in the topic and if they cannot relate the material to something they already know, the lesson/presentation will be unsuccessful. While a wide range of activities, are considered suitable for motivating interest, it is important to consider learners' characteristics and a teacher's abilities when deciding what to do.

The motivational activity gives learners a chance to FOCUS on what they already know about the subject or topic. The motivational activity serves the following purposes:

- Stimulates interest
- Involves the learner
- Draws on the learner's past experience
- Relates to the objective of the instructional plan

Use motivational activities whenever:
- Starting something NEW
- Resuming an interrupted class/session

The following are examples of motivational activities:

Before choosing your examples be sure they are related to your topic. Cartoons and films can be fun, but you don't want your students wondering why you included them.

- Use a cartoon on an overhead projector to illustrate an idea
- Write some key concepts on the board to review yesterday's lesson
- Create an atmosphere in the room . . . e.g. play music, describe a special place
- Show a film clip
- Pose a question - open-ended
- Tell a joke
- Tell a story
- Recite a poem
- Brainstorm a List
- Create a semantic map
- Display an artifact
- Demonstrate a skill
- Show a picture/photograph
- Pose a problem
- Present a rationale
- Use a transparency on an overhead
- Involve students in planning projects
- Give out stickers/novelty objects
- Present a puzzle
- Play a tape
- Be enthusiastic
- Personalize information
- Demonstrate a magic effect (trick)
- Present relevant and interesting statistics

This is an example of how a teacher may personalize the topic during the motivational activity:

Today we're starting a unit about drugs. Some of you have had drug education and others haven't, but each of us has certain expectations about it simply because of what we've heard about drug education.

This is an example of "posing" a problem:

Divide the class into groups of five or six students each and assign a project to each group. Be prepared to answer the question, "Why do people take the following drugs? Aspirin, cocaine, marijuana, valium, etc."

This is an example of using a film clip and presenting relevant and interesting statistics:

Introduce the film (name of the film) by telling learners that it is estimated that one out of four children have been affected by an alcoholic parent or relative.

This is an example of using a film clip and posing a question:

Introduce the film (name of the film). Pose questions learners are expected to answer after viewing the film.

This is an example of personalizing:

Discuss the learners view on smoking. How many people here smoke? At what age did you begin? What are some of the factors that influence people to begin smoking?

This is an example of how to present a rationale:

Inform the audience/class that this lesson/presentation has two purposes.
- To review . . . .
- To show . . . .

This is an example of using an overhead:
Make a transparency of a drug advertisement to be shown on an overhead projector. Show transparency and then ask questions relating to the topic.

Worksheet: Plan a Motivational Activity
Directions: On a separate sheet of paper, list specific examples of appropriate motivational activities for each of the following instructional events.

- to introduce the letter "m" to a group of kindergarten children.
- to introduce the persuasive essay to a group of eighth graders.
- to introduce your colleagues to an Internet training session.
- to introduce the topic of photosynthesis to a ninth grade Biology class.
- to introduce the concept of fractions to a group of third graders.
- to introduce a group of health care workers to a new therapy for arthritis.
- to introduce the Battle of Gettysburg to an eighth grade class.
- to introduce the theory of "Supply and Demand" to a 12th grade economics class.
- to introduce the dangers of tobacco to a 5th grade class.
- to introduce new vocabulary words related to food (e.g. bread, cheese, milk, eggs, butter, meat, etc.) to 10th graders in a foreign language class (French, Spanish or Russian).

The Developmental Activity

The developmental activity, often the longest part of the presentation, outlines specific steps or procedures for teaching the skill or content. It is a list of steps that you will follow in order to teach the content or skill. The list may include content to be discussed, questions to be asked, instructions for group work, workbook pages to be completed, films to be shown, etc.

You should select an instructional activity that best meets the needs of the learners and the subject matter. The instructional activity should provide opportunities for guided practice. Guided practice enables you, the teacher, to guide learners as they practice the new materials. You must explain to the students what they are supposed to be doing and why. Guided practice allows the learners to see where they make mistakes; it also shows learners how to do things, and it may affect their attitudes or values.

Once the learners have displayed evidence that they have mastered the concepts under the guidance of the teacher, you will want to provide opportunities for independent practice. Independent practice is an activity that allows learners to practice a new skill or to use newly acquired knowledge on their own. Teachers often use worksheets or writing assignments to provide opportunities for independent practice. Independent practice allows the individual learner to demonstrate their proficiencies and allows the instructor to assess learner progress.

During the developmental activity, you will want to ask questions to ascertain learner understanding. Your questions should also serve to encourage critical thinking about the topic.

In order to develop proficiency in questioning, the authors suggest that you plan your questions as you are preparing your instructional plan. Pre-planning questions will enhance the actual instructional presentation. Be sure to follow these directives:

- Write down your questions in advance. Try to think of all the possible questions you might ask. You can list these within your instructional plan or on separate index cards for easy reference.
- Plan to ask questions at different levels of understanding (literal, inferential, critical). For example, if you are discussing a short story in an elementary school classroom, you might ask your students the following questions:

Literal level -   Who is the main character?
Inferential level -   Why do you think that the main character was mean?
                           (Student must determine answer by considering details
                           of the story?)
Critical level -   What would you have done if you were the main
                           character and why? (Student must determine the answer
                           by application of story to one's own life experiences.)

- Plan to ask divergent and convergent questions. Divergent questions have more than one answer. For example: "What were some of the hardships experienced by the Pilgrims when they
arrived in America?" A convergent question has only one answer. For example: "What was the name of the Pilgrim's ship?"
- Plan appropriate follow-up questions. "Why?" and "Why not?" are usually appropriate follow-up questions. These questions provide insight into the learner's thinking process.

Expect that learners will pose questions that you cannot answer. But if you prepare questions in advance, the likelihood of this happening will be minimized. Don't bluff. Perhaps someone else knows the answer. If not, research the question and answer it at a later date. You may say, "That's a very good question, I'm not sure but I'll get back to you with an answer." You can also provide the learner direction on how to further research the topic.

The Summary Activity

The summary activity is an important component of the instructional plan. This final activity provides closure and an opportunity for the teacher to summarize what has been covered. It is also an opportunity to ascertain if the learners did in fact learn the intended skills or content. An easy way to plan the summary is to review the behavioral objective of your instructional plan. Compare the summary activity to the behavioral objective. Does the behavioral objective and summary activity match? Consider the behavioral objective that follows:

"Learners will list the causes of the Civil War in their notebooks."

An appropriate activity might be that learners work with partners to determine the causes of the Civil War and record these responses in their notebooks. You may also want to review the ideas orally or perhaps use a visual display.

Some other suggestions for your summary or closure include the following:
- "Tomorrow we will begin to focus on the areas you indicated today that you would like to investigate in this lesson."
- Conclude the activity by asking what areas of _____ can be changed by positive actions of students at home.
- Conclude by relating the individual descriptions to . . . by saying, "Although we do know about the effects on _____, knowing this may explain why people feel, behave and think differently about . . ."
- Conclude by suggesting available resources to . . .
- Conclude by emphasizing the importance of . . .
- Ask group:
       How does this information compare with . . .? or
       Knowing this information explain why an individual would . . .
- Conclude discussion with the evaluation of the benefits of . . .
- Conclude with a summary of . . .

-     Conclude by reviewing the similarities and differences between . . .
-     Conclude by reminding students that . . .

PROCEDURAL ADAPTATION: (Identify special learners in the group and describe how you plan to meet their special needs.)

An effective teacher knows how to adjust instruction to meet the needs of the learners. As discussed above, you must consider what the learner already knows to enable them to learn the new materials. The authors suggest that you ask yourself, "What do the learners already know about this topic?" and, "Why should I teach this material?"

New learning must build on prior knowledge so that the information presented makes sense to the learner. Similarly, there should be some valid reasons why certain topics are included within the presentation. In the classroom, these reasons provide a rationale for teachers (and also learners) to make sense of the materials. For example, learning how to read and write are certainly important skills to be mastered. When teachers and learners have a clear focus on why these skills are necessary, their daily activities can be viewed as contributing to the development of a broader curriculum.

Always remember that among a large group of learners, levels of prior knowledge can differ greatly. Learners within the same group have different learning experiences as well as ability levels. You can expect that your group will include gifted learners, learning disabled and learners for whom English is a second language. Given this broad range of individual differences within the group, planning effective instructional presentations becomes a much more complicated matter.

When preparing large group presentations, you will most likely prepare activities which will meet the needs of the largest group within the classroom, namely the average learners. In the classroom, it is also your responsibility to accommodate the special learners (gifted, Learning Disabled [LD], English as a second language, visually impaired, learning impaired, etc.) who may be in the group.

The instructional plan format asks that you consider adaptations to the instructional procedures. These adaptations might include more challenging assignments for the gifted learner or modified work for the learning disabled. Your adaptation may be as simple as pairing brighter learners with slower learners so that they may work cooperatively.

Classroom teachers face the great challenge of meeting the needs of an increasingly diverse student body. Students who enter the classroom may be male or female and come from various ethnic backgrounds. They come from all socioeconomic groups and from homes where English may or may not be spoken. In addition, the students may possess incredibly high levels of intelligence or be severely disabled in some way. Given the wide range of student differences, it is imperative that classroom instruction meets the special needs of all learners. In this section, you will learn more about special learners and how to adjust your instructional presentation to meet individual needs.

LEARNERS WITH DIFFERENCES

Since the 1970s, there has been a steady effort to educate children with differences in regular educational settings with their peers. The year 1977 marked the implementation of the <u>Education for All Handicapped Children Act, PL 94-142</u>. For the first time, public schools were required to identify, and subsequently provide, special education services to all children with educational, developmental, emotional, or physical disabilities (Turnbull & Turnbull, 1998). Now known as the <u>Individuals with Disabilities Education Act</u> (IDEA), the mandate guarantees all children the right to a "free appropriate public education," regardless of the severity of the handicapping condition.

By 1977, most states were already initiating programs to reform their special education laws, so the legislation did not represent a radical policy change. What it did accomplish was to intensify state efforts towards special education reform. Two decades later, special education programs continue to evolve and change. In 1997, the <u>Individuals with Disabilities Education Act Amendments</u> were sanctioned and the IDEA re-authorized. Although IDEA had been largely successful in its intention to provide all students with access to a free appropriate public education, past implementation had been impeded by three significant factors.   First, there were low expectations for disabled students.   Secondly, there was too little focus on translating research into practice.   Third, there was too much emphasis on the procedural paperwork that was tied to legal requirements.   Consequently, there was too little focus on teaching and learning and positive student outcomes.   The paradoxical effect of the federal laws has not been lost.   While the legislation served its intention of providing students with access to a free appropriate public education, the educational process has not achieved the desired outcomes.

The current focus in education is on outcomes for all students, as evidenced by the push for raising national standards.   Some educators are unsure of the validity of the new standards for students with special needs.   Some are worried about how the inclusion of test scores for special education students will reflect on their district.   Consider the English Language Arts Exam that was administered in Spring 1999 for the first time in New York State.   At the Milton L. Olive Middle School in Wyandanch, Long Island, only 13% of the regular school population tested at Level 1, considered a poor level of performance.   When special education students were added, the percentage soared to 21.5%.   The Loretta Park Elementary school in Brentwood, Long Island, reported a similar effect.   The 13% figure overall for students scoring at Level 1 at Loretta Park Elementary jumped to 22.6% with the addition of special education students (Saslow, 1999).

The New York State English Language Arts Exam was only a pilot (even for regular education students) and there is still quite a bit of query about how the scores should be interpreted.   However, the fact that special education students were included in the tally points to one significant fact: there are now higher expectations for students with special needs.

The Individualized Educational Program (IEP) and the IDEA

The cornerstone of special education is the Individualized Educational Program (IEP).   An IEP is a written document that prescribes specific instruction and services for the disabled student.   Each special education child has his/her own IEP with learning outcomes specified and the means by which the outcomes will be achieved.   The IEP is developed by school district committees that include teachers, school administrators, psychologists, social workers, special education teachers, parents and if appropriate, the students themselves.   The committee thus includes individuals who can offer unique perspectives and insight into formulating an effective educational plan for instruction.   PL 94-142 specifically included families of disabled children in the process of formulating the IEP.   PL 94-457 goes even farther in acknowledging that individual families, like individual children, have unique strengths and needs that should be considered in developing intervention plans (Sussell, Carr & Hartman, 1996).

Initially, school district committees developed Individualized Educational Programs that would pull special needs students out of the regular classroom setting.   Students were often isolated in special classes or resource rooms in an effort to provide specialized instruction and individualized attention.   The result however was the creation of a segregated school with special needs learners having minimal contact and interaction with non-disabled students.   Under the new IDEA, children with special needs, whether in special education or in the mainstream are required to learn the same information as non-disabled peers of the same age and grade.   Ongoing evaluation is conducted to review the child's performance compared to age- and grade- appropriate peers.   The child's strengths are identified as well as his or her needs. Generally the requirements for an IEP are as follows:

- The plan must encompass the general education curriculum and note any necessary adaptations.
- The plan must reflect that the child will participate in class, district, and state assessments.
- The plan must include notation of appropriate modifications needed to accurately measure what the child knows and can do.

Many states now mandate that special needs students participate in statewide testing. If the child cannot participate in some of the regular district and state assessments, the IEP is required to specify alternative measures that can be used to measure the child's progress (Autin, 1999).

For educators whose concern is the quality of education for children with special needs, the interpretation of statewide test scores may be moot. States are required by the IDEA to demonstrate that the goals established for children with disabilities are consistent, to the maximum extent appropriate, with the goals set for their non-disabled peers. The states are also required to set performance indicators to assess the progress of special needs' children in terms of academic achievement, dropout rates, and graduation rates. Under the federal mandate, the states must report every two years on the progress made towards reaching their goals. Furthermore, all state reports on children without disabilities must include a report on children with disabilities.

Is Inclusion All-inclusive?

Initial practices in special education focused on what was wrong with the student. In an effort to fix problems, students were removed from the mainstream group for individualized and intensive instruction. Special education programs were segregated and self-perpetuating systems. New IDEA initiatives focus on students' strengths and abilities as the emphasis shifts towards mainstreaming and inclusion. Mainstreaming refers to the selective placement of special education students in general classrooms for a significant portion of the school day. In contrast, inclusion refers to a commitment to educate all children, to the maximum extent possible, in the regular school environment (Rogers, 1993). Inclusion involves the development of individualized goals for students with special needs and meeting those needs within regular academic classrooms. Therefore, all teachers can anticipate having special learners in the classroom regardless of their subject area or grade level. Teachers must then make a commitment to helping special needs' students achieve their goals, even if they are different from the goals of the rest of the class.

Heckmon & Rike, (1994) observed that learning disabled students placed with non-disabled peers make greater gains in social behaviors and interactions, engage in fewer inappropriate behaviors, and achieve more of their personal learning objectives. Thus, inclusion benefits the special needs' students in a variety of ways. Improved learning results from peer modeling and increased access to appropriate social skills. In the segregated setting, the special needs students had limited access to "good models" of learning and behavior. The regular classroom setting offers wider access to varied learning experiences for the special learner. There are increased opportunities to develop friendships in larger classrooms and an opportunity to develop a sense of belonging to the larger school community.

Interestingly, inclusion offers even greater benefits for non-disabled students. The general school population develops an appreciation and awareness of human differences and learning styles by interacting with disabled students. Improved learning results for all students as teachers increase instructional accommodations within their regular instructional routines. Support personnel are present on a regular basis and available to provide assistance to anyone who may need some extra help. Socially, the non-disabled students have opportunities to develop friendships with different types of students, an excellent preparation for the future where individuals will be expected to work in an ever changing, diverse and integrated workplace.

Some educators are concerned that the rate of students diagnosed with learning disabilities appears to be growing at an alarming rate (Welch, 1996). However, figures can be deceiving. One reason for the increase in numbers is how we define learning disabled students.

Children with learning disabilities make up the bulk of students with special needs in regular education. Learning disabled students are described as having average or above average intelligence, but they have difficulty in specific content areas, such as reading, writing or mathematics. According to Hammill, Leigh, McNutt, and Larsen (1988), "Learning disabilities is a general term that refers to a heterogeneous group of disorders manifested by significant difficulties in the acquisition and use of listening, speaking, reading, writing, reasoning, or mathematical abilities. These disorders are intrinsic to the individual, presumed to be due to central nervous system disorder, and may occur across the life span." (p. 217)

The gap between a student's potential and his/her actual performance in the classroom, usually determine the existence of a learning disability. Since an average to above-average IQ suggests that a child should be able to learn with relative ease, a child who has difficulty learning is assumed to have a learning disability. The learning disability classification suggests a rather mild form of disability and parents readily consent to the label that will provide educational support to the child.

The second reason for the increase in students with learning disabilities may actually be due to a reluctance to classify students as mentally retarded. Interestingly, the increasing rate of children identified with learning disabilities runs parallel to a drastic decrease in children who are labeled mentally retarded. Thus, individuals who escape the label of retardation may be included in this group and have deficits in all learning areas. Children with emotional and behavioral disorders are another significant group with special needs. These students exhibit inappropriate behavior and emotions that interfere with learning. Consequently, learning behavior management strategies are of the utmost importance! Even a regular classroom can be noisy when the teacher is not in control. These students require a structured and positive classroom environment in order to learn effectively.

An increasing number of students in regular classrooms are classified as having Attention Deficit Disorders (ADD) and Attention Deficit Hyperactive Disorders (ADHD). These students exhibit inattention, distractability, and impulsiveness. They have great difficulty attending to and completing typical academic tasks within the classroom setting. In order to insure academic success, these students require a structured environment that will minimize distractions and enhance learning.

Students with physical disabilities are usually the smallest group of students with special needs to be found in a classroom. Below, we will address the needs of students with vision and hearing impairment. Even experienced teachers often lack expertise in addressing the needs of blind or deaf students.

Non-academic and Extracurricular Activities

IDEA mandates that children with disabilities must be exposed to the array of educational programs and services available to children without disabilities (Autin, 1999). These programs and services include:

- Music
- Art
- Industrial arts
- Home economics
- Vocational education
- Physical education and sports
- Counseling
- Transportation and health services
- Recreational activities
- Clubs and special interest groups
- Referrals to agencies and employment

Thus IDEA acknowledges that participation in activities outside the academic curriculum are especially valuable for children with special needs. These activities provide opportunities for socialization and interaction with their peer group.

Support Services and Placement

One of thorniest provisions of the IDEA is the concept of the "least restrictive environment" (LRE). The basic philosophy behind the LRE is the idea that placing a child in a separate educational environment is inherently stigmatizing. Several legal cases have confirmed that LRE does not necessarily mean that all students with disabilities must be educated within the regular education classroom or in their home school (Turnbull & Turnbull, 1998). Yes, some students are too disruptive for the rest of the class. And yes, cost is a factor and a significant one.

Many children with disabilities can have their needs met in a regular classroom, providing they have appropriate supports, services, aids, and accommodation. The new IDEA also allows services to be provided for, and on behalf of, children classified as general education students (Autin, 1999). This includes services such as training and professional development for the regular education teacher. Services, such as sensitivity training or initiating a peer buddy system, can also be provided to other students.

Professional development is also an integral part of the standards movement. It is essential to provide training when teachers who have never worked with students with disabilities are suddenly confronted with the daunting task of providing for special needs. Historically, regular and special education were two distinctly different fields with distinctly different personnel (Welch, 1996). Now that the lines are blurred, special and regular educators need to team up! Collaboration is a keynote of education reform and the emphasis is on teachers collaborating to meet the needs of special learners within inclusive classroom settings.

The National Education Association offers five helpful tips for successful inclusion:

- Team teach. Two or more teachers within the classroom ensure that the needs of all students are met. The regular classroom teacher and the special education teacher must schedule a common planning time each day.
- Screen students carefully. This is especially true for a large class. Students with special needs should be carefully screened to determine the probability of success in a large class.
- Cut class size. The maximum size for success is 28 students with two teachers.
- Achieve balance. No more than one-quarter of the class should consist of students with learning disabilities. The remaining three-quarters should be heterogeneous groups combining general education and gifted students.
- Focus. Always focus on the student not on the diagnosis or the label in the file. (NEA, 1996).

Behavior Supports for All Students

No one denies that children with disabilities can present a behavioral challenge. However, an effective teacher can monitor the behavior of all learners within the classroom and inclusion can be effective. Advocates of special needs' students are concerned that as more children with disabilities are included in the regular classroom, they will be banished again, this time for their behavior not their disabilities, because general educators do not have expertise in behavior management (Autin, 1999).

The new IDEA allows schools and districts more flexibility in dealing with truly threatening student behavior. Keeping schools user-friendly and safe is one of the goals of the education initiative. At the same time, the new IDEA requires schools to identify the behavioral aspects of children with disabilities, identify the causes of those behaviors, and implement positive behavior support plans to address the underlying causes of problem behaviors. The aim is to create a positive learning environment for all learners within inclusive classrooms.

One of the most difficult problems for educators is teaching children with attention-deficit/hyperactivity disorder (ADHD). There is no question that children with ADHD are disruptive. Some children fidget in their seats - others cannot stay in their seats. Anything can be a distraction. The following strategies are designed to accommodate the needs of children with ADHD and learning disabilities - and create a classroom conducive for learning for all students. Taught in workshops for pre-service and in-service teachers, these strategies parallel the guidelines recommended by the U.S. Department of Education (Blazer, 1995). As you examine the listing, note that the suggestions reflect sound educational practices that result in a positive learning environment for *all students,* not just those with learning differences.

Create a structured learning environment:
- Establish routines and schedules. Follow them consistently.
- Seat students within ready eye contact and away from distractions.
- Keep transition time short.
- Be sure class rules are clear. Keep them posted.

Simplify and repeat instructions about assignments:
- Keep oral directions clear and simple. For multi-step directions, stop between each one.
- When possible, have students repeat instructions.
- Keep visual information on tests and worksheets minimal. Provide a lot of blank space.

Back up verbal instructions with visual instructions:
- Write instructions on the board or provide a written instruction sheet.
- Designate a class note taker who can fill in details that inconsistent listeners may miss.

Use a positive approach to behavior management:
- Provide frequent positive feedback.
- Reinforce effort.
- Structure tasks that are challenging but not daunting - give each student tasks he or she can successfully complete.
- Be consistent with all students.
- Remember, rewards work!
- Be adaptable.
- Provide a good mix of activities that require focus and concentration and those that offer opportunities for movement and hands-on learning.
- Welcome feedback from parents. Allow parents to participate in selecting class schedules and teachers who work well with special needs learners.

Modify test-taking:
- Be flexible with time limits
- Give take-home tests where possible.
- Allow students to use a computer for essay questions.
- Substitute a research/term paper for a test.

Use technology:
- Tape record assignment instructions, lectures, and study guides to help students prepare for tests.
- Encourage students to submit work that is word processed or typed.
- Surf for software - use computer programs that help students with organization, writing, outlines, math, and visualization.
- Make use of manipulatives.
- Record your own videos. Use videocassettes to provide models of appropriate and inappropriate classroom behavior.
- Make videos part of your reward system. Reward good behavior by showing a video in class or giving out coupons for video rental (Salend, 1995).

Modify materials:
- Keep a set of textbooks that has key points highlighted for easy access.
- Break up worksheets into smaller parts by folding or using blocking paper.
- Offer parents the option of purchasing a separate set of textbooks to keep at home in case books needed for homework or study are left at school.

Tailor homework assignments:

- Reduce the volume of homework where appropriate. But be careful - strategies such as assigning only even-numbered or odd-numbered problems may enable students to create assignments, but at the risk of lowered expectations.
- Allow extended time for homework completion by means of a contract. For example, no penalty if work is submitted in 2-4 days.
- Have students keep a separate notebook for recording assignments.
- Make use of peer tutors - in fact, peer tutoring is a great way to help learning disabled (LD) or slower students keep up with faster peers, and offers a good opportunity for social interaction and modeling of social skills.

Another useful instructional technique is to use strategic approaches for completing academic tasks. All students can learn these strategies and apply them appropriately to the learning situation. For example, critical thinking skills such as interpreting implied ideas can be developed by providing a clear strategy for students to follow. Here is an example of a strategy used by a teacher to help a group of mildly behaviorally disordered students in a class for social skills to interpret pictures.

A - Action. Look for the action in the picture.

I - Idea. Guess the main idea of the picture.

D - Details. Study each picture in detail.

E - Explanation. Read the explanation with the picture (Marks, Van Laeys, Bender, & Scott, 1996).

The regular and repeated use of the AIDE strategy by learning disabled students results in improved levels of comprehension. Non-disabled students also benefit from strategies such as this one.

A similar strategy, RIDER, works to help students develop reading skills:

R - Read.   Read the first sentence.

I - Imagine.   Imagine a picture of that sentence.

D - Describe.   Describe the image, and adapt it to new information.

E - Evaluate.   Evaluate your image to be sure it is complete.

R - Repeat.   Repeat this process with each sentence.

You can come up with your own acronyms to clarify steps for interpretation, problem solving, classroom management, or any other task you can come up with. Again, these strategies will work for slower learners and everyone else too.

Team Up

One universal statement by general educators about including children with special needs is that one teacher cannot go it alone! As mentioned above, an ideal situation would be a partnership between special and regular education teachers and many schools are attempting to implement this type of arrangement. However, the cost of such collaboration is very high, and qualified personnel may not be available to achieve the ideal in inclusive classrooms.

To meet the needs of students and teachers, some school districts have employed paraprofessionals. Paraprofessionals are usually individuals with some college education, but they may be lacking teaching credentials. Some individuals pursue teaching certificates while working as paraprofessionals. However, the level of education and degree of training each paraprofessional receives, varies considerably.

Research on the effectiveness of using paraprofessionals in inclusion classrooms has been minimal. Marks, Schrader, & Levine, (1999) researched the effectiveness of paraprofessionals whom they called paraeducators. These paraeducators were working with inclusion students in elementary and middle school. The 20 paraeducators in the study ranged from 22 to 46 years of age, and 18 possessed educational degrees (BA or MA). The levels of education and training of these study participants were not typical.   The researchers found that the dual concerns of developing a positive working relationship with the classroom teacher and ensuring positive responses for both the paraeducator and the inclusion students have led many paraeducators to assume primary responsibilities for managing student behavior.   Many regular education teachers seemed to be more than happy to relinquish the task of managing the behavior of the inclusion student. The paraeducators, in turn, found satisfaction in being perceived by the teacher as the "expert" on behavior management.   Both teachers and paraeducators appeared to be happy with the model in this study, and the children seem to be faring well. However, as the researchers observed, this arrangement keeps the classroom teacher from assuming primary responsibility for the inclusion student, who after all, is an integral member of the class.

Several strategies are recommended for facilitating the best possible partnership between the teacher and paraeducator:

- Teachers and paraeducators should engage in ongoing collaborative meetings for sharing areas of expertise, and for discussing and defining areas of responsibility, including a plan for "fading" the level of support provided by the paraeducator.
- Both teachers and paraeducators need ongoing training on the goals of inclusive practices, including specific skill areas, such as curricular and academic modifications, and positive behavioral support strategies.
- Ongoing research is needed to identify strategies for more effective collaboration and delegation in the inclusion classroom (Marks et al., 1999).

Teamwork takes time!   If you work with a paraeducator, be sure to set aside time for discussion. Share ideas. At this point, paraeducators do have the expertise in behavior management. Learn from them - and share your academic knowledge.   These conversations will help paraeducators to begin to provide students with more effective learning strategies. Remember, learning and behavior are intertwined. Both involve long-range planning and ongoing partnership.

Remember that team members are not only those in the classroom. The development of an IEP can involve the school social worker, speech and language pathologist, physical therapist, counselor, as well as school administrators. Above all, do not forget the parents! Professionals, including teachers, need to establish strong bonds with families in order to understand their individual needs and enlist their active participation in their children's education.

Blind and Visually Impaired Students

Students with visual impairments can succeed in the academic setting and beyond, but their development proceeds at different rates and often in different sequences than their sighted peers.   Visual impairment creates a number of unique educational needs:

- Vision loss can result in delayed concept development, which requires specific intervention to facilitate normal development.
- Students must learn with alternative strategies that draw upon their other senses.
- Students frequently need specialized skills as well as specialized books, materials, and equipment for learning through alternate modes.
- Students are limited in acquiring incidental knowledge. They are often unaware of subtle happenings in the environment.
- Curriculum areas that require special strategies or adaptations for visually impaired students include: concept development, academic functioning, communication skills, sensory/motor skills, social/emotional skills, orientation and mobility, daily living skills, career/vocational skills, and the use of low vision (American Federation for the Blind, 1999).

The classroom environment is a highly visual place. In fact, the lavish use of visual materials is a good way of engaging children with learning disabilities as well as regular students. Our obvious dependence on visual stimulation underscores the difficulties facing children who are blind or have limited vision.

Though the task may seem daunting, remember that the keynote is teamwork. Parents of visually impaired children typically seek to take an active role in their child's education. Collaboration may involve an orientation and mobility specialist, as well as a Braille teacher. For organizing the classroom, the following guidelines are very valuable for providing blind and visually impaired children with the same quality of education and experience as sighted peers:

- Be verbal. Verbal descriptions will help the child understand what is happening in the classroom.
- Use names when calling on students.
- Provide clear, precise verbal descriptions when modeling an action.
- Explain what you are doing to help the blind child interpret situations she or he cannot see: "While the class sits quietly, I'll be right back with the blocks for our math lesson."
- Verbalize what you write on the board or on overheads. Spell out difficult words.
- Augment storybook illustrations with verbal descriptions, especially when the pictures carry the plot.
- When describing objects, think about attributes other than color: shape, size, texture, weight, and location.
- Use normal language. Trying to eliminate words like "look" or "see" (Castellano, 1999). It is not politically correct, and it is highly impractical!

You do not have to restructure the classroom routine to accommodate a blind child. You do have to help the child become familiar with the routine. For example: Help the child organize his or her desk or storage space for maximum independence.

- Adapt materials or parts of the lesson where necessary.
- Provide lots of hands-on opportunities. All children are stimulated by hands-on experience, and hands-on experience is especially valuable for children with visual impairments.
- Model movements by moving the blind child through the motions. Think of the value of Gardner's kinesthetic intelligence to a blind child.
- Offer information but not help. Like all children, blind children need time to explore and correct their mistakes.
- Understand and respect the skills of blindness.
- Provide Braille which is the equivalent of print reading and writing material.
- Remember that the sense of touch is a reliable source of information.
- Do not coddle. By using their orientation and mobility skills, blind children become more independent.
- Respect the use of sound, memory, mental mapping, and various special techniques. Sighted students as well can benefit from honing new strategies, and blind and sighted students will develop better understanding of one another.

Hearing Impaired/Deaf Students

Interpreters are the most common resource provided to deaf or hearing-impaired students in the regular classroom. Hearing disabled students generally use some form of English sign or cueing system at school, although some students communicate primarily through American Sign Language or Pidgin Signed English. Adapting the mode of communication in the classroom to integrate deaf students into all activities is a challenge. And like other adaptations to special needs, it cannot be accomplished alone. To successfully educate deaf students, team members need a) up-to-date information about the abilities of the student, b) the involvement of the interpreter if one is employed, and c) ongoing monitoring of progress to ensure that the child's language progresses at the desired developmental level (Luetke-Stahlman,1998).

Accommodating the needs of hearing disabled children involves modifications of the classroom environment as well as resources and materials:

The Listening Environment
- Try to eliminate extraneous noise. Use of curtains, rugs, and acoustical tiles can be helpful.
- Advocate the use of quieter alarms or signals for hearing children.
- Captioning at an appropriate language level is necessary! More than 60 libraries produce captioned films and videotapes indicated by "CC."

The Physical Environment
- Survey the environment for ways to enhance visual prompts and decrease eyestrain, such as aesthetic bulletin boards and breaks from long periods of focused attention.
- Check your seating arrangements. Hearing impaired students should be situated where they can see both adults and peer speakers and are separated from hallway noise or extraneous classroom noise.
- Ensure that seating facilitates communication and integration. Do not allow the child to be excluded or singled out. Semi-circles and cluster groupings that provide the hearing impaired child a good view of peer and adult speakers are ideal. In addition, the small groupings facilitate involvement in learning for all students.
- Adapting tests and grading. Choices include:
    Utilizing test study guides that offer a variety of answer forms.
    Giving frequent quizzes.
    Using alternative response forms where existing formats impede comprehension.
    Try the use of key word strategies, additional time, and the use of practice tests.
- Increase opportunities for face-to-face interaction.
- Reduce the level of abstraction when presenting information, and use attractive visual representations (for blind children, clear verbal representations).
- Make information relevant to life.
- Match the learning style of the student and the instructor.
- Identify who is speaking by using names, pointed gestures, or asking the person to stand.
- Make lavish use of technology - and individualize!

All Learners Are Gifted

Learners, who show evidence of high performance and exceptional potential, are often described as being gifted. These individuals display exceptional ability or outstanding performance in one or more of the following areas: general intellectual ability, specific academic aptitude, creative and productive thinking, visual and performing arts or leadership (Gifted and Talented Children's Act of 1978, PL 950561, section 902).

There are many misconceptions about the term "gifted" since a student may be gifted in many areas or perhaps only one.   In academic settings, the term "gifted" usually refers to an individual who demonstrates outstanding performance on academic tasks such as reading, writing and mathematics. However, researchers are beginning to recognize that individuals can demonstrate giftedness in many different ways.

One researcher who has contributed to our knowledge of giftedness is Howard Gardner. More than a decade ago, Howard Gardner (1983) introduced the concept of multiple intelligences. In Gardner's viewpoint, children are much more complex than the sum of their IQ points and test scores.

Gardner identified seven intelligences:
- **Linguistic:** sensitivity to the meaning and order of words.

- **Logical/Mathematical:** the ability to reason deductively or inductively and to recognize abstract patterns and relationships.
- **Musical:** sensitivity to pitch, melody, rhythm, and tone.
- **Bodily/Kinesthetic:** the ability to use the body to create, solve problems, and convey meaning; and to skillfully handle objects.
- **Visual/Spatial:** the ability to perceive the world accurately and to recreate and transform those perceptions mentally or concretely.
- **Interpersonal:** the ability to understand people and relationships.
- **Intra-personal:** the ability to be deeply aware of inner feelings, intentions, and goals.

Recently, Gardner added an eighth intelligence, the **naturalist**, "who is able readily to recognize flora and fauna, to make other consequential distinctions in the natural world, and to use this ability productively," as in farming or biological science (Gardner, 1995, p. 206). As examples of the naturalist, Gardner cites Charles Darwin and E. O. Wilson. He also adds, "youngsters exploit their naturalist's intelligence as they make acute discriminations among cars, sneakers, or hairstyles."

In other words, all learners (even those who have learning, developmental, or physical disabilities) can be quite competent in intelligence or "gifted" when one's definition is not constrained by the usual academic criteria. For example, children who are learning disabled can possess artistic or musical talent. Children with physical disabilities can excel at sports when competing with like peers. Children with disabilities often have difficulty in learning social skills, but when included in activities with peers, they may show keen insight into people and human relationships.

Critics suggest that gifted programs are really about snobbery and class distinctions. However, if the classroom teacher views all learners as being gifted in some way (as suggested by Gardner) we can use knowledge of individual learning strengths to enhance classroom instruction.

Here is an example of how the concept of multiple intelligences can be integrated into the classroom, giving all learners a chance to shine. Take a class trip to a park. For a lesson on parks, students can:

- Sing a song or compose an original piece of music about parks.
- Build a model of a park.
- Share artwork or writing about parks.
- Perform a solo or group dance. Be a tree or a squirrel.
- Engage in shared reading or discussion about animals that live in the park.
- Represent a dramatic play the way a worm moves through the earth.
- Interview a groundskeeper about her or his responsibilities and report their findings.
- Share their feelings about the homeless people who live in the park.
- Estimate the number of trees in the park, using a small area as a basis (Burchfield, 1996).

These are only a few of the boundless possibilities. To promote the intelligences of learners with diverse needs, teachers have to be flexible, to think in terms of extending ability not disability. Trust your own imagination, and you will help your students to develop and explore theirs. Remember that every learner has a gift. It is your job to find it!

MULTICULTURAL CONCERNS

Classrooms are becoming increasingly diverse culturally, linguistically, and economically. By the year 2000, more than one-third of our students will be from culturally and ethnically diverse families, a figure expected to increase substantially over the first quarter of the new century (Cruz, 1999; Patrick & Reinhartz, 1999).

Diversity itself can be a positive influence in our schools, encouraging exploration of different cultures, histories, and perspectives, increasing our sensitivity to others as well as providing incentive for self-exploration and growth providing that we are prepared for the challenge of teaching a diverse population of learners. The question is, how well are teachers prepared for the multicultural classroom? The answer, unfortunately, is disappointing if not discouraging.

According to a 1998 study by the U.S. Department of Education, experienced and novice teachers alike do not feel they are well prepared to teach students from diverse cultural backgrounds. In fact, only 20% felt prepared to teach students with limited English proficiency or from diverse backgrounds (Cruz, 1999). This was not a survey of teachers in upscale suburban schools or insular communities, but a nationally representative sample of full-time public school teachers representing a variety of subjects. Of special concern, more than half (54%) had experience in teaching diverse groups, and yet they still felt unprepared for the task.

Paradoxically, as the population of learners grows more diverse, the teaching force is becoming even more homogenous. Despite talk about recruiting minority teachers, only a scant 5% of the teachers at the time of the new millennium will be people of color (Cruz, 1999). The vast majority of primary and secondary school teachers are white, middle-class females as they have been in the past. At the university level, the balance shifts by gender but not by ethnicity. Gender issues play a prominent role in the theme of multiculturalism on college campuses, including sexual orientation (Rhoads, 1998). At the secondary school level, Allan (1999) notes that even the most multiculturally sophisticated teachers often overlook students who come from gay households or are personally grappling with issues about their sexual orientation.

When we include gender and sexual orientation to the perennial issue of race and the proliferation of new immigrant groups in the United States, it is not surprising that few teachers describe themselves as prepared to deal with multi-cultural issues. The scope of diversity itself is daunting! When this is combined with dire predictions, not necessarily from conservatives, that multiculturalism in education will lead to "Balkanization" and a focus on "identity politics" rather than broadening knowledge and learning, the challenge may seem insurmountable. However, in spite of the popular mythology surrounding multicultural education, and the apprehensions of many teachers, a national college study has found that students in institutions with a strong commitment to diversity expressed a similarly strong commitment to promoting racial understanding (Rhoads, 1998).

Rhoads sees identity politics as "democracy playing itself out." Karamcheti and Lemert (1991) see multiculturalism as an expression of "who matters." It encompasses giving different people a chance to speak and knowing when to keep silent. The students who recognize that appreciating diversity promotes understanding are aware that everyone matters, that everyone has something important to say. As teachers, we can allow democracy to play itself out in the classroom by giving different people a chance to speak and showing that everyone matters in an environment that is a microcosm of our society.

The apprehension that teachers experience in a culturally diverse classroom typically has a common cause: lack of adequate preparation. There is a sizable gap between the content of teacher preparation courses and the real life experience of many of our students (McBee, 1998). An analysis of the experience of 17 student teachers from five universities revealed that the presentation of material under the framework of multiculturalism perpetuated stereotypical thinking and prejudice toward certain groups. Furthermore, the basic beliefs and attitudes of the prospective teachers remained unchanged (Fry & McKinney, 1997). The student teachers showed none of the "willingness to question ourselves: the sources of our knowledge and the authority of our teaching" that is the essence of an authentic, culturally sensitive perspective (Karamcheti & Lemert, 1991).

If prospective teachers are not provided with the knowledge and insight needed to grapple with multicultural issues, we are destined to have multicultural education that goes no further than the "heroes and holidays" or "faces, facts, and fiestas" approach to teaching and learning (Cruz, 1999). As Cruz wryly observes, "Multicultural education is more than adding a few pieces of literature written by an author of color..." In fact, if there is no genuine multi-cultural perspective, who will interpret the work of this "alternative voice" without perpetuating prejudices and stereotypes (Berry, 1997)?

Banks (1996) identifies five basic dimensions of multicultural education:

- **Content integration** is the extent to which teachers use examples and content from a variety of cultures and groups to illustrate key concepts, principles, generalizations, and theories in their subject area.
- **Knowledge construction process** relates to the extent to which teachers help students to explore, understand, and determine how implicit cultural assumptions, frames of reference, perspectives and biases within a discipline influence the ways in which knowledge is constructed within it.
- **Prejudice reduction** targets the characteristics of students' racial attitudes and ways they can be modified by teaching methods and materials.
- **Equity pedagogy** exists when teachers change their teaching in ways that will promote academic achievement of students from diverse racial, cultural, and socioeconomic class groups. This includes using a variety of teaching styles to encompass the learning styles of diverse groups.
- **Empowering school culture and social structure** refers to grouping and labeling practices, sports participation, dichotomies in achievement, and the interaction of students and staff across racial, ethnic, and cultural lines.

Banks suggests that all five components need to be addressed if we are to achieve an authentic multicultural learning environment.

Professional Development Schools and Field Experiences

One approach to the problem has been the creation of Professional Development (PDS) schools (McBee, 1998; Patrick & Reinhartz, 1999). In the PDS paradigm, teacher education faculty work together with teachers, principals, and superintendents in the school setting. The keyword is collaboration. According to Patrick and Reinhartz, "When such collaboration exists, the educational systems become aligned in a seamless web of experiences." (p. 388) There is no single model of a PDS, but all provide preservice teachers with ample opportunities to implement an array of instructional strategies, materials, equipment, and technologies.

Although the PDS may be an ideal way to promote learning and academic achievement for diverse groups of students, it is obvious that the majority of teachers have come to their professional practice, and will continue to do so, without having been part of a "seamless web of experiences." However, many of the strategies used in PDSs can be adapted by teachers who create their own collaborative networks.

Among the activities recommended as part of PDS coursework are:

- Examine issues of effective instructional strategies, classroom management, and assessment in diverse cultural settings.
- Analyze textbooks and children's literature for treatment of people and issues representing diverse populations.
- Write and implement instructional plans that prepare curricula (Patrick & Reinhartz, 1999).

Evaluation of these and other activities by students is based on a variety of formal and informal methods, including reflective journals, portfolios, ratings, and documented knowledge of content and pedagogy as well as teaching proficiency.

If you are already teaching, activities such as these can be undertaken as part of a group. Have your own system of peer review. Try to make your group as diverse as possible. Solicit input and feedback from all members.

Field trips to schools with diverse populations can have a tremendous impact on dispelling myths and stereotypes about different groups and helping teachers, regardless of experience, to feel comfortable in a multicultural environment.

McBee (1998) describes a field trip to an urban New Jersey school as part of a PDS teacher preparation program. At first glimpse of the gritty streets and school security, the students teachers fell silent. After becoming acquainted with the school, its students and faculty, the silence was replaced by exuberance.

After the field trip, the students complete observation forms and written reflections. McBee notes that feedback consistently indicates that the visit helps to dispel myths and stereotypes about inner city schools, students, and learning. Reflections show that the trip has facilitated the introspection that is essential to genuine cultural sensitivity. The prospective teachers reflect on the differences between their own experience and those of the students; their reflections show insight, not judgment. The reflections serve as springboards for future discussion.

In contrast to the PDS approach, which has a flexible but defined framework for promoting multicultural competence, Fry and McKinney (1997) describe a study in which field experiences were incorporated into a language arts methods course in an elementary education program at an Oklahoma university. In addition to subject area and multicultural course content, the course included an action research component. Students were given three assignments based on their field experiences of classroom observation focusing on children's literacy development:

- Teaching a book discussion.
- Teaching a writing experience.
- Teaching a poetry experience.

The students also kept dialogue journals throughout the course.

In contrast to the experiences of students in standard multicultural courses, whose attitudes remain unaffected, the students in the Oklahoma program reported significant changes in attitudes. The students had far more favorable attitudes toward teaching in a culturally diverse urban school; in fact, two said they would prefer it. All reported feeling prepared to work with children from a variety of cultures.

Based on their findings with this group of primarily white, female, middle-class education students, Fry and McKinney (1997) cite several implications for teacher preparation programs. Some of these implications can be modified and extended for teachers already in practice, and at all levels of experience:

- **Early field experiences in culturally diverse settings** with a reflective component should be an integral part of teacher preparation.
- **Critically examining preconceptions and attitudes** about cultural issues within a diverse community of peers is essential.
- **Experience in diverse settings** is needed to understand and evaluate career options. Interest in urban teaching may be increased substantially.
- **Teachers need to develop their own personal teaching philosophy** that addresses attitudes toward teaching students who are culturally different.

Cruz (1999) emphasizes that teachers need staff development opportunities that link learning directly with practice. While you may not qualify as a candidate for "early field experiences," if your experience has been limited to relatively homogenous settings, you still qualify as a novice in the multicultural arena. And even if you are not scouting around for new career options and plan to stay in the same school, the demographics of the school may be changing around you. By visiting schools with diverse learners, you can bring your experience back to your own classroom, feeling prepared to deal with diversity.

Team Teaching and Technology

Barnitz and Speaker (1999) describe an elementary classroom that personifies diversity: the students are African American, Hispanic American, Asian American, Native American, and European American. When you take into consideration how many subgroups can be found in these five basic categories, you have an idea of the scope of diversity encompassed in one small room. The class is team taught, and the team includes bilingual teachers, an intern, parent volunteers, and cross-age tutors. This is definitely a classroom community!

Two key factors for individualizing instruction for diverse learners are team teaching (i.e., increasing the ratio of teachers to students) and technology (Patrick & Reinhartz, 1999). The truly multicultural elementary classroom described here has both. Using both electronic and non-electronic media, the teachers have incorporated several strategies designed to promote cultural sharing and appreciation as well as individual learning:

- **Thematic inquiry** units are used to enrich the students' appreciation of various cultures and motivate the reading of culture-specific literature along with other reading materials.
- **Discussion** is encouraged among students and adults because talking promotes language development and thinking skills.
- **Authentic assessments** are used to evaluate students' abilities in writing and comprehension.
- **Multimedia performances** are an integral part of the class.
- **Children work cooperatively and individually.**
- **Natural materials and cultural artifacts** related to different cultures are present in the classroom. Examples include travel brochures, toys, games, newspapers and other reading materials in English, menus, and even "antique" photographs or objects. These materials are used for role playing of authentic events.
- **Constant movement** is part of the plan as the children and adults move through different units.

This idealized classroom is based on a holistic vision of literacy instruction. Teachers meet frequently to plan activities. They are genuinely comfortable with cultural diversity and have learned to reflect on authentic literacy strategies to use in culturally diverse schools. As in the PDS model, collaboration is integral and essential. Based on the most successful strategies for creating a multicultural classroom, there are three simple rules:

- **Learn to collaborate.**
- **Learn to reflect.**
- **Be creative.**

Authentic Voices

A part of the field experiences in the Oklahoma program, the teaching students kept personal biographies (Fry & McKinney, 1997). Examining their own biographies and learning from the biographies proved an effective strategy for enhancing cultural awareness and sensitivity. Keeping a personal biography (or journal) is easy, and you do not have to be part of a formal group to share it. Remember the importance of collaboration. Experiences can be shared in any group, whether it is in a formal gathering or in a chance meeting in the teachers' lounge.

First-person accounts are helpful for teachers in the process of developing multicultural competence. They can be critical for students. Berry (1997) observes, "First-person accounts can crystallize issues, relationships, and experiences for students." When dealing with multicultural issues, it adds credibility to the voice of the group being studied, as well as avoiding a distant, abstract perspective that will only perpetuate the notion of "us" and "them.." Berry also notes, it will occasionally save an instructor from becoming too much of a preacher. Overall, the first-person account is an effective antidote to the pretense of "objectivity," which is too often no more than the filter of the dominant group.

One excellent way to convey authentic voice about culturally different groups and promote classroom discourse is the use of taped interviews. This does not mean going around with a concealed tape recorder and seeking out people of various colors and accents. It does mean doing some creative shopping and seeking out audiotapes (or videotapes) that are appropriate. For example, "Ghetto Life 101" is an audiotape on which a 14-year old African American boy from Chicago interviews his neighbors and family (Berry, 1997). Students can make their own tapes as part of class projects. So can teachers. In fact, for a high school or college class, a tape of teachers of diverse backgrounds discussing multiculturalism may provide humor as well as elicit discussion!

Few classrooms are as diverse as the elementary reading classroom employing the multicultural, multi-age teaching team. Many classrooms have only one teacher. How does a single individual with a given racial and ethnic background and single set of experiences reflect on the experiences of another? This question often arises in response to multi-cultural issues, yet if we take it to extreme, we would have no history classes. Who would interpret Plato? We have no professors who were around in ancient Greece. Berry (1997) states succinctly, "While it may be difficult to understand the experiences of others, it would not seem impossible if one is interested and dedicated enough."

These are two key factors in successfully incorporating diversity into the classroom: interest and dedication. Activities such as taking field trips to different schools, keeping journals, and sharing reflections; making an effort to learn about the experiences of others show interest and dedication. They show that everyone matters.

The Excluded Identity

Multcultural groups typically include individuals of diverse ethnicity. However, there is discussion that gays be considered a multicultural group. Sexual orientation is generally ignored as a multicultural issue at the high school level. Not only does this ignore the identities of a significant group of students, but it also ignores the gay themes and subtexts that appear in many literary works. Exploring gay themes and encouraging students to explore their own attitudes towards sexual orientation in their writing will have many positive effects in the classroom. Not only will students gain a richer understanding of certain literary works, but they may also learn to recognize, challenge and dispel stereotypes and prejudices. Furthermore, these exercises may also help students who are struggling with issues surrounding their own sexual orientation (Allan, 1999).

Multicultural education is not a new concept. In the 19th and early 20th centuries, writers such as Thoreau and Walt Whitman were urging Americans to stop looking backward to Europe and celebrate their own cultural uniqueness (Levine, 1996). Our cultural uniqueness as Americans is that we are not one culture but many. And cultural identity is a complex web that has many components within it. As teachers we have to demonstrate that all our identities matter.

Learners for Whom English is a Second Language (ESL)

Our multi-ethnic society provides unique challenges for the classroom teacher. Regular classroom settings often include students for whom English is a second language. These students are not disabled in any way but may have difficulty in performing academic tasks that require the ability to read and write in English. While bilingual instruction may be provided in some schools, the ultimate goal of these programs is to ease the transition into a regular classroom setting. It is interesting to note that bilingual students can suffer the same segregation problems faced by disabled students in school. Therefore, there is a growing awareness that ESL and bilingual students should be included in the regular classroom settings.

Many accommodations suggested for students with disabilities also work well with ESL and bilingual students. Appropriate accommodations include:

- simplifying and repeating instructions about assignments.
- backing up verbal instructions with visual aids.
- using a positive approach to behavior management.
- modifying materials.
- modifying test-taking.
- using technology and manipulatives
- adjusting homework assignments.

While some strategies and techniques are obviously targeted to the needs of special learners, innovative educators can draw upon these strategies and benefit all learners. In this chapter we examined many types of learners and emphasized the idea that all teachers should anticipate having many diverse learners in their classrooms. Diverse student bodies demand that behavior management and instructional strategies used in the classroom must facilitate learning for everyone. Many strategies that are suggested for learners with disabilities can enhance learning for everyone else as well. Remember that a well-structured classroom environment and highly focused instructional plans with clearly defined objectives are appropriate for all learners.

DETERMINING APPROPRIATE FOLLOW-UP ACTIVITIES/HOMEWORK: (Suggest two assignments to further enhance learning. Assignments may be review, preparation, application or long range.)

In classroom settings, teachers are expected to assign meaningful follow-up in the form of homework. Follow-up activities provide an opportunity to extend student learning. There are rarely clear cut policies available regarding this matter.

In order to prepare for teaching, the authors suggest that you think about suitable follow-up assignments for each instructional plan. Even if you are a student teacher and it is unlikely that you will actually assign, collect and correct assignments, always include a follow-up suggestion in your written instructional plan. Planning follow-up assignments will allow you to develop skills necessary to complete the task.

There are four types of follow-up activities that can be typically assigned: review, preparation, application, and long range.

A Review activity requires that the learner complete a task that reviews the concept taught in the lesson/presentation. For example, students may learn about personal pronouns. Typical review homework would require that students complete a worksheet reviewing personal pronouns. Workbooks are excellent sources for review homework. You may want to suggest readings as appropriate follow-up homework or you may have your students review science vocabulary by doing a word puzzle.

A Preparation activity requires that the learner complete a task to prepare him/her for a new project. For example, learners could be asked to bring in tee shirts in preparation for a tie-dying project. The art project may be part of a larger theme-based project. Older students can find newspaper or magazine articles, dealing with the weather, in preparation for a science lesson.

An *Application* activity requires that learners apply learning differently in other settings. For example, children working on math counting skills may be asked to count the number of socks in their drawer or the number of windows in their home. You may suggest the students use the techniques just taught at home.

Long-range assignments are typically used with mature learners who may be asked to read a particular book, work on a science project or prepare a research report. Long-range assignments enable learners to plan ahead, to develop time management skills and to study the topic in greater depth. Kindergarten children can collect pictures to assemble an alphabet book. Older students can use information learned to assemble a multimedia presentation.

Make sure that the follow-up activity is appropriate for the learner or audience. Be clear about the assignment. For younger learners and slower learners it is especially helpful to write the assignment down on the board. Plan ahead and determine follow-up assignments for the day/week.

EVALUATION:

A more detailed discussion on evaluation appears in Part I, Section III of this text. After the presentation, the teacher should evaluate teaching performance and student learning. The following outline can guide your evaluation.

a. **Teacher performance**: (Do a self-assessment in terms of objective, content and method. Identify two strengths and two weaknesses.)

b. **Student Learning**: (Did learners meet the objective? Why or why not?)

REFERENCES

5 tips for successful inclusion programs. (1996, November). NEA Today, 15.

Allan, C. (1999). Poets of comrades: Addressing sexual orientation in the English classroom. English Journal, 88(6), 97-101.

American Federation for the Blind. (1999). Educating students with visual impairments for inclusion in society: A paper on the inclusion of students with visual impairments [Online], 8 pages. Available: www.afb.org/education/jltlipaper.html [1999, July 4].

Autin, D. (1999, May). Inclusion and the new IDEA. Exceptional Parent, 66-70.

Banks, J. A. (1996). Multicultural education, transformative knowledge, and action: Historical and contemporary perspectives. New York: Teachers College Press.

Barnitz, J. G. & Speaker, R. B. (1999). Electronic and linguistic connections in one diverse 21st century classroom. Reading Teacher, 52, 874-877.

Berry, K. A. (1997). Projecting the voices of others: Issues of representation in teaching race and ethnicity. Journal of Geography in Higher Education, 21, 283-289.

Blazer, B. (1995). Theory into practice: Classroom adjustments to support sudents with attention and learning weaknesses. Intervention in School and Clinic, 30, 248.

Bloom, B. S. (1984). Taxonomy of educational objectives, Book I: Cognitive domain. White Plains, NY: Longman.

Broder, J. M. (1999, January 18). President is set to propose major changes in schools. New York Times.

Bronner, E. (1999, January 8). High mark for New York student standards. New York Times.

Burchfield, D. W. (1996). Teaching all children: Four developmentally appropriate curricular and instructional strategies in primary grade classrooms. Young Children, 52, 4-10.

Burns, A. C. & Gentry, J. W. (1998). Motivating students to engage in experiential learning: A tension-to-learn theory. Simulation & Gaming, 29, (2), 133-151.

Busching, B. A. & Slesinger, B. A. (1995). Authentic questions: What do they look like? Where do they lead? Language Arts, 72, 341-355.

Castellano, C. (1999). The blind child in the regular elementary classroom [Online], 12 pages. Available: www.nfb.org/regschol.htm [1999, July 4].

Cooney, T. J. (1994). Research and teach education: In search of common ground. Journal for Research in Mathematics Education, 25, 608-636.

Cruz, M. C. E. (1999). Preparing ourselves for a millennium of diversity, or enjoying the whole enchilada, collard greens, fry bread, and apple pie. English Journal, 88, (6), 16-18.

Emihovich, C. (1997, December 6). Colleges of education are at work on new ways to teach tomorrow's teachers. Buffalo News, p. C2.

Fry, P. G. & McKinney, L. J. (1997). A qualitative study of preservice teachers' early field experiences in an urban, culturally different school. Urban Education, 32, 184-201.

Gardner, H. (1995). Reflections on multiple intelligences: Myths and messages. Phi Delta Kappan, 77, 200-209.

Goodman, K.S. (1994, September 7). Standards, not!: The movement is being used as a cover for an attempt to centralize power. Education Week, 39-40.

Hammill, D.D., Leigh, J.E.. McNutt, G. and Larsen, S. (1988). A new definition of learning disabilities. Learning Disability Quarterly, 11, (3), 217-232.

Harrow, A. J. (1977). Taxonomy of the psychomotor domain. New York: Longman

Heckmon, M. & Rike, C. (1994). Westwood Early Learning Center: A framework for integrating young children with disabilities. TEACHING Exceptional Children, 26, (2), 30-35.

International Reading Association and National Council of Teachers of English (1996). Standards for the English Language Arts.

Joyner, M. (1995). NCTM's assessment standards: A document for all educators. Teaching Children Mathematics, 2, (1), 20-22.

Karamcheti, I. & Lemert, C. (1991). From silence to silence: Political correctness and multiculturalism. Liberal Education, 77, (4), 14-18.

Kendall, J.S. and Marzano, R.J. (1997). Content knowledge, The McRel standards database: A compendium of standards for K-12 education, 2nd ed. Retrieved November 2, 1999 from the World Wide Web http://www.mcrel.org/standards-benchmarks/docs/contents.html

Krathwohl, D., Bloom, & Masia. (1964). Taxonomy of educational objectives, Handbook II: Affective domain. New York: McKay.

Langley, D. (1993). Teaching new motor patterns--Over-coming student resistance to change. Journal of Physical Education, Recreation, and Dance, 64, (1), 27-31.

Lee, F. Y. (1992). Alternative assessments. Childhood Education, 69, (2), 72-73.

Levine, L. (1996). The opening of the American mind: Canons, culture, and history. Boston: Beacon Press.

Louis, K. S. (1998, Fall). "A light feeling of chaos:" Educational reform and policy in the United States. Daedalus, 13-40.

Luetke-Stahlman, B. (1998). Providing the support services needed by students who are deaf or hard of hearing. American Annals of the Deaf, 143, 388-391.

Marks, J. W., Van Laeys, J., & Bender, W. N., & Scott, K. S. (1996). Teachers creating learning strategies: Guidelines for classroom creation. TEACHING Exceptional Children, 28, (4), 34-36.

Marks, S. U., Schrader, C., & Levine, M. (1999). Paraeducator experiences in inclusive settings: Helping, hovering, or holding their own? Exceptional Children, 65, 315-318.

McBee, R. H. (1998). Readying teachers for real classrooms. Educational Leadership, 55, (5), 56-58.

McGee Banks, C.A. (1997). The challenges of national standards in a multicultural society. Educational Horizons, Spring, 126-132.

Morrison, G. S. (2000). Teaching in America. 2nd ed. Needham Heights, MA: Allyn and Bacon.

National Commission on Excellence in Education (1983). A nation at risk: The imperatives of educational reform. Washington, DC: U.S. Government Printing Office (ERIC Ed 279603).

New York State Board of Regents. (1991). A new compact for learning.

New York State Core Curriculum Guide for English Language Arts (Pre-K through 12).

Nuthall, G. (1999). The way students learn: Acquiring knowledge from an integrated science and social studies unit. Elementary School Journal, 99, 303-341.

New York State Education Department (1998, August). <u>Regents Strategic Plan</u> . Retrieved from the World Wide Web on July 5, 1999, <u>http://www.nysed.gov/STRATEGY/stratplan98a.htm</u>

Ostergard, S. A. (1997). Asking good questions in mathematics class: How long does it take to learn? <u>Clearing House</u>, <u>71</u>, 48-50.

Patrick, D. & Reinhartz, J. (1999). The role of collaboration in teacher preparation to meet the needs of diversity. <u>Education</u>, <u>119</u>, 388-400.

Rhoads, R. A. (1998). Student protest and multicultural reform: Making sense of campus unrest in the 1990s. <u>Journal of Higher Education</u>, <u>69</u>, 621-640.

Rogers, J. (1993). The inclusion revolution. <u>Research Bulletin, Phi Delta Kappan</u>, <u>11</u>, 1-6.

Saban, A. (1994). A bridge to books: Read aloud to children in primary education. <u>Reading Improvement</u>, <u>31</u>, 186-192.

Salend, S. J. (1995). Using videocassette recorder technology in special education classrooms. <u>TEACHING Exceptional Children</u>, <u>27</u>, (3), 4-9.

Saslow, L. (1999, May 30). The results are in for fourth-grade reading tests. Now what? <u>New York Times</u>, 10.

Savage, L. B. (1998). Eliciting critical thinking skills through questioning. <u>Clearing House</u>, <u>71</u>, 291-293.

Schmoker, M. and Marzano, R.J. (1999). Realizing the promise of standards-based education. <u>Educational Leadership</u>. <u>56</u>, (6). Retrieved July 28, 1999 from the World Wide Web: http://www.ascd.org/pubs/el/mar99/extschmoker.html

Stuart, A. (1997). Student-centered learning. <u>Learning</u>, <u>26</u>, (2), 53-55.

Sussell, A., Carr, S., & Hartsman, A. (1996, Summer). Families R Us: Building a parent/school partnership. <u>TEACHING Exceptional Children</u>, <u>28</u>, (4), 53-57.

Turnbull, H. R. & Turnbull, A. P. (1998). <u>Free appropriate public education: The law and children with disabilities</u>. Denver: Love.

Welch, M. (1996). Teacher education and the neglected diversity: Preparing educators to teach students with disabilities. <u>Journal of Teacher Education</u>, <u>47</u>, 355-366.

Wolk, R. (1998). Doing it right. <u>Teacher Magazine</u>, <u>10</u>, (1), 6.

Part I
Section II. Delivering the Presentation

Introduction

Good planning is important for effective teaching presentations. Once the instructional plan is thoroughly prepared, you are ready for the presentation. In this section, we will discuss some strategies that will ensure a successful presentation. You will learn how to implement the plan that you prepared. In addition, you will learn about strategies that make the presentation more effective such as the use of technology, magic (tricks) and humor.

Given the complex nature of student learning and the dynamics of classroom interaction, teachers will want to be flexible in their approach to delivering the presentation. Addressing all of the components of the instructional plan, does not guarantee that you will have a successful presentation.   For example, you may teach the same lesson content to two separate classes but the learners may be very different in each class. One class may have students who are below grade level in reading and writing. Your instruction will depend on what the learners need to know, understand and be able to accomplish. You will want to modify and adjust your instruction to meet the needs of your learners. Therefore, delivering an effective instructional presentation requires more than merely following the instructional plan. The effective teacher adjusts and modifies instruction within the context of the classroom dynamics.

Preparation for the Instructional Presentation

Preparation for the instructional event may be minimal or may require extra time, depending upon the activities you have chosen. If your presentation requires multimedia equipment, hands-on materials, or special room arrangements, you will have to arrive early and set up in advance. Poor preparation gets your presentation off to a poor start. Get there early, and be prepared.

Worksheet: Prepare for the Presentation
Directions: Ask yourself the following questions. Record your answers on a separate sheet of paper.
- Did you mentally rehearse the actual delivery?
- Did you time it?
- Did you prepare note cards with key ideas?
- Did you prepare questions that you plan to ask?
- Have you considered the types of responses you will receive from the learners?
- Did you anticipate the learners' questions?
- What issues might they raise?
- Are you prepared to answer these questions?
- Have you considered videotaping yourself? (Self-observation can be a very valuable learning experience.)
- Is the room large?
- What are the seating arrangements?
- Is the room conducive to the type of presentation or instruction you have prepared?
- Does the equipment (overhead projector, slide projector, video, etc.) work?

SPEECH ANXIETY

Beginning teachers sometimes experience nervousness or anxiety during instructional presentations.   The problem is relatively rare when making a presentation to a captive audience of second graders. However, place a school principal or college supervisor in the back of the classroom and the result can be a serious case of stage fright. Anxiety is heightened for inexperienced high school teachers and college professors who may be addressing an older and more sophisticated audience. Even the most confident presenters can become unnerved when the audience is composed of peers or a group of strangers. The authors recognize the importance of this issue and discuss numerous strategies that can be helpful to address the problem. See Essay 1 in Part II of this text for a more comprehensive discussion on how to reduce speech anxiety.

IMPLEMENTING THE MOTIVATIONAL ACTIVITY

The motivational activity is important to get off to a good start. Remember that your intent is to get the learners' attention and to stimulate their interest in the topic. You have planned an activity that you believe will accomplish this goal. The motivational activity is not usually very long and will typically last from three to five minutes.

Before formally beginning the presentation, be sure to get everyone's attention. If you begin the presentation without the full attention of your audience, you will have problems. This is especially true when dealing with younger children or adolescents.

How can you get the attention of a large group?

Writing or drawing assignments, accompanied by relevant assigned reading, can work to get students involved, as well as provide the teacher with information about the individuals in the class. Students can be excellent generators of ideas. Surveying the students' preliminary work can offer alternative perspectives on how to engage the class from the onset.

Often, the teacher can get everyone to quiet down and get ready to start by merely standing quietly in front of the group. Just assuming the "teacher stance" is usually enough to let the learners know that the instructor is ready to begin. If not the teacher can try one of these techniques:

- Pose the question: "Is everyone ready to begin?"
- Move the microphone to generate some loud noise.
- Shut the lights. (Works with young children).
- Ask everyone to stand and then be seated.
- Ask everyone to raise their hands if they are ready? (For young children)
- Comment that, "Table 1 is ready to begin." (Again for young children).

The most important thing to remember is not to begin the instructional presentation until you have their attention. This is most important for elementary and high school teachers to remember.

Your motivational activity will be successful if you remember:

- To insist that everyone look at you before you begin.
- To insist that extra books, papers, radios, etc. are put away.
- To be enthusiastic.
- To explain why you are presenting this content and its value to the learner.
- To relate this content to information the learner already knows.

IMPLEMENTING THE DEVELOPMENTAL ACTIVITY

A well-planned developmental activity will hold the learners' interest and guide them as they acquire new knowledge and skills. The developmental activity will present new information through lecture, discussion, demonstration, group work, debates, projects, experiments, etc.

Ideally, the developmental activity will present new information and then allow the learner to "try it out" in some way. In instruction, we call this "try out" or practice. If the try out is supervised by the teacher or by a classmate it is called "guided practice." If the try-out is done individually, we call it independent practice. A well-structured instructional plan should provide opportunities for both guided and independent practice.

During the developmental activity, the successful teacher will:
- Be enthusiastic/vary his/her voice to express interest and energy
- Present new stimuli for learning
- Include individual or group work within the presentation.
- Use props, pictures, or artifacts
- Guide learners' thinking/learning
- Keep the learner active (responding to questions, writing, talking, etc.)
- Provide opportunities for guided practice
- Ask a variety of questions to stimulate thinking and learning
- Provide feedback about correctness
- Provide opportunities for independent practice
- Judge and assess learner performance

You will note that the successful teacher engages the learner in active learning. Active learning is a key element in all aspects of the instructional presentation. The essays in Part II of this text elaborate on specific strategies that encourage active learning. Essay 2 discusses the use of graphic organizers during the instructional presentation. Essays 3 and 4 discuss numerous writing approaches pertinent to active learning. Essay 5 demonstrates how to use library resources so that learners can become active researchers. Essay 6 provides several classroom learning activities that foster ethical thought in the classroom and encourage active learner participation.

Effective questioning is an important part of active learning within the instructional presentation. The importance of planning and asking questions was discussed earlier in this text. The following are some additional suggestions to help you to be more effective during the presentation:
- Allow learners adequate time to think and formulate their answers.
  Wait time is important to develop thinking skills. Always give students time to think. Encourage them to explore alternate ways of looking at questions.
- Avoid shotgun questioning. Firing questions in rapid succession leaves no time to absorb concepts and ideas. You might say, "Think about this for awhile ..."
- Call on all learners but never embarrass anyone. You can ask for group responses by asking learners to show "thumbs up" or "thumbs down" to indicate their agreement with an answer.
- Use praise to encourage learners. "That's right", "Good job" and "Excellent" are phrases that encourage further participation.
- Encourage learners to expand on their answers. "Can you tell me more?" and, "Can you explain?" are ways to probe for more information.
- Encourage learners to ask questions. Often when a teacher asks, "Any questions?" the learner doesn't even know what to ask. Let learners discuss concepts with a partner and generate questions.
- Expect that learners will pose questions that you cannot answer. Don't bluff. Perhaps someone else knows the answer. If not, research the question and answer it at a later date. You may say "That's a very good question, I'm not sure but I'll get back to you with an answer." You can also provide the learner direction on how to further research the topic.

IMPLEMENTING THE SUMMARY ACTIVITY
The summary activity provides an opportunity for the teacher to review the main ideas, concepts and skills covered during the presentation. This activity provides closure. Even if time is running short, the

summary activity should never be eliminated from an instructional presentation. You may find that you modify it in some way, but you should never skip it.

During the summary activity, the successful teacher does the following:
- Reviews what was learned.
- Provides practice for retention.
- Provides closure or ending.
- Provides a preview of the next instructional presentation (if applicable).
- Assigns or recommends follow-up learning experiences.

THE EFFECTIVE USE OF TECHNOLOGY IN AN INSTRUCTIONAL PRESENTATION

Technology enhances learning because it allows the learner to actively construct knowledge using a multi-sensory approach. Learners who use multimedia resources for learning employ all their senses as they interact with information and repeatedly experience learning with what they see and hear.

Originally, a multimedia presentation simply meant the use of more than one form of media in a presentation. For example, using audio-tapes, slides and a short video would meet the requirements for a multimedia presentation. Today, with the use of computer technology, multimedia has come to mean the integration of various media presented via the computer. This type of multimedia technology is becoming extremely popular since it appeals to all learners and audiences.

Professional development requires continuing research and interactive learning in order to remain current. Technology provides numerous opportunities for instructors to conduct timely research right from their own homes and offices. The very latest information is available for research purposes over the Internet. In addition, professionals can converse with other experts in the field via e-mail. Never before have such timely information resources been accessible to so many so readily. As a result of these developments, technology is changing the way we acquire knowledge. Individuals from all over the world can communicate and network with other teachers and learners. Thus, the power and capability of technology allows professionals from all disciplines to keep up with new developments in their field.

Audiotapes, videotapes, slides, filmstrips and computer software are readily available for use in presentations. Some educational publishing companies provide these as supplemental materials for use with their textbooks. Commercial materials may be costly but should be explored because these are usually of a very high quality and target the exact aspect of the topic that you wish to explore. Catalogs such as National Information Center for Educational Media (NICEM) and The Multimedia and Videodisc Compendium are available in libraries and audiovisual centers. These catalogs provide extensive listings of available materials according to titles and subject areas.

As a teacher, you should always be on the alert for suitable instructional materials. If you observe a colleague using an effective type of media be sure to get the title and publisher into your own files. Keeping a file of suitable types of media will allow you to have an extensive resource for instruction. When creating your file be sure to make note of title, date and publisher so that you can locate and retrieve media resources efficiently.

Once you have located a particular type of media for use in instruction, you must ascertain that it is suitable for your target audience. First, you must analyze the learners. "What do they already know?", "What do they need to know?" and, "How does this type of media bridge the gap in their knowledge?" are appropriate questions to ask. Thus, determining learners' prior knowledge is key to appropriate selection.

During your presentation it is important to relate the technological medium to the instructional objectives which you have determined. If a film or computer graphic is fun and interesting but quite unrelated to your purposes then its effectiveness will be minimized. Require that the learner participate actively with the media presented. For films or audiotapes provide a structure in the form of questions to be answered after the tapes are played. Provide feedback so that learners are assured that they have acquired the knowledge that you determined to be most significant.

After using media of any type, be sure to evaluate its effectiveness and make plans for revising its use in the future. If, you use a particular type of media and you are not pleased with the results, you must reflect on how to make better use of the media. Consider whether or not the media was a good match for the curriculum. Did the film or graphic maintain learner interest? What was the level of learner participation? Did the media meet the needs of the audience? Did the media present material in an unbiased manner? Did the media help students meet the instructional objectives?

Sometimes an instructor or teacher is unable to find suitable media for instruction. If this is the case, you may want to modify some existing materials. For example, show only a small segment of a video if it pertains to your audience. An alternative strategy is to create your own media. For example, you can make your own films using a camcorder, tape poetry using a tape recorder, or prepare an instructional program on the computer.

Using Computer Presentation Software

Computers have significantly changed the way we manage data and acquire information on a daily basis. The computer has been hailed as the answer to education's woes, but in actual classroom settings, one will rarely observe its use for daily instruction. Computer presentation software can assist teachers in providing multimedia learning experiences at all levels of schooling. This section describes the use of computer presentation software for classroom instruction, including the advantages and disadvantages of this approach.

Few teachers take advantage of the power and interactive capabilities that the computer has to offer. Teachers are notorious for resisting the computer. Much of this resistance is based on a lack of training and expertise in its use. Teacher resistance to computer use may be attributed to: 1) poorly designed software applications, 2) frustration in learning to use the computer, 3) a belief that computers do not enhance learning, 4) a perception that the computer is competition for students' attention, 5) unsupportive administrators, and 6) fear of looking stupid in front of students (Hannafin & Savenye, 1993).

No doubt, teacher resistance to using technology is attributed to the difficulty in mastering a new skill. Novelli (1993) noted that it typically takes from five to seven years for teachers to go from technophobe to master. By the fifth year, teachers report being able to move from drill and practice and tutorial software to more advanced technologies. While this report seems discouraging, the good news is that software applications have become increasingly user friendly and that many teachers are interested in using computers in creative and exciting ways.

Technology supports multimedia instruction as a powerful aide to learning. Peoples (1992) noted that the research on visual learning is very persuasive. Peoples indicated that empirical studies suggest that 75% of the information learned come to us visually while only 13% come through auditory pathways. In addition, the use of visual aids increases the likelihood that an audience will be persuaded by 43% (Peoples, 1992). The audience perceived teachers who used visual aids as being more professional, more persuasive, more credible, more interesting, and better prepared. While we remember only 20% of what we hear and 30% of what we see, we remember 50% of what we see *and* hear. Perhaps the research most relevant to classroom instruction is that learning is improved by 200%, retention is improved by 38%, and time to explain complex subjects is reduced by 25% to 40% when visual aids are used (Peoples, 1992).

Research suggests that only 5% of college and university faculty are currently using computers to aid classroom instruction or to enrich student learning (DeSieno, 1995, p. 47). College faculty seem to believe that computers, CD-ROMS, and high-speed networks require too much time/effort and yield few results to warrant the financial investment. Apparently, at the college level there is the perception that technology does not meet the curricular needs of the faculty and students.

There are college faculty, who believe that digital technology can make information more vivid, more instructive, and more focused upon the immediate needs of students. In a pilot study, teachers at Wright State University who expressed a desire to use technology more effectively in their classroom presentations were provided with equipment and training to become familiar with hardware and software. Hardware included a 486-notebook computer, external monitor, ink-jet printer, and Asymetrix' Compel multimedia presentation software. Other equipment purchased for group use included a color scanner and color ink-jet printer, two LCD panels with overhead projectors, a scan converter, a portable CD-ROM drive and a portable external sound device. A study by Sammons (1995) assessed the usefulness of this method of teaching and found that students rated the use of technology very highly. Students were especially impressed with the fact that the computer presentations made the class more organized and supported the content, made the material more legible, made the lectures more interesting and helped them understand the material, and helped them pay attention and clarified information.

The term multimedia includes "materials taken from various audio and visual mediums and combined by means of an electronic device" (Botterbusch, 1994, p. 14). In this case the electronic device is a computer. Multimedia can be applied to instructional settings in three ways, according to Speziale (1993, p. 16), teachers using it to enhance classroom presentations, students using commercially available multimedia products to conduct research, or students creating their own multimedia reports. (p. 16) McGraw (1992) notes, "what multimedia does is to attract and hold attention. It is also very effective for explaining difficult concepts in any field, especially when used in interactive modes." (p. 51)

Presentation media, according to Sullivan and Wircenski (1996), are vehicles for supporting the message you are conveying to your audience. They note five primary benefits to using media in your presentation:

- To organize your information. Key points that are displayed can be used as a guide as you lecture.
- To capture and focus the attention of the audience. Just as a picture is worth a thousand words, an audience can understand the message much more easily if they can see the points you are making. Information can be delivered in the form of images through the use of graphs, figures, and pictures.
- To supplement and reinforce the key points of your topic. Lecturing while presenting visual information reinforces your message.
- To stimulate audience interest. Students do get bored. Effective use of technology can help stimulate interest. (p. 91)

What Teachers Can Do With Computer Presentation Software

Improvements in computer technology, combined with presentation software products, provide teachers with the ability to create professional looking multimedia presentations. Teachers who are familiar with traditional media such as the overhead projector and 35mm slides can easily learn to use presentation software with a computer. Presentation software supports the creation of visuals in a variety of forms such as overhead transparencies, 35mm slides and computer-based projection slides.

Overhead Transparencies

The use of overhead transparencies for classroom presentation is certainly nothing new. However, the ability to create professional looking multicolored transparencies is typically out of the reach of the average classroom teacher. Some commercial publishers may provide colorful overhead transparencies with their textbooks but these may or may not suit the specific instructional needs of the teacher. Using presentation software, it is possible for classroom teachers to design transparencies with graphics and texts to meet specific instructional needs. A color ink jet printer will print a transparency that is ready to use in the classroom.

35mm Slides

Although 35mm slides have been available for quite some time, they are still very effective for instructional purposes. For a small class or an audience of 300, slides are the best medium to see clearly (other than film). Color slides make dramatic presentations because of the contrast of color and the dark background. Teachers who may be limited by time and budgets often favor slides. Commercial publishers may offer slides as supplementary materials in conjunction with their textbooks. If not, teachers can create their own slides for classroom use. Charts and drawings that demonstrate concepts and clarify ideas are often included in the instructional package.

Teachers can make their own 35mm slides with a camera or with presentation software. Visuals created with presentation software can be converted into 35mm slides by sending files via mail or modem to a slide production facility. If your computer is equipped with a film recorder, 35mm slides can be easily produced. A film recorder is a combination of a computer screen and a 35mm camera directly connected to your computer. This set-up allows for complete control of your slide production while keeping costs low. However, the initial investment in equipment is expensive.

Computer-based Projections

Computer-based projections are becoming increasingly popular among teachers at all levels. In this case, a presentation is delivered directly from a computer (laptop or desk model). For a small class, a large screen monitor may be sufficient for viewing. Video projectors with large screens or multiple monitors placed strategically throughout a classroom may be used for larger audiences. Another option is to connect a LCD panel with an overhead projector to your computer. This set up allows you to project any image from your computer via an overhead projector onto the projection screen.

Computer-based projections allow teachers to produce high-quality state-of-the-art presentations. Graphics, texts, videos and sound can also be added. The use of computer-based projections allows new information to be entered into the presentation at any time, even during classroom instruction. However, teachers must have access to presentation software and must know how to use it. Displays may be time-consuming to develop but the results are certainly worthwhile.

Teachers who use computer-based projections can also project other types of computer software as well. Wonderful educational programs are available on disks and CD-ROM. Computer-based projection makes the delivery of these visuals simple and easily accessible for classroom use.

Selecting Presentation Software

You will want to select presentation software that allows the user to create multimedia presentations with text and graphics. Many software applications allow the teacher to generate outlines, handouts and notes in addition to slides and computer-based projections. Some popular software titles are the following: *Microsoft PowerPoint, Kid Pix, and Hyper Studio.*

All presentation software applications share common features necessary for effective classroom presentations (McGraw, 1992). If you plan on purchasing software for presentation in your classroom, make sure that the application can:

- **Create and edit text.** These features should be similar to the editing features found in popular word processing programs. They must include spell check and search features that allow you to create error-free presentations.
- **Create masters or backgrounds.** This feature insures that you create a cohesive presentation with appropriate background color, slide orientation, frames or borders, and page numbering
- **Create graphics.** Graphics make a presentation more easily understood and meaningful. The software should give you the capacity to draw rectangles, squares, ovals, circles, lines, and arrows. These can be selected, re-sized, duplicated, aligned, and grouped.
- **Create charts and graphs.** The latest software enables the user to create charts and graphs using a spreadsheet-like feature that plots the data into the chart format. These elements can be styled and re-sized.
- **Import text and graphics.** Existing data or graphics can be imported into new presentations so that you do not have to recreate your work.

- **Sort slides.** This feature allows you to view the overall presentation. This is an especially important feature if you want to change the order or delete something.
- **Create formats for overheads and slides.** Pre-defined formats mean that you do not have to enter these settings each time you create a presentation. The overall size, size of margins, and desired media are preset.
- **Incorporate color schemes.** Presentations can be created in black and white or color and then produced in shades of gray or color. Color schemes allow you to define background, foreground, and accent colors used consistently throughout the presentation.
- **Project slides from the computer.** This feature allows you to display your presentations through the computer working with an overhead projector, through a device that projects directly to a screen or through the computer screen itself. Software packages refer to this as the video show, slide show, or video projection. Handouts can be produced from slides that are appropriate.
- **Incorporate multimedia and animation.** The video show mentioned above is similar to multimedia but it lacks animation. Animation is the apparent movement of text and graphics. Some software such as PowerPoint enables you to approximate animation. Other software enables you to combine desktop presentation images with interactive video.

Presentation software is available for both Mac and PC-compatible computers. You must consider what features are most important to you, such as animation, video, and sound capabilities. Perhaps ease of use is most important. Talking with colleagues who have used specific software will help you sort out what software best meets your needs.

Guidelines for Preparing Presentations Using Technology

When creating your presentations for the classroom, the following guidelines are suggested to provide the highest quality product and one that is most conducive to the learning environment (McFarland, 1995; McGraw, 1992; Sammons, 1995; Strasser, 1996).

- The first slide your class will see sets the tone for the entire presentation. The title should be interesting and descriptive. Appeal to your audience with graphics, color, and layout. Color can be used to enhance communication. A soft, non-intrusive background such as gray or pastels is best. Eyes may become fatigued when exposed to highly saturated colors for a long period of time. Use consistent color schemes and appropriate colors for specific functions.
- When creating slides, be consistent with type fonts and sizes, uppercase text, margins, borders, and color. Number slides to give the audience an idea of the length of the presentation, i.e., "Slide 1 of 10."
- Do not put too much text on a single slide. Limit slides to a single concept or one idea. Short phrases or bullets help to make a point or reinforce an idea. Some recommend that text lines be limited to six or seven words with no more than six lines per slide. Do not fill more than seventy-five percent of the slide with text.
- Do not right justify text because it creates too much space between words.
- Use bullets and other shapes to add interest and emphasis and make bullets another color to catch the audience's attention.
- Use legible text fonts and sizes. Roman, Helvetica, and Modern are easy to read and appealing. Avoid script fonts because they are difficult to read.
- Make sure the typeface is large enough that the students in the back rows can easily read the text. Twenty-four point or larger is good for titles, subtitles should be 18 points or larger, and body text no smaller than 14 points.
- Do not place irrelevant information on the slide. Do not get carried away with graphics and clip art. Graphics and other illustrations should be secondary to the message you are getting across to students. In addition, text and visuals should complement each other offering different yet related

information. When the text and visuals convey the same message, the learner may become bored or confused.

- Reveal enough information to make your point and no more. Most presentation software include a feature that allows you to display only one slide line at a time while dimming the previous points. Slides should be displayed for no more than 45 seconds. However, a student assessment revealed that enough time was needed to take notes. Too much information too quickly will defeat the learning process. Students need "absorption" time when review information is passively presented to allow them to integrate the new knowledge. A maximum of three items should be presented on a given presentation screen at any time.

Guidelines for Implementing Technological Presentations

The guidelines for implementing a technological presentation are similar to those for a standard oral presentation. The speaker must capture the attention of the audience within the first two minutes. With computer technology, you do not need a full script but can use an outline, included in many presentation software packages, that you can expand and develop. Slides and notes should not be read to the audience but may be used as a guide. You might want to do a trial run before displaying it in the classroom. This will help to eliminate any typos, embarrassing errors, or illegible text.

Some of the limitations of computer-based or slide presentations are that it may be difficult for students to take notes in class if adjustable lighting is not available. It can be distracting for students if the instructor does not know how to handle the equipment and wastes time. The student assessment by Sammons (1995) revealed that some students are concerned that classes will become depersonalized and the instructor will lose his or her personal teaching style and control over the class. These students also disliked it when teachers only read from their slide notes. A preferable style was to include only key points on the slide and use the traditional teaching style to elaborate on them. While these students suggested greater use of computer-based projection presentations, they did not want it used in every class.

A major disadvantage of using slides is that they require a darkened room. Students are unlikely to sit in the dark for too long without getting bored or daydreaming, and it is difficult to take notes. It also inhibits teacher-student interaction. Another disadvantage is that slides are relatively inflexible. They cannot be added or eliminated during a presentation.

Recent trends in technology make it simpler for teachers to implement multimedia presentations in the classroom. Technology is more accessible and user friendly. Presentation software applications offer teachers unique opportunities to prepare professional looking overhead transparencies, 35mm slides and computer-based projections. Thus, the use of computers to enhance classroom presentations offers exciting possibilities to teachers who are willing to learn its full capabilities.

Worksheet: Evaluate Overhead Transparencies/Slides

Directions: Complete the following checklist to guide your creation and use of overhead transparencies and slides. Check the statements that are true for you.

I use overhead transparencies/slides for the following reasons:

_____ To stimulate interest in the topic

_____ To maintain the group's attention

_____ To provide an outline for the audience

_____ To emphasize important ideas

_____ To clarify difficult concepts

_____ To indicate a sequence

_____ To provide notes

_____ To summarize main ideas

My preparation of visual materials includes the following:

_____ I use a computer to generate visuals and graphics.

_____ I create special transparencies using an ink jet printer.

_____ I create special transparencies using the photocopy machine.

_____ I create special transparencies using pens and markers.

_____ I create visuals that can be seen from the entire room.

_____ I create visuals that are well organized, attractive and colorful.

_____ I create visuals that are directly related to the topic of this presentation.

_____ I create a sufficient number of visuals to enhance learner understanding.

My use of overheads includes the following:

_____ I refer to the visual(s) during instruction.

_____ I use the visual(s) to enhance discussion.

_____ I allow adequate time for learners to examine and comprehend ideas and concepts.

IS YOUR INSTRUCTIONAL PRESENTATION ENTERTAINING?

Have you ever considered being on stage? Dreamed of being a stand-up comic? Or maybe a Shakespearean actor? Of course not, you have decided to be a teacher. Well you may be surprised to learn that teachers are very similar to entertainers.

In this section you will learn to reflect upon the role of teacher as entertainer. Given the seriousness of academic learning and the emphasis on achieving high standards you may wonder how such a metaphor can be applied. You are probably thinking that the classroom is not usually associated with fun, humor, pleasure, or entertainment…and there are educational critics who support this view.

Lindsley (1992) bemoans the fact that educators are trying to make learning something that is supposed to be easy and fun. Accordingly, Lindsley believes that discipline has to be put back into learning and points out that the first definition of discipline is "teaching, instruction, tutoring." (p. 22) The words "teaching," "instruction," and "tutoring" suggest "work," "effort" and "toil," a view of schooling that is generally accepted in our society. Most students and teachers will concur that learning in today's classrooms is usually neither fun nor easy.

Proctor, Weaver, and Cotrell (1992) note that entertainment within instructional settings suggests shallowness and histrionics and is often used as a pejorative. Some teachers who have adopted an entertaining teaching style are labeled as "entertainers" or "showmen". The authors lament that:

> By entertaining students we tend to relieve them of the responsibility of learning, of attending, and participating...we are not an entertainment industry! If one goes into the classroom to be entertaining, learning suffers. (p. 147)

Although many instructors have mixed feelings about pairing entertainment with instruction, most award-winning teachers use forms of entertainment such as humor, storytelling, and dramatic double takes in their classrooms. It is interesting that students positively associate entertainment with teacher effectiveness. Proctor et al. (1992) observe that today's MTV students are media-saturated individuals who expect to be entertained and not bored. Therefore as educators you need to understand entertainment, why it works, and how to use it effectively.

If you are thinking of incorporating some entertainment into your classroom instruction, you must consider appropriate forms of entertainment for use during the instructional procedures. Using humor during the motivational activity is always effective in getting students' attention. Humor interspersed throughout the instructional development can also be effective if used appropriately. Sometimes humor during the summary activity can also work. However, will students remember the humor and forget the important content?

Proctor et al. (1992) observe that classroom experiences imitate a spiral (a concept borrowed from the Soviet psychologist Vygotsky) and that entertainment approaches complement the processes of teaching and learning. "The spiral highlights student improvement through the practice and understanding that results from new conditions of learning. Also, each cycle of the spiral affords opportunities for teachers to practice, reconsider, integrate, and refine their entertainment strategies." (p. 148) Thus, the authors see entertainment as the bridge or binding element between student learning and teacher presentations, "...entertainment is a common element that does not separate students from the sociocultural setting." (p. 148) If today's students are media-saturated and expect to be entertained and not bored, then the degree to which this is accomplished heightens, reinforces, and augments effective learning. The authors developed a construct of instructional entertainment by exploring what it means to entertain, by examining students' reactions to instructional entertainment, and by describing ways in which teachers can be entertaining without sacrificing academic rigor.

According to Proctor et al. (1992) entertainment does not include diversion, amusement, or frivolity. They note that the Oxford English Dictionary defines "entertainment" as "to hold mutually, to hold intertwined" (p. 149) and that this could be a description of the instructional process itself. The teacher does not have to choose between content and audience. Entertainment can be used to mutually hold both.

Students do believe that entertainment belongs in the classroom and enthusiastically support its use for enhancing the learning process. Proctor et al. (1992) describe a student survey used to determine attitudes about the relationship between entertainment and education. Survey results indicated that students respond positively to entertaining teaching strategies and equate entertainment with effective instruction. In short, students want teachers who are entertaining. Based on their research, Proctor et al. (1992) believe that teachers can use entertainment in the classroom without sacrificing academic rigor.

Proctor et al. (1992) provide several suggestions for making instruction more entertaining. For example, lectures can and should contain elements of humor and drama. Stories, personal anecdotes, self-disclosure, and narratives are effective instructional techniques that also entertain. Audio-visual materials entertain and instruct. A feature film can easily be linked to conceptual material. Other media such as music, art, and poetry can be used in the same way. Proctor et al. point out that research demonstrates that combining audio and video stimulation enhances learning. Games, exercises, and "structured activities designed to illustrate a specific point" can help students connect abstract concepts with concrete situations. However, these activities must be well planned and have a clear purpose. Even exams can become more entertaining by using cartoons, sketches, graphs, and diagrams to relieve the tension that often accompanies test-taking.

Teaching is similar to giving an on-stage performance in that the instructor seeks to communicate effectively with the audience (namely, students). There are however, many teachers who believe that their job is to educate, not entertain. Teachers must realize the need to attract and hold their students' attention--just as an actor does on stage. But teachers must be careful not to confuse the two roles. Because entertainment has a connotation of acting, Tauber, Mester, and Buckwald (1993) warn that a teacher should not be a phony in front of his or her students. They warn against "putting on an act" that students (especially mature students) can perceive as being insincere. In reality, performing in the classroom involves projecting various aspects of your genuine self. When students relate well to the teacher, they will be receptive to learn. According to Tauber et al. (1993), "All teachers want their students to value what they teach. According to the taxonomy for the affective domain of learning, it is a prerequisite to valuing. Therefore, before students can possibly have a commitment to something (value it), they must first be willing to give controlled or selected attention to it--both physically and mentally." (p. 21)

Jerome Bruner, as cited in Tauber et al. (1993), advocated the use of "dramatizing devices" to cultivate students' attention in an interesting way. For children, natural attention holders are those persons whom they perceive to be attractive, popular, successful, or interesting. Pop stars and athletes are effective models because they are able to capture a youngster's attention--the first step in learning. Tauber et al. suggest that effective acting skills can be the great equalizer for teachers to compete with such models for getting and maintaining students' attention.

Tauber et al. (1993) compare teaching with acting and suggest that several strategies are common to both. One common strategy is to "know your lines." For actors, "knowing their lines" means not just memorization but internalizing the meanings and understanding the character's motives. For teachers, this means knowing content so that you can creatively decide how to deliver those lines and make them meaningful. Students view the world outside the classroom as interesting and stimulating. Therefore any effort to relate classroom instruction to the real world will pique students' interest.

Actors and teachers must use body language and voice effectively. Body language is a means of communicating non-verbally. Many students are visually oriented and thanks to television relate to the world by images they see and sounds that they hear. Tauber, et al. observe that actors understand the significant potential of expressive body language and use their bodies as natural vehicles of expression. "Body language punctuates the verbal language that the lecturer speaks. Through body language, teachers are able to raise the intensity level of the subject they are teaching. This intensity, in itself, is entertaining and focuses the students' attention." (p. 23) Experienced teachers convey many messages non-verbally. Student behavior is often controlled by non-verbal cues such as a glance. You have observed teachers who take a stance in front of the room and wait for the class to be ready to begin. Without uttering a single word, students quiet down, take out notebooks and prepare to begin the lesson. Mature students have learned to recognize the non-verbal cue of the teacher. Younger students learn these cues from teachers who insist that the class respond to specific behavior cues. Similarly, voice and vocal expressiveness can be an instrument to convey discovery, to clarify and emphasize any idea expressed, and to increase a sense of excitement and interest. "By subtle, natural variations in the pitch, rate, volume, or quality of the voice, the speaker can communicate the varying importance of ideas as well as the emotional connotations." (p. 23) Voice can also be used to monitor student behavior and encourage student initiative. Unfortunately, many teachers use voice in a negative manner to reprimand and correct students' poor behavior. Remember to use positive behavior statements and praise throughout the instruction to promote a positive learning environment.

Another strategy that can be borrowed from acting is the use of space. Classroom teachers can learn much from actors in this area. Actors know where to stand and how to move for effective communication. Effective teachers incorporate more movement into their classroom behavior than do ineffective teachers. This movement allows the teacher to deliver instruction from all parts of the room. Instead of standing in one place at the podium, effective teachers move about, engaging students in the back of the room, monitoring student attentiveness and on-task behaviors. Teachers who make maximum use of their classroom space project confidence and comfort with teaching. This, in turn allows students to feel more comfortable. According to Tauber et al. (1993), "this free use of space also allows us [teachers] the license to be more animated in our lectures. Effective use of space translates into a more entertaining lesson as the student is forced to 'follow a moving target,' raising the level of interest and attention." (p. 24)

Moving around the classroom can be done effectively if the teacher knows the material well enough that part of the instruction can be delivered away from the podium and notes. This brings us back to the importance of "knowing your lines."

A characteristic identified with award-winning teachers is self-disclosure (Tauber et al., 1993). Self-disclosure is a form of vulnerability that comes from knowing one's material very well, thus giving the teacher the confidence to be vulnerable. Using a real-life personal situation to illustrate a point in class, demonstrates two things to students:

> First, we demonstrate that despite our differences in age and life experience (among other things), we are human beings, able to understand and empathize with the problems students potentially face. Second, we show that the subject matter does have a practical application in one's own life. This gives the theory value in the eyes of students and allows them to conclude that the subject is worth learning. Real-life examples may come from two sources--actual personal experiences, or experiences of others. Both represent self-disclosure. (p. 24)

However, the authors warn against excessive self-disclosure that may give students too much access into the teacher's life outside the classroom. The developmental level and sophistication of the class have to be considered as to what are appropriate examples to offer without creating an uncomfortable level of openness.

Keiper and Evans (1994) reinforce the position of Tauber et al. (1993) that effective teaching must include "performance." Keiper and Evans recognize that planning is an essential element to teaching. They note that having clearly stated objectives, an instructional plan with appropriate methodology, and an evaluation strategy is the obligation of teachers. However, performance is also essential. According to Keiper and Evans, entertainment means "the successful completion of an action, the effective carrying out of an assumed task." (p. 22) Using techniques to improve the performance of teaching enhances the total learning environment and stimulates the senses, making learning seem more natural and pleasant. Teachers who would be performers need to be passionate about their subject matter and then add effective methodology to that knowledge base. The student's desire is directly related to the enthusiasm, excitement, and energy that the teacher brings to the presentation. "Like it or not, as educators we are salespeople, and every day we must enter the classroom ready to sell our wares to the students." (p. 22)

Keiper and Evans (1994) restate Tauber et al.'s (1993) view about the importance of verbal and body language. They note that you cannot make the body be quiet. The way teachers walk into the room, the stance taken when addressing individuals, the use of hands, and facial expressions say much about how teachers feel about themselves, their subject, their job, and their students. The authors cite research by Arnold and Roach that indicates when there is a conflict between verbal and nonverbal or visual messages, the nonverbal messages were accepted as truth over the verbal. This same research asked students to list the positive visual behaviors of their instructors. Among these behaviors were:

- maintains eye contact with students, especially with those individuals asking questions or making statement;
- scans the class constantly, as if talking to each student and reading to see if 'they got it';
- moves to various locations in the room to emphasize points of importance;
- teaches to the back row first by making broad gestures, not close-into-body movements that cannot be seen by those in the rear;
- animates the lecture with movement, especially facial expressions that indicate an interest in the subject and an appreciation that the students are present and listening;
- never stands behind the podium for the duration of the lesson; and
- smiles! (p. 23)

For some teachers, poor classroom performance is often due to bad habits and laziness. Teachers who want to develop an entertaining technique will have to undo old habits and take a risk. Taking courses in speech and drama is one way to learn these strategies, but teachers can begin with some basics. For example, teachers can view videos such as <u>Stand and Deliver</u> or <u>Dead Poets Society</u>, two movies about effective teachers. Turn the sound off and concentrate on how the actors use their body during instruction. The actors' enthusiasm and sincerity are communicated through the visuals. To improve vocal technique, teachers can tape their own lessons and then listen to them critically to see what characteristics need improvement. Developing a wider range and variety in pitch, modulation, and rate will lead to a more interesting presentation with greater attention on the part of the students. Videotaping and analyzing your teaching performance is an excellent strategy for improving teaching performance. Be sure to get some tape on students' reactions during class as well. Student reactions can be particularly informative about teacher effectiveness.

Javidi, Downs, and Nussbaum (1988) compared award-winning and non-award winning teachers at the secondary and higher educational levels to determine their different dramatic styles. These researchers completed a significant amount of research in the area of instructional communication. Their own review of the literature finds that "a teacher who is dramatic within the classroom leads his or her students in identifying relevant material presented during lectures." (p. 278) They note, however, that the literature does not indicate how teachers can incorporate dramatic style behaviors into their classroom performance. Effective teachers were studied to provide models for other teachers interested in improving their communication behaviors. Most of the research was done at the collegiate level, so the researchers included secondary teachers to see what the differences or similarities might be.   Three behaviors were evaluated by Javidi et al. (1988)—use of humor, self-disclosure, and use of narrative. Their research indicated that the award-winning college teachers incorporated more humor and used self-disclosure and narratives more often to clarify the course content. Award-winning high school teachers were similar to the collegiate teachers. The high school teachers, however, used humor less frequently than the college teachers, and lower-grade high school teachers used humor less frequently than the upper-grade teachers. The researchers believe this may be due to the fact that the lower-grade teachers were more content-oriented and less concerned with style to convey course material. However, it may be that younger students fail to grasp the fine nuances of humor and therefore lower grade teachers don't find it an effective strategy. Another possibility is that younger students may require firmer discipline to keep them on-task and teachers may fear that the use of humor will detract from learning in the classroom. Non-award-winning teachers at all levels used the three behaviors less frequently. An ineffective teacher is one who is "not very lively or animated, does not signal enough attentiveness or friendliness, does not have a very precise style...is not very relaxed, and does not use a dramatic style." (p. 286) The authors believe that the link between communication and positive classroom outcomes is very important. Seeing and observing effective teaching helps train new teachers and aids all teachers in the modification of their classroom behavior.

Gorham (1988) also studied nonverbal teacher behaviors and notes that interpersonal perceptions and communicative relationships between teachers and students are crucial to the teaching-learning process. Implicit communication can be referred to as having three major referents--pleasure-liking, arousal, and dominance: "The more a person, object, or situation elicits pleasure, the more it is liked. The more arousing a pleasurable entity is, the more it is liked. The more submissive a person feels in a relationship, the less variation there will be in liking, despite large variations in pleasure, arousal, or both." (p. 40) Gorham's review of the literature found that "like", as opposed to "dislike", is expressed and understood in terms of behaviors that reduce physical or psychological distance. Arousal is partly conveyed by shifts in body position, vocal expression, and facial expression. Power is communicated through size, expansiveness, control, and relaxation. People who talk more are perceived as being more powerful. All of these behaviors are nonverbal and play an important role in the teaching-learning relationship. The more immediate a teacher was, the more she or he was perceived as effective. Behaviors such as vocal expressiveness, smiling at the class, and having a relaxed body position were particularly meaningful. Teachers who verbalize positive results of on-task behavior are perceived as more immediate than those who verbalize the negative consequences.

immediate a teacher was, the more she or he was perceived as effective. Behaviors such as vocal expressiveness, smiling at the class, and having a relaxed body position were particularly meaningful. Teachers who verbalize positive results of on-task behavior are perceived as more immediate than those who verbalize the negative consequences.

Since the purpose of teaching is for students to learn, the use of instructional entertainment has little value unless students are learning more. Gorham's (1988) research sought to identify verbal teacher immediacy behaviors that were related to increased student learning. Immediacy behaviors are those which enhance verbal and nonverbal closeness and reduce psychological distance between teacher and student. Her study found a substantial relationship between immediacy and learning. "Both the total verbal and nonverbal immediacy scores and the overwhelming majority of the individual immediacy items were significantly correlated with both affective learning and perceptions of cognitive learning for the total sample. The same pattern for total scores was evident in the results broken down by class size." (p. 46) As others have found, a teacher's use of humor appears to be of particular importance. Other behaviors related to increased student outcomes are praising students' work, actions, or comments and frequency of initiating and/or willingness to become engaged in conversations with students before, after, or outside of class. Self-disclosure by the teacher, among other behaviors, contributed to student-reported cognitive and affective learning. Nonverbal behaviors such as vocal expressiveness, smiling, relaxed body position, gestures, eye contact, and, to some degree, touch, were all associated with students' perceptions of learning. Another interesting finding by Gorham (1988) was that as the class size increased, the use of self-disclosure was more strongly related to both perceived learning and affective learning. Gorham posits that:

> [T]he physical closeness of teachers and students in small classes enhances perceptions of immediacy and fosters an atmosphere in which behaviors in the second set are relatively common. As class size increases, however, teachers become more differentiated in terms of their efforts to decrease psychological distance. A similar pattern emerges for nonverbal immediacy behaviors. Eye contact, smiling, and vocal expressiveness are important teacher behaviors regardless of class size, whereas gesturing, smiling at individual students, relaxed body position, and movement around the classroom become more important factors as class size increases. Taken together, these data indicate an enhanced responsibility of teachers in larger classes to utilize specific verbal and nonverbal approach behaviors, strategies to reduce psychological distance between teachers and their students and are likely to affect learning outcomes. (p. 51)

Gorham believes that the interrelationship between student learning and teacher immediacy is a logical one. Teachers who exhibit these behaviors reduce psychological distance by recognizing individual students and their ideas and viewpoints, by incorporating student input into course and class interactions, and by enhancing their humanness through self-disclosure and humor.

Entertainment was not the main focus of McKinney's (1998) research. McKinney (1988) was concerned about improving the quality of teaching to maximize students' learning, thinking, curiosity, enjoyment, and satisfaction. She observed and talked to teachers to determine the components of effective teaching. McKinney's study is based on personal use and experience as she interviewed 12 nominees and winners of teaching awards (on the university level) and asked them to answer the question, "What makes you a high-quality teacher?" McKinney found that the five components of quality teaching are fairness, application, challenge, entertainment, and services (FACES). She notes that although these components seem basic, teachers often neglect them. These components should be incorporated into the classroom and also be emphasized in other phases of teaching such as class preparation, office hours, informal involvement with students, advising, writing tests and assignments, and curricular planning.

McKinney (1988) acknowledges that the entertainment component is more controversial than the others. She notes that some teachers believe entertainment and teaching are mutually exclusive. While pure entertainment is inexcusable, substance with entertainment, she says, is unbeatable. She quotes an outstanding teacher who said:

I have found that the formula for good teaching is simple: 1) Have something substantive to say; 2) Know how to say it. Having the former without the latter is irrelevant; having the latter without the former is vacuous. The first point has to do with good training in graduate school--the substantive material of our discipline. The second is much more elusive and is, quite frankly, dramaturgical. Teaching is a performing art like music or art, and it must be done well with a sense of timing, good humor, passion and enthusiasm for insight and understanding. (p. 300)

McKinney believes that a fun, exciting, enjoyable, and stimulating teacher leads to less absenteeism, increased learning, and more attentiveness on the part of students. She also suggests that wearing diverse and visually interesting clothes and altering one's vocabulary will also convey a sense of enthusiasm.

Worksheet: Evaluate Your Entertainment Value

Directions: Complete the following checklist to determine if you are an engaging teacher. Check the statements that are true for you.

_____ I sometimes use games to get acquainted with students in class.
_____ I create a classroom atmosphere that is positive and conducive to self expression.
_____ I maintain eye contact with students, especially those individuals asking questions or making statements.
_____ I scan the class constantly and individualize instruction as if talking to each student.
_____ I make sure that the students follow along with my presentation.
_____ I move to various locations around the room to emphasize important points.
_____ I use broad gestures and movements that can be easily seen by everyone in the room.
_____ I use appropriate facial expressions.
_____ I am dynamic and demonstrate interest in the topic.
_____ I collect and share favorite jokes with students.
_____ I encourage students to collect humorous stories and share them with each other.
_____ I post humorous stories and cartoons on bulletin boards.
_____ I use cartoons and amusing stories to illustrate points in my instructional presentation.
_____ I reduce test anxiety by scattering humorous questions or inserting funny cartoons on the test.
_____ I smile during my instructional presentation.

Learning Activities:

- Take a trip to a local public library. Find a book on jokes, riddles and topical humor. With your course curricula in mind look for material that works well with your instructional topics. Create a file of fun and entertaining teaching ideas to use in your presentation.
- Read the comic strips every day. Cut out cartoons and comics that illustrate and relate to key ideas in your lecture or presentation. Most materials can be used legitimately by teachers for personal use in the classroom. Be careful not to violate copyright laws.
- Videotape yourself during your classroom presentation. Rate yourself as an entertaining teacher. Are you effective? Why or why not? Make a list of some ideas for improving your presentation style.

USE MAGIC TO DAZZLE YOUR STUDENTS

Getting students motivated in the classroom is not always an easy task for the teacher. An important element of teaching to get students interested in the topic and to relate the material to something they already know. Magic can help students focus their attention on the material to be covered, stimulate interest in a way that involves them as learners, and activate prior knowledge. Magic can be an especially effective tool when the teacher is introducing something new into the classroom. Magic has been used successfully with all types of learners, including students with disabilities (Frith and Walker, 1983).

McCormack (1985) observes that magic is an excellent means of introducing students to math and science concepts. Magical stunts have been used in the business world to introduce new products, to illustrate key features of a product or service, and to initiate organizational change in a way that employees will remember (Randall, 1991; Stone, 1991). In the corporate world trainers have used magic to effectively instruct corporate employees (Wheatley, 1994). The classroom teacher can use magic as an effective means of capturing the attention of students, motivating them, and reinforcing specific lessons and content that are important (McCormack, 1985).

Magic has a certain mystique. One only has to see the looks on the faces of children (and adults) as a magician performs to know that magic can cast on a unique spell on people. Yet little is known about how magic came about. Currently, an estimated 30,000 Americans practice magic as a hobby (Copperfield, 1994). The fascination it generates creates new avenues of communication that can be very productive in teaching situations (Frith & Walker, 1983). David Copperfield (1994), the great magician, points out the "Magic has captured the passion of curious minds everywhere...Magic caters to a spirit of reverence and mystery, and it is the magician...who must carry the torch of wonder. His art speaks to a primordial emotion inside us all." (p. 6)

Many people think that magic takes years of study and practice. While this is so for the great magicians such as Houdini and David Copperfield, anyone can learn, with a little practice, some simple magic tricks that will captivate an audience. Randall (1991) provides an example of a magician who can teach a client an illusion in twenty minutes. Many simple tricks and illusions can be purchased for little money at most magic stores. Windley's (1978) book, geared for teachers and parents, is filled with magic tricks that are designed to transmit information as well as entertain students.

Parrott (1994) suggests some basic guidelines on how to become a competent classroom magician:

Become acquainted with magic as a motivational tool. Learn tricks that will maintain the students' interest and hold their curiosity. Finding some books on magic and visiting a local magic shop will introduce you to tricks that you feel comfortable with, that won't take too much time to learn, and that correlate with your teaching style. Start slowly with one trick until you reach an expertise level that you are comfortable with. You don't have to be an expert to use magic successfully. Neither do you have to be an expert to look impressive. Once you understand the simple laws that are behind most magic tricks, you will learn other tricks more easily. After the initial introduction of a magic trick into your classroom, the reaction of students will reinforce your self-learning.

Use magic and humor together. The combination of the two is a very effective classroom motivator. Most teachers know the value of humor in their classroom and have used jokes successfully.   Humor has long been recognized as a means of bonding with an audience, but it has other benefits as well. Physically, humor and laughter help us relax and lower pulse and blood pressure. Emotionally, humor decreases anxiety and causes a more positive attitude and increased motivation. Socially, it helps us open communication lines, cross cultural barriers, and deal with awkward or difficult moments (Parrott, 1994, p. 36).

Parrott also notes that:
Humor can be a planned teaching strategy, a spontaneous event that may help explain a point, or a part of extracurricular activities. The alleged benefits include increased attention and interest, student/teacher rapport, comprehension and retention of material, motivation toward learning, satisfaction with learning, playfulness, positive attitudes and classroom environment, productivity, class discussions, creativity, generation of ideas, quality and quantity of student reading, and

divergent thinking. Other benefits include decreased academic stress and anxiety, dogmatism, boredom, and class monotony. (p. 37) Many magic tricks are very humorous. You can increase the humor quotient by placing them at appropriate times within the context of your class. See the creative potential in magic. Many magic tricks are public domain. The teacher can adapt them so that they are more appropriate for use in the classroom or for a certain lesson. Magic can be a means of expanding students' thinking about an idea or concept. Use it as a means of teaching students to question what they are seeing. Magic can also be a means of relaxing your class when you want to introduce material that may be more emotionally charged, such as AIDS awareness. The right combination of humor, magic, and seriousness can make for a compelling presentation.

The main objective in the classroom is to present information to the students. Use just enough magic so that you gain the students' attention and reinforce a lesson. Make sure the magic trick is relevant to the material you are presenting. The teacher wants students to remember the lesson, not the magic trick.

Surprise is an important element in magic. Magic gives students a "hook" by which to remember something by. The element of surprise adds to this hook.

McCormack (1985) notes that when an abstract concept is paired with magic, the teacher is combining verbal information with visual surprise. Students can retain this information more easily.

Magic is not only for the elementary classroom. Dr. Kathleen Schmalz uses it successfully at the college level and in a variety of content areas. For example, magic can be used successfully in the following subjects—math, science, social studies, health and foreign language.

The different ways magic can be used in the classroom are as follows:
- To improve communication within the group. (Use the trick as an icebreaker to get students to open up and share with one another.)
- To introduce concepts or ideas that are particularly relevant to the curriculum.
- To dramatize key concepts that may otherwise be perceived by students as too boring or unimportant for their attention.
- To teach complex or abstract ideas in a way that students can remember them more easily.
- To encourage students to think more creatively.

Typical magic tricks that can be used in the classroom included card tricks, rope tricks, coin tricks or perception illusions. A simple card trick that always fascinates audiences is to get a volunteer to pull four aces out of a deck of cards. This trick can be used as an ice-breaker for a new class or as an adjunct to a lesson. This trick can also be used to stimulate a class discussion on probability in math class. For example, ask students to predict what is the probability of drawing four aces from a deck of cards. They can discuss the probability and then you can perform the trick.

Rope (or scarf) tricks can be used to demonstrate how health programs (or economic programs) are cut and restored or how different concepts are related to each another. Using money or coins, you can teach a lesson or idea about the financial costs of a war in some social studies class. Show an empty hand and one holding a nickel to the audience. Then magically change the nickel to a quarter to make your point. Perception illusions--changing sizes, colors, or locations of objects--can be used to get students to think about things in a different way. What they think they see maybe different than what others are seeing.

Most magic tricks are accomplished through techniques of misdirection, sleight of hand, or other gimmicks. Magicians are pledged not to reveal the secrets of their success. However, you can have your class try to figure out how a magic trick was performed. This can be used in conjunction with the type of material you are introducing. Remember that the information presented with the magic trick will have real staying power. Overusing it can dilute its effects and take energy away from what you are really there for-- to teach.

From experience, I can tell you that magic is an effective means of motivating students and getting them interested in classroom material. I believe you will find that it enhances the presentation of your material and makes for a more relaxed classroom. Magic books, tricks and resources are available at magic shops, magic clubs, or your local library. Caution... remember to tell your students that one trick they cannot learn is to make their homework disappear.

Suggested Activities

If you think magic tricks are only for the elementary classroom, think again. People of all ages are fascinated by illusion. Here's an example. You are teaching a course in economics. What is a cash cow? A cash cow is a product that generates instant money. Making a cow appear in the classroom can be difficult, to say the least, but you can make the money appear. Kushner (1997) gives the example of a Chief Executive Officer (CEO) faced with the task of telling his employees they had to work harder to make more money. Now, everyone is interested in making money, but who wants to hear the obvious. So instead of stating the obvious, the CEO showed them the unexpected.

The magician puts all sorts of stuff into an empty pan, lights it on fire, and covers the pan. When the cover is lifted, instead of a stew of junk it is a pure white dove, ready to fly away.

The CEO consulted a trainer who knew some magic techniques. Instead of a dove, the trainer wanted money to appear in the pan. Here's the secret. It's called "spring money." It is fake money made of compressed paper that springs up when it is released.

On the day of the presentation, the CEO gave his speech about turning a little money into a lot. You can guess the rest. The pan was lit, the cover removed, and money poured onto the stage. The CEO was a big hit because he had discovered a secret. Some magic tricks are very easy to do.

In other words, you don't have to be a magician–or a CEO–to perform magic. Illusions can be used to encourage students to see things in different ways.

Mathematics

Many students still view math as the class where there is only one way to see things and only one right answer. A card trick or two should help to change apathy resulting from misconception to delight derived from illusion. The trick is called **The Card and the Orange.** It can be accomplished under the noses of even the most skeptical spectators (Tarbell, 1971, p. 276-284).

Present your orange to your audience for examination and then let a spectator hold it during the experiment. A spectator chooses a card which is then torn into pieces. You wrap the torn pieces in a handkerchief, keeping one corner to give to the spectator. Another audience member holds the handkerchief which - supposedly - holds the torn pieces of card. When you jerk the handkerchief, the pieces vanish. Then the orange is sliced open and Voila! Inside the orange is the card, completely restored except for that little corner. Which always manages to fit perfectly.

Social Studies

You are conducting a lesson on government spending. For this class, you can use the **Dove Pan**, the same one the CEO used on his sales force. If you really want to be dramatic, you can do a great job destroying the junk you put in the pan. Your students will probably love that! This trick is even easier than the card trick because it comes in a kit. No need for sewing or gluing your paraphernalia. The price of the kit ranges from $42.50 to $57.50 depending on size. And the trick takes a mere 10 seconds to learn.

You can tell your audience you are holding a copy of the annual fiscal budget. Or some top secret documents the government doesn't want anyone to know about. An exorbitant military budget. Perhaps for some new type of plane the Pentagon knows will never get off the ground. It would not be the first time the government was pulling a sleight of hand!

Language Learning

Kushner (1997) describes **The Magic Coloring Book** as a "great trick for showing how different people perceive things differently." (p. 368) You can use it as a metaphor for understanding a new language and a new culture. The trick involves an "ordinary" coloring book. Hold it out to your audience, flipping the pages so the audience can be sure to see them. On the first flip, the pages are blank. Second flip and the page contains the outline of a drawing like a real coloring book. Third flip, and the pictures are all colored in. You can keep right on flipping, changing the image each time. This one costs a mere $8.95 and takes 20 seconds to learn.

You can come up with a snappy dialogue about how the blank page represents the first stage of L2 learning, when the new language seems incomprehensible. The outline represents the basics, like grammar and syntax. Full color image, and you are now a fluent speaker in your new, rich, colorful language.

Further Suggestions:
- Visit a local magic shop to find some tricks that could be used effectively with the students in your class.
- Review your course materials and curriculum topics for the academic year.
- Identify topics and subject areas that might be appropriate for using magic.
- Visit the public library or teacher store to find books with science or math tricks. There are some clever tricks that can easily be mastered by the classroom teacher.

REFERENCES

Copperfield, D. (1994). A delicate sleight of hand: Magic and the history of illusion. Omni, 17, (2), 6.

Frith, G. H. and Walker, J. C. (1983). Magic as motivation for handicapped students. Teaching Exceptional Children, 15, (2), 108-110.

Gorham, J. (1988). The relationship between verbal teacher immediacy behaviors and student learning. Communication Education, 37, (1), 40-53.

Keiper, R. W. and Evans, H. M. (1994). 'Act well your part:' Teachers and the performing arts. Clearing House, 68 (1), 22-24.

Kushner, M. (1997). Successful presentations for dummies. Foster City, CA: IDG Books Worldwide, Inc.

Lindsley, O. R. (1992). Why aren't effective teaching tools widely adopted? Journal of Applied Behavior Analysis, 25, (1), 21-26.

McCormack, A. J. (1985). Teaching with magic: Easy ways to hook your class on science. Learning, 14, (1), 62-67.

McKinney, K. (1988). Faces: Five components of quality teaching. Teaching Sociology, 16, (3), 298-301.

Parrott, T. E. (1994). Humor as a teaching strategy. Nurse Educator, 19, (3), 36-38.

Proctor, R. F., Weaver, R. L., and Cotrell, H. W. (1992). Entertainment in the classroom: Captivating students without sacrificing standards. Educational Horizons, 70, (3), 146-152.

Randall, V. (1991). How he turned the magic of business into the business of magic. Nation's Business, 79, (6), 11.

Stone, Judith. (1991). Tricks of the trades. Discover, 12, (8), 29-31.

Tarbell, H. (1971). The Tarbell course in magic. Brooklyn, NY: D. Robbins & Co., Inc.

Wheatley, W. J. (1994). Abra Cadabra! Mastering the Mystique of Magic. Training and Development, 48, (8), 15-19.

Windley, C. (1976). Teaching and learning with magic. Washington, D. C.: Acropolis Books Ltd.

Part I
Section III: Evaluating Classroom Presentations

Introduction

You have prepared the instructional plan and delivered the presentation. The next question is "How did it go?" Was the presentation effectively delivered? Did the students learn the material? Was the presentation effective?

In this section you will learn about evaluating instructional presentations. First we discuss strategies that you can use to re-examine the instructional event to identify areas that can be improved. Secondly, we discuss some long-term evaluation strategies that teachers use such as portfolios. We will also discuss evaluations of teaching performance that are conducted by principals and other supervisory personnel.

Teacher evaluations tell us something about the quality of instruction. Evaluation of teaching performance is important, but only as it relates to student learning. Student assessment reveals what students have learned as a result of the instructional event. Positive student learning outcomes are assumed to be a result of effective teaching. Angelo and Cross (1993) observed that "The quality of student learning is directly, although not exclusively, related to the quality of teaching. Therefore, one of the most promising ways to improve learning is to improve teaching." (p. 7)

In this section you will also learn how to evaluate student learning. Evaluations of student learning occur naturally during instructional presentations, as well as, after instructional events. We will discuss the concepts of traditional and authentic assessment as they relate to student learning in the classroom.

EVALUATING YOUR INSTRUCTIONAL PRESENTATIONS
Strategies for Self-evaluation

Perhaps the most important type of evaluation that will enhance your teaching performance is self-evaluation. Self-evaluation is the process of examining one's own teaching performance for the purpose of improving teaching effectiveness. Airasian and Gullickson (1997) described teacher self-evaluation as the process "in which teachers make judgments about the adequacy and effectiveness of their own knowledge, performance, beliefs, or effects for the purpose of self-improvement." (p. 2) They noted that the teacher is at the center of the evaluation process and is responsible for examining and improving his or her own practice.

Airasian and Gullickson (1997) observed that teacher self-evaluation is the most common type of teacher evaluation, however, it usually goes unnoticed. Consistent and sincere self-reflection provides opportunities for teachers to enhance and refine their teaching skills. After each instructional presentation, effective teachers take some time to reflect upon their performance. Teachers will want to consider the following questions after the instructional presentation:

Did students achieve the learning objective?

Did the instructional presentation hold students' attention?

Were students actively engaged in the learning process?

Did the learner acquire the intended knowledge or skill?

Was the content adequately presented and learned?

Was the instructional strategy appropriate and effective?

Self-evaluations enable teachers to eliminate instructional strategies deemed less desirable and to increase the use of desirable strategies in future presentations. Good teachers are reflective and can recognize when an instructional strategy is not working for them. Trying alternative teaching strategies enables the teacher to discover what works well in their classroom. Journal writing, student evaluations, videotapes, self-assessment checklists/inventories and teaching portfolios are all useful strategies for self-evaluations by teachers. Each of these strategies allows the teacher to review instructional practices in order to determine teaching effectiveness. Using these strategies on a regular basis, teachers can become more reflective practitioners and further refine their presentation skills.

Journal writing is particularly helpful for purposes of self-evaluation. Keep a notebook or a journal handy to record thoughts and insights you may have about students, teaching methods and curriculum. A review of the journal will be helpful, in preparation for the next presentation. Journal writings are especially helpful in planning for a new academic year. Very often, the best ideas for a new approach, comes immediately after the old approach has not been as successful as you would have liked. Keeping good ideas in a journal will ensure that they are not forgotten.

Ernst (1998) found that journal writing helped to improve her teaching skills. The art teacher observed that "I am often surprised to find the forming of an idea (beginning portfolio reviews, artist's share or conducting parent workshops) is hidden in my journal pages sometimes months or even one year before it actually takes place in the artist's workshop." (p. 34)

Reread your journal regularly to remind yourself to implement the new ideas. As you record your insights over time, you will marvel at your growth as a teacher and how much you have learned about teaching through the experience of journal writing.

Student evaluations of teaching effectiveness can assist the teacher in reflection and self-evaluation. Teachers can collect feedback from students in various forms. At the conclusion of a lesson or unit, teachers can ask students to report on the learning strategies that worked best for them. This information can be collected in either oral or written form and may be anonymous. What the teacher does with the information is important.

Student evaluations can be taken seriously and used to revise future classroom learning. Words of caution though, student evaluations of teaching performance are readily influenced by many factors. Teven and McCroskey (1997) reported that college students who perceived their teachers as caring, tended to give more positive evaluations. These same students also evaluated course content more positively and reportedly learned more in the class. The authors suggested that students who perceive that the teacher is caring will be more likely to attend class and listen more attentively during instruction.

Student evaluations may be easily influenced by perceptions of teacher enthusiasm. Lang (1997) reported that teacher ratings on student evaluations soared when professors used a more enthusiastic tone in class. In addition, a more enthusiastic tone by the professor resulted in students giving higher ratings for the class textbook and teaching aids (even though these were the same in the unenthusiastic class presentations). An occasional disgruntled student notwithstanding, student evaluations can provide good information to help promote self-reflection on one's teaching performance.

Student performance data also provides information for teacher self-evaluation. Students' scores on exams, written reports and projects provide evidence of student learning. Teachers will want to reflect on students' performance and consider reasons why students achieve or fail to achieve. While poor student performance is not always indicative of poor teaching, it does suggest a need to re-examine teaching strategies. Teachers may find that alternative approaches to instruction may more adequately address students' needs.

Videotaping and self-evaluation is perhaps one of the best ways to improve one's presentation or teaching skills. Although the process of viewing oneself in action is rather intimidating, it is a wonderful strategy for self-evaluation. Most teachers have access to a camcorder and can arrange for a student to assist in the videotaping. Ask the camera operator to focus on your teaching performance. If you can't find anyone to run the camera, just set the camera on a tripod in the corner of the classroom and let it run.

If you decide to videotape your instructional presentation, you will want to review the tape soon after the lesson. As you view the tape, take note of your teaching style. Review your written instructional plan along with tape and look for the following:

- Were you able to follow your original plan?
- Did students achieve the learning objective?
- Was your voice loud, clear and engaging?
- Was body positioning effective for the lesson?
- Did you use of the classroom space effectively?
- Did you ask higher level questions in addition to those that require simple recall?
- Did you randomly call on students by name?
- Did you engage students' by your use of questions?
- Did you praise students who knew the right answers? How did you handle incorrect responses?
- Did you encourage students to ask their own questions?
- Were you enthusiastic?

Worksheet: Evaluate Your Videotaped Presentation
Review your written instructional plan along with the videotape. Check the statements that are true for you.
_____ I followed my original plan.
_____ Students achieved the learning objective.
_____ My voice was loud, clear and engaging.
_____ My body positioning was effective for the lesson.
_____ I used the classroom space effectively.
_____ I asked higher level questions in addition to those that required simple recall
_____ I randomly called on students by name.
_____ I engaged students' through effective questioning strategies.
_____ I praised students who knew the right answers.
_____ I handled incorrect responses appropriately.
_____ I encouraged students to ask their own questions.
_____ I was enthusiastic.

After viewing the tape, decide on two or three aspects of your presentation that could be improved. Make a plan on how to improve these presentation skills. Work on these and then videotape your teaching again. Do you notice improvement in those areas? Do you notice other areas that need to be addressed? Regular use of videotaping and self-reflection will provide excellent feedback and help improve your teaching performance.

   Checklists (sometimes called inventories) are also helpful for self-evaluation of presentation skills or teaching performance. A checklist can be described as a listing of criteria to evaluate a product or process. Some checklists require the rater to make evaluative judgments about the quality or how well the criteria were met. Other checklists are simpler to complete and require the rater to merely identify the presence or absence of stated criteria.

   Checklists are easy to complete and can be used regularly for purposes of self-evaluation of teaching. We have provided a sample checklist for your use. Teachers may want to modify this checklist by adding additional criteria that are appropriate for specific content area.

After completing the checklist for self-evaluation, be sure to write yourself a prescription for improvement. Try to implement the prescription in subsequent instructional presentations. Also remember to review past prescriptions to be sure that you continue to improve your presentation skills.

The following checklist will be helpful in performing self-evaluation after instructional presentations. You may want to keep several copies of this checklist in your instructional plan book.

Worksheet: Evaluate Your Presentation Skills

Teacher: _____   Date: _____

Topic/Subject: _____   Class/Audience: _____

DIRECTIONS: Rate yourself on a scale of 1 - 4 in each category. One is the lowest and four is the highest.

TOTAL SCORE: ___ out of 100

The Motivational Activity

_____   Gains and holds learners' attention

_____   Tells learners what they are expected to learn

_____   Reminds learners of related knowledge skills

The Developmental Activity

_____   Presents new stimuli for learning

_____   Guides learners' thinking/learning

_____   Provides opportunities for guided or individual practice

_____   Provides feedback

_____   Judges or appraises the performance

_____   Asks higher level thinking questions

_____   Engages learners in activities

The Summary Activity

_____   Helps generalize what is learned

_____   Provides practice for retention

_____   Matches the behavioral objective and/or provides evidence of learners' understanding

_____   Provides closure or ending

General Performance Criteria

_____   Is enthusiastic

_____   Paces the lesson/presentation

_____   Handles behavior problems effectively (if applicable)

_____   Voice is loud/clear

_____   Is flexible during the lesson

_____   Elicits learner/audience responses

_____   Supportive of learner/audience responses

_____   Acts assertively/leadership quality

_____   Capitalizes on learner/audience interests

_____   Vocabulary is understood by learner/audience

_____   Instructions are clear to learner/audience

Prescription for Improvement:

Worksheet: Evaluate Your Presentation Skills (Sample)

Teacher: _____Mr. Charming_____   Date: ____June 8, 2001____
Topic/Subject: __Social Studies/Battle of Gettysburg__   Class/Audience: ___Grade 11___

DIRECTIONS: Rate yourself on a scale of 1 - 4 in each category. One is the lowest and four is the highest.

TOTAL SCORE: <u>88</u> out of 100

The Motivational Activity

4	Gains and holds learners' attention
4	Tells learners what they are expected to learn
4	Reminds learners of related knowledge skills

The Developmental Activity

4	Presents new stimuli for learning
4	Guides learners' thinking/learning
4	Provides opportunities for guided or individual practice
2	Provides feedback
3	Judges or appraises the performance
2	Asks higher level thinking questions
4	Engages learners in activities

The Summary Activity

4	Helps generalize what is learned
3	Provides practice for retention
4	Matches the behavioral objective and/or provides evidence of learners' understanding
4	Provides closure or ending

General Performance Criteria

4	Is enthusiastic
4	Paces the lesson/presentation
4	Handles behavior problems effectively (if applicable)
4	Voice is loud/clear
4	Is flexible during the lesson
4	Elicits learner/audience responses
1	Supportive of learner/audience responses
3	Acts assertively/leadership quality
2	Capitalizes on learner/audience interests
4	Vocabulary is understood by learner/audience
4	Instructions are clear to learner/audience

Prescription for Improvement: Need to work on being supportive of the students' answers. Be sure to say "Good answer" or "Good thinking" to encourage more participation. Also, try to relate concepts of student interests.

LONG TERM STRATEGIES FOR SELF-EVALUATION

Teaching Portfolios

Teaching portfolios can be useful for self-reflection over a longer period of time. If you want to evaluate your instructional practices over the course of a semester or an academic year, you will want to assemble a teaching portfolio.

A teaching portfolio is a compilation of artifacts and evidence that illustrate your professional accomplishments both in the classroom and elsewhere. Teaching portfolios are designed to display a teacher's knowledge, talents and proficiencies. Portfolios are one way to present information. Teachers are probably familiar with student portfolios that exhibit samples of students' best work. Teaching portfolios exhibit samples of the teacher's best work. Teaching portfolios can showcase and demonstrate a teacher's excellence and effectiveness in classroom performance.

Teachers may develop portfolios for a variety of reasons including career advancement. When applying for a new position or promotion, a portfolio summarizes a candidate's strengths and provides potential employers with more information than might be collected during the ordinary interview process.

Currently, many college teacher preparation programs are using teaching portfolios with their pre-service teachers. The teaching portfolio is a strategy that allows the teacher candidate to demonstrate what he or she has learned in preparation for classroom teaching. New teachers are encouraged to share their teaching portfolios with prospective employers. Hurst, Wilson and Cramer (1998) described the efficacy of this approach. They noted that originally they used teaching portfolios within the college classroom setting, but soon learned that students were taking their portfolios along on job interviews. Many students in their program obtained teaching positions because of their teaching portfolios. The teaching portfolios revealed much about the pre-service preparation of new teachers, including field experiences, coursework and extracurricular activities. Hurst, Wilson and Cramer (1998) also observed that the process of creating the portfolio refined the teacher's professional and personal goals. The portfolio process encouraged reflection and created an awareness of the teacher's professional journey. They noted that the portfolio process documents teaching strengths, competencies and clarifies goals and objectives for the educator.

Research by Borko, Michalec and Timmons (1997) also examined the use of portfolios by student teachers. Their findings suggest that the very process of assembling the portfolio was helpful and encouraged student teachers to think about their strengths and limitations. The process also helped student teachers become more realistic about their teaching and identify ways to improve. In particular, writing an educational philosophy helped the student teachers clarify and refine their ideas about teaching and to connect their philosophy to their teaching practice. In this study, the researchers found that portfolios functioned differently than journal writing. Journal writing fostered reflection on daily classroom experiences. Portfolios encouraged student teachers to take a broader perspective of their teaching experience, to synthesize the experience and examine it.

While teaching portfolios are increasingly popular for career advancement, they are also useful for more experienced teachers. After securing a teaching position, teachers can continue to develop their portfolios as a strategy to document growth and professionalism. Classroom teachers can display their portfolios for parents to review at open school night or other school-wide events. School district officials may want to review teaching portfolios for purposes of promotion and tenure decisions. Updating and maintaining a teaching portfolio is a strategy that fosters professional growth. Given the recent popularity and the impact of teaching portfolios, it is likely that the use of portfolios may eventually become a standard practice for evaluating teachers.

Each teaching portfolio is unique. Hurst, Wilson and Cramer (1998) observed that the contents of individual teaching portfolios vary according to one's philosophy, values, viewpoints and teaching experiences. In addition, the teaching portfolio provides a multidimensional representation of teachers that highlights their varied abilities and interests. A portfolio reveals much more about an individual teacher than a resume or vita.

When assembling a portfolio, the teacher must review his or her professional experiences in order to select those artifacts and documents that reflect one's own teaching. The very act of reviewing one's experiences is a form of reflection and a unique strategy for self-evaluation. Barnett (1992) suggested that teachers select artifacts that demonstrate acquired knowledge, skill and competency. It is also important to pay attention to how the artifacts are presented.

The length of one's teaching portfolio will depend upon an individual's experiences. The quality of the portfolio is truly more important than its length. Fewer artifacts may be more desirable, since an overstuffed scrapbook-type portfolio may overwhelm the reviewer, who may be a potential employer.

A typical portfolio might include the following materials:

- A short biographical sketch
- An essay describing one's educational philosophy
- A description of teaching experiences
- Documents such as copies of degrees, licenses, certificates of certification
- Letters of recommendation, honors and recognition
- Instructional plans
- Unit plans
- Photos of creative projects such as bulletin boards, student assemblies, class events
- Evidence of continuing study
- Publications and conference presentations
- A videotape of the teacher engaged in teaching

The first step in assembling a teaching portfolio is to gather together evidence and artifacts related to professionalism and growth in teaching. As teachers examine the evidence, they should think about what each piece reveals about their teaching. For example, a well-written unit plan suggests that the teacher is highly organized and able to plan instruction. A photo of an attractive bulletin board can demonstrate a teacher's creativity. A certificate of academic recognition demonstrates a teacher's intellectual strengths and abilities. A description of a class project using the Internet illustrates that the teacher is comfortable using technology. A teacher-made written exam demonstrates one's ability to assess student learning.

Hurst, Wilson and Cramer (1998) observed that the teaching portfolios provide evidence of good teaching. When preparing the teaching portfolio teachers will want to consider:

- The purpose of the portfolio
- The audience
- Major responsibilities as a teacher
- Major accomplishments as a learner
- Major achievements as a teacher
- Major achievements as a scholar

Suggestions for Organizing Teaching Portfolios

Once you have collected your artifacts and materials, you will have to consider how to organize and present your portfolio. Teaching portfolios are often assembled in book form, but electronic portfolios are becoming increasingly popular and common. An electronic portfolio can be assembled with a computer program such as Microsoft PowerPoint or HyperStudio. Electronic portfolios can appear on the Internet as WebPages. To get an idea about electronic portfolios you may want to surf the net to find some samples already posted on the Web.

While what to include within the teaching portfolio is a personal decision, Hurst, Wilson and Cramer (1998) offered the following suggestions for assembling the portfolio:

- Strive to make the portfolio a reflective collection of artifacts.

- Provide a personal touch, but keep the portfolio professional.

- Keep the portfolio a reasonable length and size so that it is not burdensome to read.

Most portfolios group artifacts to provide a coherent presentation. Hurst, Wilson and Cramer (1998) suggested how a teacher can organize a portfolio. The teaching portfolio can include the following sections:

- Table of Contents – to help the teacher organize materials and to assist the reader
- Resume – to provide an overview of the teacher's preparation and experience
- Statement of Philosophy – to clarify one's beliefs about teaching and learning.
- Official Documents – to provide evidence of certification, test scores, awards.
- Letters of Recommendation – to support teaching effectiveness
- Evaluations by Supervisors – to provide evidence of one's teaching ability
- Photographs and visuals – to illustrate a teacher's work with students or creative project
- Self–Goals – to illustrate what the teacher hopes to achieve
- Goals for Students of Tomorrow – to illustrate what the teachers hopes for his/her students
- Student and Parent Sentiments – to provide evidence of rapport with students and parents
- Samples of College Work – to illustrate one's ability to write instructional plans, reports, IEP's, etc.
- Thematic Units – to demonstrate one's ability to plan instruction
- Learning Activities for Students – to illustrate ideas for instruction
- Original Ideas – to demonstrate creativity
- Examples of Students' Work – to show the type of work students produced in the classroom.
- Personal Data/ Autobiographies - as the teacher may feel appropriate
- Reflections – to demonstrate decision making and growth
- Inspirational Items – to illustrate ideas that have an impact on the teacher

Evaluating Your Teaching Portfolio

As you can see, developing and maintaining a teaching portfolio is a useful strategy for long-term professional development. Time and effort invested in the portfolio process can result in personal growth and afford an opportunity to display one's accomplishments over the course of a semester, an academic year or one's career.

Once you have assembled your teaching portfolio, you will want to evaluate the quality of the project. Rubrics, a form of authentic assessment, are helpful in evaluating portfolios. The rubric on the next page was created to evaluate the teaching portfolios of undergraduate students. The rubric was created by the faculty in the Department of Teacher Education at the College of Mount Saint Vincent, Riverdale, NY. You can use this rubric to evaluate your own teaching portfolio. If you wish to create your own rubrics, you will find some guidelines later on in this text.

Evaluation by Principals and Supervisory Personnel

Principals and other supervisory personnel determine the effectiveness of instruction by evaluating teaching performance. The most common form of teaching evaluation is that of the classroom observation. However, other forms of evaluation such as teacher mentoring or peer coaching may also be used in school settings.

Mayo (1997) noted that there has been a major shift in teacher evaluation during the last ten years. In the past, teacher evaluation strategies attempted to measure teacher competency for purposes of retention and tenure. The current approach emphasizes teacher evaluation as a means to foster development and growth. Mayo (1997) suggests that, "The evaluation system should give teachers (a) useful feedback on students' needs, (b) the opportunity to learn new teaching techniques, and (c) counsel from principals and other teachers about how to make changes in the classroom." (p. 269)

In the following section, we will examine how school principals and supervisory personnel evaluate the teacher's performance and discuss various approaches that are commonly found within school settings.

Portfolio Rubric

	Exceptional Performance	Satisfactory Performance	Limited/minimal Performance
Organization	Content is organized in a logical and unique pattern which is immediately apparent to the reader.	Content is organized in a clear and recognizable pattern.	Content is disorganized.
Originality/ creativity/ variety	Selection & preparation of content is unusual, creative & varied reflecting student's unique perspectives.	Selection & preparation of content shows some variety and originality	Selection & preparation of content shows little or no variety & originality
Goal-setting/initiative	Meaningful goals are established; growth and progress are well documented.	Some attempt at meaningful goal-setting and documentation is evident.	Little or no evidence or goal-setting or progress toward goals.
Comprehensive-ness	Content documents exceptional growth in knowledge, professionalism, and implementation.	Content documents adequate growth in knowledge, professionalism and implementation.	Content does not satisfactorily document growth.
Problem solving	Content indicates that student wrestles with problems, uses various resources, and applies a large and varied repertoire of strategies.	Content indicates adequate use of resources and strategies when attempting to solve problems.	Content reflects student's sense of helplessness and frustration when faced with problems, and his/her lack of effective strategies.
Reflection	Reflections are multidimensional with a wide variety of supporting observations.	Reflections are multidimensional with sufficient supporting evidence.	Reflections are single in focus or too global; lack supporting evidence.
Writing	All written products demonstrate correct vocabulary, grammar, sentence structure, and mechanics.	Written products may vary somewhat in vocabulary, grammar, sentence structure, and mechanics.	Written products contain persistent errors in vocabulary, grammar, sentence structure and/or mechanics.

Classroom Observations

The classroom observation is the most commonly used technique that provides an opportunity for a principal or school supervisor to view teaching performance in the classroom. Teachers are routinely observed to determine levels of teaching effectiveness and judged on the quality of their instructional presentations. The purpose of these evaluations is to insure that effective teaching and learning occurs within the classroom.

Informal teacher evaluations take place every day as the principal and other school staff notice a teacher's attendance, manner of dress, professional attitude and work habits. They observe the teacher's ability to interact with students, parents and colleagues. Without even stepping a foot into the classroom, a good administrator knows whether or not effective instructional planning and implementation are occurring in the room. Invariably, those in charge make mental notes about how well teachers are teaching and whether or not they fit into the existing school culture.

Classroom observations are more formal evaluations of teacher presentations. Principals and other supervisory personnel visit classrooms to formally observe teacher presentations. After the formal classroom observation, a written report that describes the teacher's ability to plan and implement a lesson is prepared and placed into personnel files. It is common practice that new teachers are observed three to six times during the academic year. For more experienced and tenured teachers, classroom observations may occur with less frequency. The number of formal classroom evaluations conducted during the academic year varies according to school district policy and teacher contracts.

Typically, classroom teachers know when formal observations of their teaching will occur, although this is not always the case. Sometimes, especially with novice teachers, the principal or supervisor will come into the classroom unannounced. Good teachers are never concerned about unannounced classroom visits because they are always well prepared for class with clearly written instructional plans. Announced formal observations are much more likely to occur.

Formal classroom observations are usually announced a week or two in advance. The principal or supervisor expects to observe the teacher engaged in the act of teaching. If the teacher has scheduled an exam (or planned a field trip, or scheduled a guest lecturer) on the announced date, the date may be changed so that the observer can observe some meaningful classroom instruction. Remember that the purpose of the formal classroom observation is to see the teacher engaged in the act of teaching and the students engaged in learning.

Many principals and supervisors prefer to meet with the teacher in advance to discuss the upcoming lesson. These pre-observation conferences help the observer understand what will be happening during the instructional presentation. The pre-observation conference is an opportunity for the teacher to explain his/her approach to instruction. For example, if a teacher will be using a cooperative learning strategy, he or she may want to explain why they chose this strategy and its value for student learning. A teacher might also want to share with the observer his or her rationale for class seating, method of homework collection or strategy for handling inattentive students. The pre-observation conference is an excellent opportunity for the observer to learn more about the unique characteristics of the students in the class. It's also an opportunity for the teacher to learn more about the upcoming formal observation.

It is extremely important that the teacher arrive prepared for the pre-observation conference. Being prepared means knowing what you plan to teach and how you will teach it. Even if the teacher has not finalized the ideas for the lesson, a well-prepared teacher has a good sense of what will be happening in class on the day of the formal observation. Teachers who are new to the school will want to inquire about the assessment format that the principal or supervisor plans to use. Some administrators have forms that delineate criteria for teacher evaluation. If so, the teacher should ask for a copy of this form. Knowing the criteria for assessment tells the teacher what the administrator will be looking for during the formal classroom observation.

Formal classroom observations are opportunities for teachers to display their best teaching practices. Good impressions can be made during formal observations. Teachers should try to be creative.

For example, teachers can demonstrate their ability to use technology or incorporate the fine arts. Uninspired presentations suggest that the teacher failed to put sufficient effort into instructional planning and teaching. Therefore, in preparation for formal observations, teachers are encouraged to look for creative teaching ideas in magazines or on the Internet.

Some teachers find that formal observations produce anxiety. Formal observations create less anxiety for teachers who adequately prepare and implement lessons on a daily basis. For well-prepared teachers, the presence of a principal or supervisor makes little difference.

On the day of the formal observation, the teacher should arrange to have everything prepared for the lesson. Time wasted in setting up materials can suggest poor planning by the teacher. The teacher should provide the principal or supervisor with a typed instructional plan. When there are clearly written instructional plans, it enables the observer to follow along. The plan should clearly indicate the instructional objectives and procedures. The Instructional Plan Format, suggested in this text, allows the observer to develop a broad understanding of the instructional process by delineating multiple aspects of the lesson, including students' prior knowledge, instructional rationale, learning standards, and follow-up activities. In addition, adaptations for special learners are also described.

During formal observations, most school administrators choose to sit in the back of the classroom in an unobtrusive manner. The presence of supervisory personnel may influence students to be on their best behavior. During the lesson, the observer will take notes to record his or her impressions of the instructional presentation. Some observers write copious notes, while others seem to write very little. These notes assist the observer in writing his or her final report on the lesson.

Most supervisors remain in class until the instructional sequence reaches a natural ending. In high school settings, the ringing of a bell may signal the end of class and thus the end of the lesson. In elementary classrooms, the transition from teaching math to writing stories will signal the end of the math instructional sequence. Occasionally supervisors may depart before the teacher believes that the lesson is concluded. As long as the time for instruction was appropriate for the level of the learner, teachers should not view this early departure as a sign that the lesson did not go well. The supervisor may simply have another appointment or feel that he or she had observed for a sufficient period of time.

After the formal observation, the principal or supervisor will schedule a conference to discuss the instructional presentation with the teacher. Typically, the observer has prepared a written report as well. Ideally, the conference should be a dialogue between teacher and principal or supervisor. However, that is not always the case.

The conference usually begins with the principal or supervisor describing positive aspects of the observed lesson. For example, the observer may comment on the way that the teacher gained student interest or the effective use of cooperative learning. During the conference, there will also be some suggestions for improving the instructional presentation. Even if the observer feels that the lesson is just about perfect, many supervisors feel that they must make suggestions for improvement. A teacher should not be discouraged if the supervisor seems to have more than one suggestion. Suggestions may merely indicate different ways of doing something, not necessarily better, just different. Other times, suggestions will help the teacher think differently about their teaching style.

Michael Lorber (1996) observed that administrators tend to evaluate instructional presentations from a particular perspective: "As a consequence of their educational philosophy and their experiences, they have a mental picture of how the ideal teacher should look and operate. A good part of your rating will depend upon the extent to which that picture is matched by you and your performance." (p.297)

At the conclusion of the post-observation conference, teachers receive a written copy of the observation report, and another copy is placed in the personnel file. Teachers usually sign each copy to indicate that they have read the document before it is placed in their personnel files. There also may be space on the document for the teacher's comments or response. If a teacher feels that the observer's report does not accurately represent what had occurred during the formal instructional presentation, he or she may wish to add some explanation to the document. However, if the teacher and observer discuss the instructional presentation during the post-observation conference, the teacher will know exactly what will be included in the final report. New teachers are advised to keep copies of their written reports for their teaching portfolios.

Some schools generate annual reports on all school personnel. Formal observations of instructional presentations may be included in annual reports on teachers. The annual report, documents teaching skills but may also include the evaluation of other less tangible factors such as one's attitude, attendance and collegiality. Annual reports usually contain recommendations for the following year's employment.

Concerns and Objections to Formal Classroom Observations

Many school administrators have concerns about assessing teacher competence by formal classroom observations. One concern relates to the fact that the formal observation merely provides a snapshot view of learning within the classroom. A second concern is that district level assessment instruments focus on direct instruction and may not adequately describe teacher effectiveness in holistic classroom environments (Searfoss and Enz, 1996).

Marvin Marshall (1998) observed that formal classroom observations are often perceived as negative experiences because evaluator suggestions are often viewed as criticism. He noted that the very nature of the process sets up a situation in which the principal or supervisor knows what works and the teacher does not. Marshall suggested that schools use evaluation strategies that build relationships and foster growth. He suggested that supervisors first ask teachers to describe effective teaching and learning. Secondly, supervisors should ask teachers how their own class activities move them towards effective teaching and learning. This can be accomplished by self-evaluations by teachers. Third, Marshall suggested that teachers themselves devise plans to become more effective in the classroom. Teacher ownership of the plan is important. Marshall noted, "Using this new approach transforms the principal's role from a cop to a coach and results in building relationships – the basis of all school interactions; fostering growth - a prime purpose of schools; and instructional improvement- perhaps the most significant of educational reform." (p. 119)

Edwards (1995) reported on the Danville Public School system in Virginia that replaced its traditional classroom observations with a plan that they believed would encourage real professional growth for teachers. The first step was for each teacher to reflect upon his or her performance and write a self - evaluation. The self-evaluation was reviewed collaboratively by teacher and principal and a plan for growth was developed. Edwards noted that the results were quite impressive, supporting the idea that teachers are capable of making professional choices about their own growth and development.

TEACHER MENTORING

School districts are increasingly adopting mentoring programs to help novice teachers develop their teaching skills. Teacher mentoring typically pairs novice teachers with more experienced teachers. The experienced teachers collaborate with the new teachers and serve as in-school resource personnel.

Danielson (1999) noted that mentoring is currently recognized as a critical element in teacher development and that the first few years of teaching is especially important if teachers are to develop expertise in their field. She observed that novice teachers need mentoring because teacher preparation programs, regardless of their high quality, cannot provide an independent teaching experience since all practice teaching must be in someone else's classroom. Thus, pre-service teachers don't truly experience what it is like to be fully in charge until they are assigned to their own classroom. The need for mentoring is especially important since novice teachers are often presented with more challenging teaching assignments than their experienced colleagues. These assignments usually include numerous preparations, the most challenging students and no permanent classroom.

Danielson (1999) described the elements of effective teacher mentoring programs. In addition to providing the novice teacher with a buddy and a resource person, the mentoring program should provide adequate training for the mentor and compensation to ensure the mentor's commitment to the program. In addition, novice teachers must engage in self-assessment, reflection, and formative assessment as they seek to refine their teaching skills.

Although self-assessment and reflection are useful, outside mentors can provide novice teachers with valuable insight. As mentors observe novice teachers, they can suggest strategies for classroom management and discipline techniques. Alternative strategies for instruction can be explored. Novice teachers can also observe mentors to learn new skills and expand their teaching repertoire.

If a school does not have a mentoring program, novice teachers may be able to find suitable mentors on their own. Novice teachers should seek out experienced teachers who will be willing to answer questions and share expertise.

James B. Rowley (1999) identified six essential qualities of a good mentor. Novice teachers will want to keep these qualities in mind as they seek to identify suitable mentors.

> The teacher is committed to the role of mentoring.
> The teacher is accepting of the beginning teacher.
> The teacher is skilled at providing instructional support.
> The teacher has effective interpersonal skills.
> The teacher is a continuous learner.
> The teacher is hopeful and optimistic.

Asa Hilliard, a noted teacher, psychologist and historian, believes that only successful teachers should mentor new teachers. Hilliard observed, "If I were searching for good teachers, I would look for those who have experienced extraordinarily powerful results with children" (Checkley and Kelly, 1999, p.59).

When a novice teacher identifies such a master teacher, who is willing to share his or expertise, then he or she has found a mentor. The next step is to develop a relationship with this person so that the learning process can begin.

PEER COACHING

Peer coaching is a form of teacher evaluation that is growing in popularity. In peer coaching programs, teachers collaborate and observe each other's teaching strategies. Peer coaching suggests a more collegial relationship among the teacher participants. Some school districts have implemented peer coaching programs as a form of teacher evaluation for experienced teachers.

Although peer coaching usually focuses on the development of experienced teachers, sometimes novice teachers are included in the group. Peer coaching is viewed as a way to improve teaching.

Pierce and Hunsaker (1996) noted that there are many advantages to using peer coaching as a support system. Besides increasing collegiality, peer coaching enhances each teacher's understanding of teaching concepts and strategies. Teachers who participate in peer coaching feel comfortable in trying new instructional approaches if the environment is friendly and non-evaluative.

One component of peer coaching programs is the peer observation. Peer observation is an excellent strategy to help teachers refine their teaching skills. Teachers share teaching ideas and invite partners to sit in on class presentations. Colleagues ask for suggestions and discuss alternative instructional strategies that might be effective for diverse learners. Teachers, often find that observing the teaching/learning situation from the back of the room, provide another perspective of student and teacher behavior.

Showers and Joyce (1996) worked with school districts to organize faculties into peer coaching teams. They provide some guidelines and warn that peer coaching programs should not become only teachers evaluating teachers.

- All teachers involved in the peer coaching process must consent to being participants.
- Verbal feedback should be omitted as a coaching component. When team members give verbal feedback there is a tendency to become evaluative and supervisory. Instead, teacher teams should focus on planning, developing curriculum and instruction as they pursue shared goals.
- When pairs of teachers observe each other, the one who is teaching should be considered the "coach" and the observer the "coached". This allows observers to learn from their colleagues not evaluate them.
- The focus must be on learning from each other. This is accomplished by planning instruction, developing support materials, watching one another work with students and developing an understanding about how teacher behaviors impact student learning.
- The focus of peer observation should always be on collaborative problem solving.

Even if a school doesn't have a peer coaching program, teachers can still participate in this process on an informal basis. A teacher can ask a colleague to be a partner for peer observations. Colleagues can share ideas for making instruction more effective. Shared curriculum planning results in a richer learning experience for students in the classroom. As schools recognize the value of collaborative experiences for classroom teachers, the use of peer coaching as a strategy for teacher evaluation will become more commonplace.

Reflections on Teacher Development Programs

The foregoing discussion on how to improve classroom practice, assumes that teachers are eager to improve their teaching performance and professional skills. Strategies such as self-reflection, portfolio development, or videotape analysis can and should be used by individual teachers on a regular basis. The fact is that most teachers do engage in these self-improving activities.

In an effort to assist teachers in their professional development, school districts often provide special programs for teachers. Unfortunately, many of these programs are workshops of short duration that address a single topic, such as technology or writing across the curriculum. While the intent is admirable, research suggests that teachers often fail to implement new approaches to teaching and often return to traditional methods. Joyce and Showers (1988) attributed the limited use of innovative strategies to weak in-service programs. Fullan (1982) observed that most in-service programs are short term and do not provide ongoing support for developing new skills.

Pierce and Hunsaker (1996) indicated that teachers are often not involved in decisions about teacher development programs. They noted that, "The professional development agenda is rarely the teachers' agenda, the consultants come and go, but there is no support system to help teachers work through the 'bugs' that arise during the implementation." (p. 101) Therefore, they suggested that teachers and school administrators work together to design teacher development programs. Teachers must be involved in the change process, if schools are to change in meaningful ways.

Ann Lieberman (1995) also believes that teachers must discuss, think about and experiment with new practices, if we expect them to change the way they work. She suggested that teachers assume roles as leaders, peer-coaches and researchers within their schools as they problem-solve and make decisions. The goal is to create an environment where professional learning is expected, supported and an ongoing process within the school.

EVALUATING STUDENT LEARNING IN SCHOOL

As teachers seek to develop effective presentation skills within the classroom, one can anticipate that student learning will be enhanced. However, how will teachers assess this student learning? What strategies are effective in determining whether or not students have acquired the intended knowledge or skills?

Within classroom settings, students are regularly evaluated to determine levels of understanding, competencies, and abilities. Some of these assessments are informal while others are formal. Informal student evaluations occur daily and may or may not be documented by the classroom teacher. Teachers make daily informal assessments of their students in terms of attitude, behavior, cooperation and ability to fit into the established school culture. Teachers also evaluate student learning informally during instructional presentations. Teachers notice which students seem to master the learning and which students have difficulty.

Formal evaluations are assessments that are planned and usually result in a tangible score, grade, written report or project. Some formal evaluations are traditional such as teacher-made and standardized tests. Other formal evaluations may be authentic assessments such as performances or experiments.

Teachers use data collected through both formal and informal strategies to create a profile of student learning. In the following section, we will first present an overview of traditional and authentic student assessment practices. Secondly, we will discuss a variety of ways to assess student learning during and after instructional presentations.

TRADITIONAL STUDENT ASSESSMENTS

Standardized tests, teacher prepared examinations, and written papers form a basis for traditional student assessments. Traditional assessments measure student achievement by one's ability to perform well on these tasks. Individual scores are most commonly recorded in school records such as report cards and student record cards.

Traditional student assessments usually provide quantitative indicators of student academic achievement. For example, students may be assigned letter grades such as A, B, C, D or F. Other letters may also be assigned to represent achievement, such as "S" for "satisfactory," "U" for "unsatisfactory" or "I" for "incomplete." Sometimes numerical indicators of academic achievement such as 70, 82, 89 or 90 are used. Numerical indicators provide a wider range of grading possibilities providing teachers with more flexibility in grading. Some teachers prefer number grades and feel that numerical grades more accurately describe levels of student achievement.

Usually, student report card grades are computed by averaging number grades on a variety of academic tasks. The averaging of numerical data suggests that grading is a rather objective non-biased strategy to evaluate student learning. However, the subjective nature of the grading process cannot be ignored. Letter or numerical grades in student records or report cards usually include subjective data collected informally by the teacher during the term. Subjective data include student participation and cooperation for which a grade may be assigned.

Student report cards usually include subjective data in the form of teacher comments. Teacher comments are commonly included on student record cards. Teacher comments provide a means to describe student academic achievement more fully than the use of numbers or letters alone. For example, a student who receives a grade of "C" in biology may be considered as having put forth less than adequate effort. However, the teacher's comment, "Good effort," tells us that this student is working diligently to reach the established learning standards. However, a comment such as "Not working up to potential" suggests that the student is not exerting very much effort into his/her studies.

Kim and Kellough (1991) note that, "Teachers' comments should be useful, productive, analytical, diagnostic, and prescriptive, for the continued development of the learner." (p. 393) Unfortunately, some teachers write comments that are unprofessional and these may remain on permanent student records. Examples of unprofessional comments include statements such as, "Edward is lazy" or "Shelly is disruptive." These statements are not useful, productive, analytical, diagnostic or prescriptive. A more professional comment might be, "Edward needs to put more effort into class assignments" or "Edward will benefit from attending extra help sessions." Note that these comments are much more useful and prescriptive in nature. Concerning the student with disruptive behavior, the comment might become, "Shelley has ability in biology but has difficulty sitting still during large group instruction." This comment provides more information about Shelley and her difficulties in class. It also suggests that Shelley might do better in a class where she can be more active and engaged in hands-on learning experiences.

Since teacher comments do provide clearer descriptions of student achievement, school report cards usually include teacher comments. Elementary teachers who have 20-30 students may be required to fill in report cards manually, but most school districts have computerized the process. Teacher comments are usually provided in a long list and teachers can select an appropriate comment to be included on a student's report card. Sometimes teachers find that comments on the list do not accurately describe the students in their class. Teachers can request that additional comments be added to the list. Be sure to inquire about adding comments if the ones provided do not seem appropriate for your students or discipline.

New teachers who approach student assessment for the first time will probably need some guidance. Each school has its own procedures for reporting student achievement and teachers should be knowledgeable of those procedures before the academic year begins. Consider, for example, the novice third grade teacher who constructed and graded math tests on a regular basis. When asked to complete the report cards in early November, she discovered that the school expected her to give separate grades in computation and problem solving. Knowing this in advance, the teacher would have given two different types of tests and recorded grades differently. Therefore, we advise new teachers to review a sample student report card before planning instruction and constructing classroom tests.

In an effort to determine what students have learned at various stages, schools rely heavily on standardized testing strategies. Standardized tests such as Scholastic Aptitude Tests (SAT) and the California Achievement Tests (CAT) are examples of standardized tests used in school. There are also many different types of exams currently required by state educational agencies who are interested in whether or not students are meeting the newly created state standards. Standardized tests compare students with one another in order to determine student mastery of knowledge.

Johnson, Dupuis, Musial, Hall and Gollnick (1999) observed that standardized assessment tools for student evaluation may be of at least two types.   "The first type includes national and /or state-developed instruments such as the Iowa Test of Basic Skills or the California Achievement Test batteries. These may be used for a broad examination of student performance in direct comparison with other students at any given age or grade level.   The second type of standardized assessment still compares student performance among peers but is more closely related to classroom activities. This assessment entails the regular classroom testing with tests constructed by the teacher." (p.461)

Johnson et al. (1999) indicate that national and/or state developed instruments are problematic because they fail to measure higher levels of cognitive learning and fail to examine affective and psychomotor abilities. National and/or state instruments are typically limited to pencil and paper performance and fail to give a complete picture of what a student has actually learned or accomplished. The second type, teacher-made assessments usually have poor or no test validity and/or reliability, although they do monitor students' day-to-day learning in the classroom. Teacher-made assessments usually form the basis of student evaluations on report cards.

Teachers are expected to produce an evaluation of students at the end of each academic term. This end-term evaluation usually appears in the form of a report card grade. Report card grades can tell us something about student learning. Grades can reveal whether or not students have mastered course content. Student growth can also be evident in examining student report cards. However, final report grades are often inflated or deflated by factors not related to student learning. For example, consider how class attendance, students' attitude and willingness to cooperate with class procedures, may raise or lower students' report card grades. Numerical value may be assigned to these factors and averaged into report card grades. Therefore, given the complexity of factors that comprise the teacher's determined final grades, report card grades are not always reliable indicators of student learning.

Criticism of standardized and teacher-made tests have led educators to consider assessments that are more related to real or authentic learning. In addition, new national, state and local initiatives in the form of learning standards require students to demonstrate self-direction, collaboration, complex thinking, quality performance, and community contributions (Johnson, et al., 1999). None of these student competencies can appropriately be measured with traditional assessment strategies. As a result, schools have increasingly moved toward the use of authentic assessment strategies to formally evaluate student learning.

AUTHENTIC ASSESSMENTS OF STUDENTS' LEARNING

Schools are increasingly concerned about true evaluations of student learning. As a result, teachers are using authentic assessment, a term used to describe evaluations within real life situations. Authentic assessments are sometimes called performance-based assessments. Hansen (1998) observed that, "performance based learning experiences" is a collective term that describes how students are asked to learn differently, to perform cognitive and affective skills, and to engage in meaningful learning activities. Therefore, assessment strategies must be genuine, useful, applicable, practice-based, transferable and demonstrable.

Despite the recent interest in authentic assessment, it is not a novel concept. In fact, most of us have experienced various forms of authentic assessment. Examine the following activities that are examples of authentic assessments.

Written essays. Essays demonstrate how well students can use facts in context and present them in a meaningful way. A good essay demands analysis, synthesis, and critical thinking skills.

Oral discourse. Like written work, oral discourses or interviews require students to synthesize knowledge, draw conclusions or make decisions, and justify choices. As part of the learning process, discourse enables students to polish their speaking skills and feel comfortable with public speaking.

Exhibitions and event tasks. In physical education class, an exhibition might be a lay-up or jump-shot in basketball. In science, the exhibition might be an experiment or a science fair project. Substitute "presentation" for "exhibition" and the task can apply to any discipline. In a hands-on presentation, students tend to take their time and pay attention to detail. They are also more likely to retain the knowledge embedded in the task.

Portfolios. This is the most popular form of authentic assessment. In fact, in spite of the many forms authentic assessment can take, portfolios are sometimes seen as synonymous with authentic assessment. Portfolios range from selective-to-comprehensive and provide an excellent measure of progress over an extended period of time.

Johnson et al. (1999) indicated that authentic assessment activities must resemble actual classroom and life tasks. They note that the characteristics of authentic assessment are:

- The assessment closely resembles the way the student will encounter the task or use the knowledge in real life.
- The teacher and the student constantly examine what has been learned, and they jointly determine the limits of that learning.
- The assessment has the learner display learning in a variety of contexts, not just one.
- Assessment provides for active collaborative reflection by both teacher and student. (p.462)

Lund (1997) also outlined several characteristics of authentic assessment. Although the focus is physical education, these characteristics hold true for virtually all disciplines:

- Authentic assessments require the presentation of significant tasks designed to represent performance in the field. Ideally, they can approximate something the person would actually be required to do in a given real world setting.

- Authentic assessments emphasize higher level thinking skills and more complex learning. They are designed to show how well a student can <u>use</u> knowledge, not memorize a set of responses. Lund uses the example of game play in physical education which requires students to apply cognitive knowledge (rules and strategies) for successful participation. However, rules and strategies are not limited to physical education and games which can be incorporated into authentic assessment in other disciplines.
- The criteria used in authentic assessment are emphasized in advance so that students understand how they will be evaluated. Rubrics that list assessment criteria help students to focus on key elements as they work toward mastery in a particular discipline. Because students know the criteria, they are expected to evaluate themselves. An accurate self-assessment is an important skill to master in any field.
- Authentic assessments are so firmly embedded in the curriculum that they are almost indistinguishable from instruction. Therefore, assessment is ongoing rather than summative. Instructional alignment tends to be high when learning and assessment is intertwined in pursuit of a common goal. This is the essence of the learning organization, an environment in which many of our students will be employed. A common business term is "quality improvement."
- Authentic assessment changes the teacher's role from adversary to ally. <u>Assessment</u> comes from a root meaning, "to sit with." In a best case scenario, the relationship is similar to the mentor/protege relationship that is used in many professional settings.

Teachers, who wish to initiate performance-based instruction and assessments within their class, will find the following guidelines offered by Hansen (1998) most useful.

- Start with objectives. Indicate exactly what your students will be able to do as a result of instruction.
- Provide models and examples of the expected performance. Students need to have some idea of what they are expected to do. Just telling them is not enough. Models and examples clarify student understanding.
- Identify ways to exhibit, display or perform student learning.
- Engage students in their work. Remember that if performance is required then students must be active learners.
- Performance-based learning is both product and process. When examining student work, the end product is important but the process is also very important.
- Establish meaningful assessment criteria or rubrics to measure performance. Criteria are the standards of the performance, the degree of mastery or the success in task completion.
- Use a graduated scale for assessments. Allow for revision, adaptation and modification, which are true indicators of real learning.

In the following discussion, we will examine how teachers use traditional and authentic assessments to evaluate student learning. We will examine how these assessments occur during and after instructional presentations.

EVALUATING STUDENT LEARNING DURING INSTRUCTIONAL PRESENTATIONS

While most evaluations of student learning occur after the instructional event, teachers actually monitor student learning while they teach a lesson. Usually this evaluation is informal in nature, but more formal evaluations can also occur during a lesson.

As the instructional presentation progresses, the teacher monitors students' progress towards meeting the prescribed instructional objective. Through question and answer strategies and observation, teachers determine whether or not students are learning. For example, when the teacher poses a question, an incorrect response signals a lack of understanding on the part of the student. Similarly, an incorrect answer for a math problem signals a failure to learn a mathematical concept. Correct responses from students suggest that learning has in fact occurred.

It is also possible to use more formal assessments of student learning during instructional presentations. Formal evaluations usually involve judging some product of student learning that can be produced during the lesson. For example, when students take a quiz during a lesson, correct responses provide evidence of student learning. Other class activities can also provide opportunities to observe student learning. Activities may reflect traditional or authentic assessments of student learning. Complete the following worksheet to determine your understanding of traditional and authentic assessments.

Worksheet: Identify Authentic Assessments
The following list of activities can be used during an instructional presentation. Determine whether the strategy is a traditional or an authentic assessment. Write "T" for traditional and "A" for authentic. Check your answers below.

_____   Give a quiz or self-test based on the lesson content during the lesson. Students can exchange papers with their peers, grade, and discuss the quiz among themselves to clarify understanding.

_____   Write a one-minute paper during the summary activity. Ask students to summarize the main points of the lesson in a short paragraph or two. The teacher can collect the papers or have students exchange papers and discuss.

_____   Assign blackboard work that requires students to solve a problem or create a model related to the day's topics. Ask for students to come to the board to solve an application problem based on the lesson content.

_____   Ask students to write a journal entry that requires a reflection or application of the lesson content. Students can keep a learning journal to summarize and reflect on the new content. Ask students to relate the new lesson to previously learned content.

_____   Ask students to debate or discuss concepts that require an understanding of the lesson content. Pose an issue that has two viewpoints for discussion. Allow students time to prepare arguments in small groups in order to get the greatest student participation in the exercise.

_____   Ask students to demonstrate processes or skills that were taught during the lesson. For example, demonstrating a basketball jump shot in physical education class is one type of demonstration. In science class, the students might demonstrate critical thinking skills as they perform experiments.

_____   Ask for individual or group presentations that incorporate the key concepts of the day's lesson. For example, provide five minutes for students to work with partners in order to summarize the key points of the lesson. Then ask for some groups to share their summaries with the class.

_____   Present problem solving activities and experiments that require students to apply knowledge presented during a lesson. Once again mathematics and science problems are appropriate. Social studies or health issues can also be used in this way. English literature provides many opportunities for applying knowledge as well.

As you reviewed the list, you may have noticed that all of the activities are examples of authentic assessments with the exception of the quiz in bullet #1. The others are considered authentic assessment strategies. Each authentic assessment strategy requires that students demonstrate what they know and what they are able to do. The tasks are also embedded within the curriculum, so that the assessment is naturally intertwined with instruction.

EVALUATING STUDENT LEARNING AFTER INSTRUCTIONAL PRESENTATIONS
Student learning is commonly evaluated after the instructional event has passed. Testing is one way to evaluate student learning after instructional presentations. However, other forms of evaluation such as observational assessments, portfolios and rubrics are also very effective ways to evaluate learning after instructional presentations. In this section, we will explore these strategies.

Using Testing to Evaluate Student Learning
Teacher-made tests and examinations are probably one of the most popular means to evaluate student learning after instructional presentations. Tests provide the classroom teacher with information concerning whether or not students are learning. However, Kim and Kellough (1991) indicate that tests can serve several purposes in addition to measuring student achievement:
- To review and drill to enhance learning
- To motivate students
- To provide information regarding student promotion, guidance, and counseling
- To assess and aid curriculum planning
- To measure teacher effectiveness

Many educators discover that testing is a strategy that ensures student learning. Frequent testing requires that students study and review course content on a regular basis. It is helpful to keep in mind that if you test, the students are more likely to study…usually. Smaller sections of content material can be studied more deeply, therefore, a more effective strategy is to give shorter tests more frequently. Kim and Kellough (1991) observed that frequent tests reduce test anxiety and increase the validity of final grade determination.

New teachers are often pleasantly surprised to find that textbook publishers provide examination packets aligned to class textbooks. Teachers can use these prepared exams by simply photocopying the appropriate pages from the teacher's manual. However, as novice teachers gain experience, they soon realize that publisher-prepared examinations rarely test exactly what was covered during class instruction. As a result, most teachers find it necessary to construct their own exams that will reflect the content covered in class. While publisher-prepared tests may not exactly meet the teacher's needs, these tests can serve as a resource for sample questions.

Once teachers have decided to construct tests for their class, they need to consider the type of exam that is best suited to their students and to the subject area. If the major objective is to help students develop critical thinking and writing skills, then the teacher will probably want to include essay questions on the exam. If the main objective is that students acquire specific content related to the subject matter then objective test questions may be suitable. Many teachers include both objective type questions and essay questions on teacher-made tests. The objective questions allow the teacher to evaluate whether or not students have learned a broad range of content and are easy to grade. Typically, students are given a choice of essay questions and the number of questions is usually limited in number. This strategy, of combining objective test questions and essays, is effective. Test grading will then become more manageable for the teacher.

Gronlund (1985) noted that objective tests encourage students to develop comprehensive knowledge of specific facts and if properly constructed, can encourage the development of higher level thinking skills. Objective test questions are popular among classroom teachers because such tests are easy to grade. Test questions that require one correct response are classified as objective. True-false, multiple choice, matching and fill in the blank questions are included in objective tests. Lorber (1996) observed that these test questions "are 'objective' only in the sense that there is no need to make value judgments about the answers. They are clearly either right or wrong." (p. 255)

Objective tests allow the classroom teacher to test a broad range of information. Easy grading is especially attractive for high school teachers who may have as many as 150 test papers to correct. Although the preparation of a good objective exam is difficult and time consuming, many teachers feel that time saved in grading is worth the effort. Gronlund (1985) indicated that objective test questions minimize the likelihood of students bluffing and that high reliability is possible with well-constructed tests.

Lorber (1996) outlined some general rules to guide teachers in the construction of good objective test items:

- Keep the objective clearly in mind.
- Keep the language simple.
- Ask students to apply rather than to simply recall, information.
- Make sure each test item is independent.
- Do not establish or follow a pattern for correct responses.
- Do not include trick or trivial questions.
- Be sure that there is only one correct or clearly best answer.
- Avoid trivia. (p. 255-258)

Jones (1979) also provided some suggestions on how to construct a good objective test. Accordingly, Jones suggested that teachers attempt to:

- Measure important knowledge.
- Keep the level of readability below the grade level of the students being tested.
- State the test items in a positive form. Negative words like "not" compound verbal logic.
- Underline or capitalize key words to make the test item easier to read.
- Ascertain that information from one item should not be useful in answering another item.
- Refrain from lifting statements verbatim from instructional materials, since out of context statements lose their meaning and may result in ambiguous items.

Jones (1979) was also concerned about the appropriate use of objective tests. Therefore, Jones identified circumstances under which objective tests are best used:

- When students have the appropriate and required reading ability to comprehend the questions.
- When writing skills are not the main learning objectives.
- When the course content lends itself to a paper and pencil measurement.
- When the time available for test construction is greater than the time available for test scoring.

There are various types of objective test questions including true-false, matching columns, fill-in-the-blanks, and multiple choice. Students are familiar with all of these types of questions that are typically used in school. Students often prefer formats that provide opportunities for "guessing" at the correct answer. We will examine each type of objective test question and provide some guidelines for test construction.

True – False Test Questions

Students often prefer true-false questions. True-false exams present statements that students judge to be accurate or not. A large number of true-false questions can be answered within a short period of time. True-false questions allow the teacher to test a broad range of content. Test scoring is quick and can also be machine scored. True-false questions can be difficult to compose and students have a fifty-fifty chance of merely guessing at the right answer.

Kim and Kellough (1991) provide some guidelines for preparing true-false statements:

- First write out the statement as a true statement; then make it false by changing a word or a phrase.
- Avoid negative statements.
- Include only one idea within the statement.
- Use approximately an equal number of true and false statements on the test.
- Avoid the use of word clues such as always, never, all and none.
- Avoid words that have different meaning for different students.
- Avoid using the exact words from the lecture or textbook.
- Avoid trick test items.
- Use modified true-false questions. A modified true-false question provides space for students to explain why a response is false.

Arends (1994) noted that well-written true-false statements indicate clear choices and the answers are unambiguous. It will take some practice before you are able to consistently construct well-written true-false questions for use in the classroom. You will probably find it helpful to use textbooks and teacher guides as resources for test items. However, be judicious in your selection of test questions so that the test is a valid measure of student learning.

The Matching Test

Matching tests usually present the learner with two columns of information that are related in some way. Matching tests are commonly used to measure recall of facts, ideas, definitions, people and dates. For example, one column can list the names of people, and the other column can list their accomplishments. Concepts and definitions can be matched. Events and dates are another possibility that can be matched. Matching tests are fairly easy to construct, easy to grade and can test a broad range of knowledge.

Some guidelines for preparing matching test questions may include the following:

- Limit the types of information within the columns. Mixing dates, concepts and people can result in a less challenging task. Be sure that the choices are not obvious and logically deduced.
- Provide a greater number of choices in the answer column to reduce guessing.
- Keep the number of items short (10-12 items are appropriate for secondary students and 5-7 for elementary students).
- Indicate whether or not an answer can be used more than once.
- Indicate how students should mark the correct response. Drawing lines is a typical strategy used with young children. Older students are usually asked to write a corresponding letter or number next to each item in column one.
- Be prepared to listen to student reasoning as to why they chose one response over another. (You may have to be flexible if the student's rationale is valid).

Fill-in-the-blank or Completion Tests

Fill-in-the-blank tests (sometimes called completion tests) present students with a statement in which one or more words are missing. Blank spaces indicate the placement of the missing words. Students usually find these tests rather challenging because they require that students recall exact terminology and concepts in order to answer the question. Fill-in-the-blank tests are fairly easy to prepare and grade but once again the teacher must be careful to avoid ambiguity. Questions that have more than one correct response are problematic on completion tests. Completion test items require that students fully recall a key word or phrase. According to Lorber (1996), completion items are problematic because they stress rote memorization and students, under the stress of the testing situation, may have difficulty recalling key ideas.

Lorber (1996) does however provide some guidelines for completion tests:
- Prepare items that can be completed with a single word or a short phrase.
- Be sure that only one word or phrase can correctly complete the statement.
- Place the blanks close to the end of the sentence so the student guided towards the correct response.
- Make all blanks approximately the same length.
- Use no more than two blanks in one test item.

Teachers can help students to recall concepts on completion tests by providing a word bank of possible answers. The word bank changes the nature of the academic task to resemble more of a matching exercise. However, if the word bank is sufficiently large, the completion items can still be challenging. Students for whom English is a second language will find a word bank especially helpful when taking completion tests. Word banks are an excellent way to adapt testing materials for special needs students.

Multiple Choice Tests

Teachers often prefer to give multiple choice questions on classroom tests. These test questions can be scored by machine if students use the appropriate forms and number 2 pencils. Most schools have simple-to-use scanners available for teachers to use. Students seem to like multiple choice test questions and often refer to them as "multiple guess." Students are comforted by the fact that they can take an educated guess and not have to leave the response blank.

Most evaluation experts consider multiple choice test items to be the best type of objective test item (Arends, 1994). If well-written, multiple choice test items can require higher level thinking skills.

According to Arends (1994), multiple choice items are composed of three components: a stem, a correct answer and distracters. A stem is a statement that poses a question. The correct answer solves the problem or answers the question correctly. The distracters are several statements that are believable, but incorrect.

Arends (1994) observes that good multiple choice test items are difficult to write. The stem must include adequate information for the student to understand the problem being posed but not reveal the correct answer. The distracters must be believable yet must be recognized as being clearly incorrect.

The following guidelines for constructing multiple choice test items are offered by Kim and Kellough (1991):
- Be sure that the stem is a statement that provides meaningful information.
- Use language that is easy enough for the poorer readers to understand.
- Arrange items from shortest to longest, when the length of choices vary.
- Consider using alphabetical order to arrange single word choices
- Distracters should be plausible and related to the correct alternative.
- Arrange choices in a list rather than paragraph form.
- Be sure grammar is consistent.
- Use four or five choices to reduce the possibility of guessing.
- Express the stem in a positive form.
- Be careful with using "all of these," "one of these," "all the above" and "none of the above." These responses can cue the correct response.
- Be sure there is only one correct or best response.
- Be sure that the stem means the same to all test takers.
- Be sure that the stem does not include clues.
- Consider using charts, diagrams and visuals as well as verbal questions.
- Check the position of the answers so that responses do not form a particular pattern.
- Provide space for students to include a rationale for their response.

- Keep a tally of students' incorrect responses when correcting exams. Analysis of incorrect responses is helpful in subsequent test writing.
- Begin your own multiple choice test item bank for analysis and improvement of test questions.

Following these guidelines, it is possible to become proficient in writing clear, well-formulated multiple choice questions to test students' understanding of instructional content.

Essay Tests Questions

Essay tests questions are simpler to compose but much more difficult to grade. Lorber (1996) observes that well-written essay test questions require that students gather, organize, interpret and evaluate data, draw conclusions, make inferences and express these ideas in writing. Students who are capable of critical thinking and possess good writing skills definitely have an advantage with essay test questions. Essay tests require much more time for grading.

Lorber (1996) offers some suggestions for constructing and administering an essay test:

- Be definite about what is expected from students. Include sub-questions to clarify what is expected.
- Describe the task clearly.
- Specify grading criteria. What must be included in an answer to get A?, B?, C?, and etc. For example, if students are discussing causes of the Civil War, how many should be discussed? Three? Four?
- Write out a sample A-quality response to guide your grading.
- Review content in class to fully prepare students.
- Provide sufficient time for students to answer questions.
- Compare student essay responses to your own A-quality model.
- Grade all responses to one question and then go back and grade all responses to the next question. This strategy provides greater consistency in grading.

When constructing essay test questions, be sure to use words and phrases that will adequately describe what you expect of the students. Consider the following words that may be used in an essay question: explain, describe, discuss, and define. Both teachers and students must have the same understanding as to the meaning of each word. Teachers can clarify what is expected in the correct response by providing sub-questions within the essay. For example, consider the following essay question: "Discuss American foreign policy during the Cold War." The question is broad and may elicit a wide range of responses from students, some of which the teacher did not intend. You could ask the question so that it is more focused. Ask, "Discuss American foreign policy during the Cold War. Cite the two strengths and three weaknesses and give examples of each." Student responses will probably be closer to what the teacher expected.

Responses to essay questions allow teachers to examine students' handwriting, grammar and spelling. Poor performance on essay questions can indicate gaps in students' understanding of content as well as writing difficulties. Secondary teachers who rely heavily on objective test items may be missing important information concerning students' academic needs. Teachers should always collect samples of students' essay writing early in the term to inform class instruction. Students, who lack the reading and writing skills needed for academic success, require assistance. The classroom teacher can help these students in a variety of ways. For example, supplying textbooks with grade level content, but low readability levels can support poor readers. Structuring writing assignments so that preliminary drafts are collected on a scheduled basis can support poor writers.

Teachers will find the following worksheet helpful in evaluating teacher-made tests.

Worksheet: Evaluate Teacher Made Tests

Directions: Complete the following checklist to guide your construction of teacher made tests. Check the statements that are true for you.

Physical Appearance

_____ Typed

_____ Easy to Read

_____ Free of spelling and grammar errors

_____ Sufficient space for students to write answers

_____ Place to write student name

_____ Place to write the date

Test Directions

_____ Test directions are clearly stated

_____ Questions are numbered

_____ Points for each question are indicated

Test Content

_____ Test covers materials presented in class

_____ Students know what to study

_____ Knowledge is measured in a variety of ways (Fill-ins, multiple choice, matching, essay)

_____ Students have a choice of essay questions

Length of Test

_____ Length of test is appropriate for student grade level

_____ There is adequate time for students to take the test

Grading

How to Help Students Take Tests

Teachers can help students perform better on tests and enhance students' learning. Announcing tests well in advance is always helpful. Both elementary and secondary students need adequate time to prepare and review content materials. Students have commitments such as athletic events, music recitals, and family gatherings. If students know when to expect exams, they can schedule study time appropriately. For younger students make sure that parents are also informed about test dates. Parents can help their children study and thus enhance learning. Teachers should provide some review of content during class time.

Teachers who spend time reviewing content before exams enhance student learning. During review sessions, teachers should emphasize important concepts and ideas that students need to know for the test. If the purpose of classroom tests is to ensure student learning, then a comprehensive review session is always necessary. For older students, teachers can verbally provide an outline of key ideas to study, however, younger students will usually need a written study guide. Teachers will find that telling students what they are expected to know for the test will usually result in higher test grades and greater student learning. For older students, Lorber (1996) suggests that major tests be scheduled on Monday with formal review sessions held on Friday. This approach gives students an advantage because it gives them the weekend to study. Lorber further suggests that students should know how many sections and questions are on the test and the type of questions, such as true-false, multiple choice or essay. He suggests that providing sufficient information about the test will reduce test anxiety for students.

When administering classroom tests, teachers should review test directions with students. Younger students and special learners may have difficulty understanding how the teacher wants the answers recorded. A review of test directions can also help the teacher with grading. Consider for example, that some students draw lines to indicate correct answers on a matching column while others record the corresponding letter next to each item. As the teacher grades each paper, he or she will have to figure out each student's answering technique. Grading takes longer when several students mark their answers differently, or on opposite ends of the page, as the teacher has to search for responses.

Remind students to budget their test time wisely. Instruct students to skip questions that they do not know and return to those later on. Students should pay close attention to questions that carry greater credit and allocate adequate time to respond.

Encourage students to take an educated guess when they don't know the answer. During review sessions, teach students how to analyze multiple-choice questions by giving examples, and teach the students to re-read the question stem. Direct students to look for words listed in the option that are also in the question.

Planning is important when responding to essay questions. Instruct students to preview all essay questions and determine how many questions must be answered. If there are no choices, students should be allowed to respond to questions in any order. Students will want to answer first those questions about which they are most confident. If students have difficulty with a question, suggest that they leave it and return to it later on. When students return to a difficult question, they often recall more about it. Teach students how to create brief outline notes before writing responses to essay questions. A brief outline can help students organize their thoughts and, hopefully, the result is a clearer presentation of their response. This approach to answering essay questions will reduce students' level of test anxiety.

Remind students to review the test answers before handing it into the teacher. Students should make sure that they answered all required questions. Caution students about changing answers unless they are confident that the change is correct.

Consider giving students an opportunity to acquire bonus points on classroom tests. Bonus points can be assigned for recalling some extra content discussed in the textbook or perhaps mentioned in class. Sometimes a film or video related to the topic can be placed in the school library for student review. The idea that one can earn bonus points for responding to some question, based on the film, can be motivating. Bonus points can be used to encourage students to probe more deeply into a subject area and the result is better learning.

OBSERVATIONAL ASSESSMENTS

Observational assessment is a useful alternative to traditional methods of evaluation such as testing. Experienced teachers learn much from observing and interacting with students in and out of the class. Through observation, teachers can identify students' strengths and weaknesses, their efforts and their attitudes.

Lapp, Flood and Farnan (1996) indicate that observations of student performance are natural, subtle and the least threatening of all informal assessment techniques. All types of student learning and class activity can be observed. Teachers may choose to record observations with checklists or in journals. Lapp et al. suggest that, "when used in conjunction with the information yielded by other assessment techniques, (observations) can be the basis for sound instructional decision making." (p. 393) Nevertheless, are observational assessments by classroom teachers an authentic form of assessment? According to Lapp, Flood and Farnan (1996), observation can be a valid assessment technique in settings that simulate authentic situations. Classrooms are authentic settings for the observation of student learning.

Observational assessments are enhanced through student-teacher conferencing. Conferencing broadens teacher observations to include the student's perspective. Learning logs and journal entries can also inform teachers' observational assessments. In this section, we will examine how student-teacher conferencing and journal writing can assist teachers in observational assessments of student learning.

STUDENT-TEACHER CONFERENCES

Student-teacher conferences provide insight into student learning in every subject area. Conferences are commonly used among reading and writing teachers. However, other content area teachers will discover the use of conferences helpful as well. If you are considering using student-teacher conferences as a means of evaluation, you are probably thinking, "When will I have time to confer with students about their learning?" and, more importantly, "What will we talk about?"

It is a good idea to set up conference time on a regular basis. If you have a small class, you may be able to schedule conferences once every two or three weeks. Larger class sizes may prevent you from implementing such a plan. However, you may want to confer with everyone at least once early in the school year. Then you can confer on a regular basis with students who seem to be having difficulty in the course. Conferences can be scheduled during free periods or class time. If class time is used for conferencing, provide a meaningful class assignment for everyone, create a schedule and meet with individuals in a quiet spot within the classroom.

The purpose of student-teacher conferences is to gather information on student learning. The teacher should thus structure the conference to that end. The following guidelines can be helpful in conducting student-teacher learning conferences:

Listen: First and foremost, the teacher should listen to what the student has to say about his or her learning in a specific subject area. Allow the student to tell you about what they feel they understand well and enjoy about the class.

Respond: Ask some probing questions in response to what the student has shared. Ask the student about areas of difficulty or concern. Inquire about how students prepare for class and study for tests. Allow the student time to share their learning experiences.

Observe: Ask students to perform some type of task that will provide insight into student learning. For example, a math teacher might ask a student to solve a math problem. A science teacher may ask a student to explain a scientific process. Since many students have difficulty with literacy skills, a teacher may ask a student to read a passage aloud from the textbook and explain it in their own words. By directly observing students engaged in these types of tasks, the teacher will better understand student ability and competency.

Plan: The next step is to create a plan to help students become better learners. Based on the discussion and observation, the teacher will be able to help the student find helpful strategies to enhance learning. For example, if the student has difficulty passing class tests, the plan might be to attend review sessions after school. Instruction in notetaking and study skills might also be appropriate. The teacher plays an important role in developing the plan and may have to find suitable resources to assist the student. For example, if a student has difficulty reading the textbook, the plan might be for the teacher to find an alternative textbook that is easier to comprehend. It is most important that the student agrees with the plan and its usefulness. Review sessions after school may be a good idea if the student has transportation home. If transportation is not available, perhaps an alternative strategy such as a study group within the neighborhood might be a good idea.

Take Notes: The teacher should keep a log that records: the student's name, date of conference and plan. The log is helpful in recalling the strategies that were planned and evaluating progress. The student should also write down the plan in his/her notebook as well. Reviewing the log on a regular basis and at future conferences will keep everyone on task.

The framework offered above should be considered flexible and adjusted to meet the individual needs of students. As teachers use student learning conferences, they will find that the approach benefits both teachers and students alike.

Clark & Wilson, (1994) suggest that teachers can gain insight into student problem solving, communication, reasoning and connection skills through observational assessment. Some of their suggestions can be used during student conferences to help teachers evaluate student learning. They offer the following framework to guide teacher observations:

<u>Problem solving</u>
- How does the student develop strategies for problem solving and critical thinking?
- Does the student understand the problem-solving/ critical thinking process?
- Is the student capable of presenting good problems or asking good questions?

<u>Communication</u>
- What is the quality of the student's oral communication?
- What is the quality of the student's written communication?
- Is the student able to reflect on and clarify his or her ideas?

<u>Reasoning</u>
- Is the student able to use conjecture?
- Is the student able to use counterexamples?
- Is the student able to construct simple arguments?
- Is the student able to thoughtfully evaluate the arguments and conjectures of others?

<u>Connection</u>
- Does the student demonstrate the ability to make connections among related topics?
- Is the student aware of the link between a class activity and its real world application?
- Is the student aware of the relevant connections between this curriculum content area (e.g., mathematics, social studies) and other disciplines.

As you can see, student-teacher conferences are an excellent strategy to provide insight into student learning. Conferencing with students is helpful in evaluating students' learning at all levels of schooling. In addition, teachers gain valuable insight in student learning processes and can focus instruction to meet individual needs.

EVALUATING STUDENT LEARNING THROUGH JOURNAL WRITING

Journal writing serves two purposes in the classroom. First, journal writing enhances student learning (sometimes referred to as "writing to learn"). Secondly, journal writing informs teacher observations about student learning, thus helping teachers assess student learning. While individual student-teacher conferences can reveal much about student learning, teachers can only confer with one student at a time. However, when students write in their journals, the teacher can gather information from every student at the same time. Journal writing can be accomplished in a short period of time and on a regular basis. Therefore, classroom teachers will find that student journal writing is a powerful tool to help students learn and to assess student learning.

The varying terminology that appears in the literature, (namely response journals, learning logs, journal writing, writing to learn, etc.) requires that we clearly define the term "journal writing." For our discussion, journal writing refers to student writings that require students to reflect upon and write about their engagement in learning experiences. Learning experiences may be reading, writing, oral discourse, viewing a film, listening to a lecture, performing an experiment or any other academic task that occurs within classroom settings.

The educational literature is rich with descriptions of how teachers can use journal writing in the classroom. Researchers have described various types of writing journals to serve a variety of purposes. Response journals, typically used in English class, are journals in which students respond to a reading assignment by writing a reaction or response. Students can be asked to reflect upon the actions of a main character or to consider a different ending to a story or event. In this type of journal, students can also ask questions about the reading material. The teacher can then respond to students' questions. For example, a student may not truly understand the main character's motivation for rebelling in school. The teacher can respond by explaining the main character's motivation or use this information to direct further instruction for the class. (Chances are others in class also have trouble with this concept). Given the broad range of written responses that might be generated, response journals can be used in any subject area that assigns required reading.

Another type of journal that can be used in any subject area is the double entry journal. Double entry journals can be used during reading activities, when viewing a film or while engaged in a learning activity such as performing a science experiment. Double entry journals are journals that require students to take notes on the left side of the notebook page while engaged in the learning activity. Students may record specific events in a story or record their observations. After the learning activity is completed, students use the right side of the notebook page to write additional responses or to pose questions.

Double entry journals are effective when used to assess student learning in the classroom. Elizabeth Lee (1997) used double-entry learning logs in her English classroom as a form of student assessment. She used the logs to assess the thinking, writing, speaking and listening in her collaborative classroom environment. Lee observed that one benefit of using learning logs was that students felt free to express their concerns and to experiment with learning. For Lee's students, the logs were records of their preparation and effort to learn, their reflection on how they make sense of content, and their extension and reformulation of knowledge.

A third type of journal is the learning journal, sometimes called the learning log. Learning journal entries can be used to respond to readings, lectures, films or demonstrations. The learning journal requires that students reflect and analyze content as they record and comment on a course of study, linking learning to prior knowledge and students' learning styles (O'Rourke, 1998). The common thread that connects these different types of journals is that students are expected to reflect upon and write about their engagement in learning experiences. By reading student reflections, teachers gain insight into student learning processes and collect information to assess student learning. Let us examine how journal writing can function within subject area classrooms.

Cutforth and Parker (1996) reported on their use of journal writing in elementary physical education classes. They found that engaging students in journal writing allowed the teacher to learn about students' physical education experiences. In addition, the teacher wanted to assess whether or not students achieved the affective learning goals of respect, responsibility, sensitivity toward others, cooperation and fair play. According to Cutforth and Parker (1996), journal writings revealed feelings about students' own work and how the class was taught. Students commented on difficulties that they are experiencing and satisfaction gained from mastering skills. Students' personal and social growth was also documented in their journals. Cutforth and Parker learned that participation in physical education class was not the same for every student and that background, aptitude and attitude may have determined how a child experienced gym class.

Charlene Root (1996) used journal writing with her secondary art students. She expected that journal writing would have profound effects on her students. Interestingly, her research showed the greatest effect was on the teacher, herself. Root discovered that writing journals affected her assessments of students' artwork. According to Root as she learned more about her students, the way she evaluated their artwork began to change. As Root learned more about her students' struggles and what they were attempting to convey visually, she saw their finished artwork in a different light. Root observed that the students' work had greater value to her after reading their journals. In addition, she noted that the journal allowed her to trace students' artwork from conception to completion. Relationships between Root and her students became closer as a result of the additional communication afforded by the journal writing in art class.

Barbara Dougherty (1996) implemented journal writing in her high school algebra class. She observed that, "As students analyze arguments, compare and contrast ideas, and synthesize or assimilate information in writing tasks, they are forming a cohesive knowledge base that pulls together otherwise isolated fragments." (p. 556) To focus students' journal writing, Dougherty used three types of journal prompts: mathematical content, process and affective/attitudinal prompts. Mathematical content prompts required students to focus on mathematical topics and their relationships. Process prompts required students to reflect on why they chose or preferred a particular strategy and to consider the ways in which they learned. Affective or attitudinal prompts asked students to view themselves as mathematicians and problem solvers. Dougherty suggested that carefully constructed journal prompts allow teachers to gather better assessments of students' understanding of math concepts. In addition, students can use their journal responses to assess their own growth in learning mathematics.

Journal writing also seems to be an effective strategy to use with students who are not native English speakers. Holmes and Moulton (1997) examined the use of dialogue journals with college students who were second language learners. Students in this study reported increased fluency and motivation to write in English after using dialogue journals in class.

Given the successes of these classroom teachers, you can understand the popularity of using journal writing within the classroom. Most likely, you are also thinking, "How can I use journal writing within my own classroom?"

How to set up a journal writing program in your classroom

Teachers who wish to use journal writing in their classes must first decide on what they hope to achieve. If you hope to gather information to assess student learning, you will want to follow these guidelines:

- Provide a separate notebook or ask students to purchase one for their journal writing. It is important that all journal entries be kept in one place. Numerous entries scattered throughout students' notes will not allow the reader to understand patterns and changes that occur in the learning process over time.
- Remind students to bring their journal notebook to class each day. Daily journal writing is usually best as students develop the habit of recording their thoughts and ideas. Provide time during class for students to write in their journals.
- Determine the purpose of the journal and explain this purpose to the class. If you want to discover what students have learned, ask them to explain concepts, ideas, or reading selections in their own words. When teachers fail to set a purpose for the journal entry, students are free to write whatever they please. Free-writing in students' journals is not a bad idea, and you may want to encourage such writing at various times throughout the term. However, if your purpose is to assess student learning, you will want to provide appropriate questions or prompts for your students.
- Indicate the number and frequency of entries that students are expected to produce. Students usually need some guidelines to direct their journal writing. Most students will not diligently write in their journals each day. It is probably reasonable to expect two or three entries each week. Daily journal writing can be encouraged, but insisting on such a routine could result in students becoming quickly bored with the activity. Setting a number and frequency for journal entries also will help students define the task more clearly.
- Explain when and how journals will be collected. It is important to collect journals regularly and provide students with feedback. Reading numerous journals and responding to students' writing can be a laborious task. It is unreasonable to think that a teacher will be able to read every student's journal each day. A high school teacher may elect to collect certain groups of journals on alternating weeks. An elementary teacher may read everyone's journal once every two weeks. It is important to find a schedule that works for you and then communicate that schedule clearly to your students.
- Explain how journals will count as part of the overall grade. Determine how much credit will be assigned to each student's journal and how individual journals will be assessed.

The problem of how to assess journals is rather complex and discussed in the following section.

How should teachers assess student journal writing?

If student journals allow teachers to assess student learning processes, should teachers evaluate the quality of that learning by grading students' journals? Burniske (1994) observed that teachers are conditioned to respond to student writing. Furthermore, teachers feel that their response must take the form of correction, evaluation and grading. Burniske suggested that the teacher's response should be shaped by the purpose for the writing. So therefore, teachers should ask themselves, "For what reasons, am I using learning logs or journal writing?" The answer to the question will help the teacher decide on how to assess student journals.

Ava Chandler (1997) addressed the problem of how to grade student journals. She suggested that assigning a grade for journal writing is problematic and may not produce learning but merely grades. Chandler suggested that grading a journal is a destructive activity that penalizes students and inhibits learning. Therefore, she suggested that journals not be evaluated, but simply assigned as part of a student's grade. In Chandler's class, students received credit for completion of the journal and no credit for failure to complete. Chandler readily admits that this was not the perfect answer, but it did take the sting out of teacher comments, questions and responses that are made on the journal and it eliminated the evaluative aspect. (Here again, teacher comments need to be useful ones that can contribute to student learning.)

Burniske (1994) observed that most teachers are preoccupied with the assessment of writing and that is a problem. The goal of journal writing should be to encourage writing and thinking, not the acquisition of grades. Burniske's approach was to respond to student journals in a written letter format and not write comments in student journals. On a separate piece of paper, Burniske wrote each student a letter discussing the contents of the journal. Burniske did assign a grade for the journal that was based primarily on effort, with points subtracted for lateness. Journal writings that included lengthy, insightful or extra entries merited an "A" in Burniske's class.

One problem, with assigning journal writing, is the amount of paperwork produced. Teachers who have large numbers of students often find reading students' journals to be a time-consuming task. However, Ross (1998) observed that journals are only as much work as the teacher wants them to be. While teachers must read the journal, the teachers can determine the quantities of comments and type of feedback students receive. Reading the journals, helps the teacher learn how students are progressing and which questions the students have about class work. The teacher does not have to respond to every entry nor does he or she have to assign an evaluative grade to journal writing.

Ross (1998) also discussed the assessment of student journals and encouraged teachers to decide on a grading policy that works for them. Spelling, grammar and punctuation may be overlooked if the teacher decides to grade on the basis of content. In addition, students can also read and respond to each other's journals. This strategy provides feedback and allows the students to learn from one another.

Chandler (1997) suggested using a shared reading strategy for responding to students' journals in the classroom. In a shared reading strategy, students read each others journals and respond to each other. If time allows, students can receive responses from many different classmates. Shared reading strategies can be used as a regular practice or as an occasional alternative to teacher response. The shared reading strategy is advantageous for students by:

- Eliciting more responses to journal writings, instructor and peers.
- Reinforcing the importance of students' writing, thinking and sharing.
- Exposing students to multiple viewpoints and interpretations of the same issue.
- Reinforcing common understandings.
- Allowing students to see and discuss common misunderstandings.

In conclusion, journal writing provides a powerful means to assess student learning. The use of journals within the content area classroom does present some challenges to the teacher. These challenges include how to manage the volume of students' writings and the problem of assessment. However, the advantages of using journal writing are many. First, students' learning is enhanced as they reflect, analyze and internalize what they read and learn about in class. Secondly, the teacher gains a better understanding of students' learning as these journal entries provide insight into thinking and learning processes. Lastly, journal writing provides opportunities for teachers and students to share ideas, attitudes and understandings in a personal way. This type of sharing is not usually achieved through student-teacher interactions during regular instructional presentations.

STUDENT PORTFOLIOS

Student portfolios are becoming a standard practice in elementary and secondary school classrooms. Generally, portfolios are defined as meaningful collections of students' work over time. Wolf and Siu-Runyan (1996) define portfolio more specifically as, "a selective collection of student work and records of progress gathered across diverse contexts over time, framed by reflection and enriched through collaboration, that has its aim the advancement of student learning."(p. 31) A similar definition is offered by Meyer, Schuman and Angello (1990): "A purposeful collection of student work, exhibiting to the student and others the student's efforts, progress or achievement in selected areas and including, at a minimum: a) student participation in selection of portfolio content; b) the criteria for selection; c) the criteria for judging merit and d) evidence of student self-reflection." (p. 3)

As described above, the portfolio concept is particularly attractive to teachers who wish to document student growth and accomplishment over time. The idea of displaying what one knows and/or is able to do by a portfolio is not new. Artists and journalists have traditionally used portfolios as a means of displaying their work for the purpose of assessment.

Portfolios can serve many purposes, other than assessment. Tierney and Readence (2000) observe that portfolios can serve the following purposes:

- To engage students in self-assessment
- To engage students in periodical evaluations and goal setting
- To serve as a means of collecting, analyzing and developing plans based on students' work
- To screen students on the basis of what they have done

Student portfolios also serve to inform our teaching in the classroom. When teachers help students develop portfolios about their learning, they gather important information about students. This information enables teachers to redirect, refocus and refine their approaches to instruction. Tierney and Readence (2000) confirm that portfolio assessment is intricately tied to teaching and learning. Portfolios are learner-based assessments that yield "a unique and multifaceted profile of a student." (p. 481) They note that portfolios consistently yield more and better information about student learning, student abilities, student interests and development. Not only do students receive a positive view of themselves, they become invested in their own development.

DeFina (1992) suggests a set of assumptions that can be made about all portfolio assessment:

- Portfolios are systematic, purposeful and meaningful collections of students' work in one or more subject areas.
- Students of any age or grade level can learn not only to select pieces to be placed in their portfolios but can also learn to establish criteria for their selections.
- Portfolio collections may include input by teachers, parents, peers and school administrators.
- In all cases, portfolios should reflect the actual day to day learning activities of the students.

- Portfolios should be ongoing so they show the students' efforts, progress and achievements over a period of time.
- Portfolios may contain several compartments or subfolders.
- Selected works in portfolios may be in a variety of media and may be multidimensional. (p. 13-16)

Wolf and Siu-Runyan (1996) suggest three distinct portfolio models can be found in schools: ownership, feedback and accountability portfolios. The primary purpose of each differs. Ownership portfolios are personalized and emphasize student choice and self-assessment. The main purpose of ownership portfolios is to allow students to explore, extend, display and reflect upon their learning. Feedback portfolios are comprehensive collections of students' work and teacher records co-constructed by student and teacher. The main purpose of feedback portfolios is to guide teachers and students in identifying effective teaching and learning strategies and to communicate this information to parents. Accountability portfolios are selective collections of student work, teacher records and standardized assessments that are submitted by students and teachers according to established guidelines. The purpose of this last type of portfolio is to evaluate student achievement for accountability and program evaluation.

Other researchers have also identified portfolio models. Valencia (1998) described five different models of portfolios according to purpose, audience, participants and structure. These five models include showcase, documentation, evaluation, process and composite. According to Valencia, showcase portfolios highlight students' best and meaningful work and to engage students in ownership and thoughtful reflection. Students assume total responsibility for constructing these portfolios and therefore decide on the structure of the project. While students are the primary audience for showcase portfolios, teachers and parents review these portfolios as well.

Documentation portfolios provide a systematic record of student progress. Valencia (1998) observed that documentation portfolios include student work but also teacher observations, anecdotal records and interviews. Teachers usually select evidence to be included, but students may also be involved in the process. While this type of portfolio is often found in primary grade settings, they can be used with older students as well.

The third type of portfolio identified by Valencia (1998) is the evaluation portfolio. Its primary purpose is to evaluate student learning in a systematic manner and to communicate that evidence to others. School districts may require this type of portfolio to collect information to supplement standardized test data. The group who requested the information and scored according to a set of evaluation rubrics usually structures evaluation portfolios.

Valencia (1998) described a fourth type of portfolio, called the process portfolio. Process portfolios focus on the process of learning. The writing process is often presented in this type of portfolio. Samples may include notes, numerous drafts and finish pieces of writing as well students' reflections on their work. Process portfolios inform instruction and document student growth.

The final model described by Valencia is the composite model that includes elements of the other models. Accordingly, the composite model has three components:

- Student-selected work: work selected by the student, often accompanied by a reflection.
- Teacher-selected work: work selected by the teacher that helps describe a particular student more fully.
- Common tools: specific assessment tasks or strategies designed to assess specific learner outcomes and used by all participating teachers on a regular schedule (Valencia, 1998, p. 39).

Unless a particular portfolio format is dictated by the school system, a teacher's choice of portfolio model will largely depend on its purpose. The actual portfolio model may evolve as students and teachers collect evidence of student learning and growth. Teachers are encouraged to keep an open mind as they begin this process and they will discover what works best for their particular discipline and age group.

A Practical Approach for Implementing Student Portfolio Assessment

Once you have decided to use student portfolios in the classroom you need to devise a plan for implementation. What artifacts will be collected? Where will the items be placed? How will the items be organized and displayed?

Student portfolios are a collection of "artifacts of student learning." "Artifacts of student learning" are those concrete, tangible records of student work that provides evidence of learning. Graded classroom tests, written reports, student artwork, and other work samples are examples of artifacts that provide evidence of student learning. When teachers, students and parents examine these artifacts, they know that learning has occurred. The type and the quality of the selection also inform the type of learning that has occurred. High test-grades, well-written reports and creative science projects suggest high levels of academic achievement. Conversely, low test grades, poorly written papers and poorly designed science projects suggest low levels of academic achievement, Hamm & Adams (1992) suggest that comprehensive student portfolios might contain:

- Samples of students' written compositions.
- Journal entries, personal reflections and reactions to work.
- Problem solving attempts, strategies, and outcomes.
- Ideas about projects and exploration.
- Artwork, audio and videotapes, photographs or other creative expressions.
- Selected samples of specific content presented over time.
- Computer readouts and disks.
- Student logs and collected data.
- Group recordings and assignments.
- Projects from rough drafts to finished products.

Students are intensely involved in the selection of artifacts of learning. Although, teachers will probably want to indicate specific items that must be included in the portfolio, there should be many opportunities for student selections as well.

For example, a high school biology teacher may indicate that students must include unit exams and lab reports within their portfolios. However, the students would determine additional materials selected for inclusion. One student might include learning logs, reflection papers and photographs of a science fair project. Another may select to include a videotape and written analysis of a field experiment within the portfolio. Students should largely determine the actual form that the portfolio takes. All students should be encouraged to include photos of them and classmates involved in learning within the classroom. Teachers can assist in this process by taking photographs of students engaged in learning on a regular basis. Usually younger students will need more teacher guidance in the process of selecting and assembling their portfolio. However, as students gain experience they will become more independent in developing their own unique portfolios.

Classroom teachers will want to select an appropriate vehicle for displaying the portfolio artifacts. A large binder, an accordion folder or perhaps a set of folders will work best for your class. Teachers may allow older students to decide for themselves on how to display their portfolio. However, for students just beginning to develop portfolios, teacher guidance in how to display and present their work will be helpful. Regardless of the form used in developing students' portfolios, teachers will find that there will be a plethora of artifacts collected. Therefore, students with the help of their teacher, need to select only those artifacts that truly describe what they have learned, accomplished and achieved over the academic year.

A more innovative approach is an electronic portfolio or digital portfolio. Computers have the power to provide educators, administrators, parents, and students with an individual database on each child (Newsome, 1996). This application of technology creates an individual database with evidence of student learning that can be continually revised and updated. This database can be available to individual students, teachers and parents. Models of student portfolios can be placed on the Internet for community review. All stakeholders can then have access to and understand the types of learning experiences that occur within the local classrooms.

For elementary and secondary teachers, it's a good idea to assemble the first draft of student portfolios after the first few months in school. Students can probably get this draft ready for parent-teacher conferences that occur usually around the first marking period. The portfolio can become the focus for parent-teacher discussions of student academic progress. A second draft can be assembled mid-year and the final version completed at the end of the academic year. Mid-year drafts should be sent home for parental review and teachers can include a place for parents to record their comments about student achievement. The final versions of the portfolio will provide students with a wonderful record of learning achievement and memories about an entire academic year.

Are Portfolio Assessments of Student Work Valid And Reliable?

In an effort to use portfolios as an assessment instrument, educators have sought to use scoring guides, rubrics and checklists to determine a level of performance. Producing a single score to describe student performance suggests that portfolio assessment is valid and reliable. However, do portfolios actually measure what we intend? If so then they are valid assessments. For example, portfolios are used to show growth in students' writing ability. Does the portfolio actually demonstrate student growth in terms of writing? Possibly, but as Ward and Murray-Ward (1999) suggest, the selection of the contents and scoring procedures are a primary concern regarding the validity of portfolio assessment. Valencia and Calfee (1991) suggest that paying careful attention to portfolio tasks can ensure validity. Is the portfolio task representative? Does it match the objectives and the purpose of the portfolio?

Are portfolios reliable? Do they consistently give the same results when scored a second or third time? MacGinitie (1993) indicated that portfolio assessment scores lack reliability for the following reasons:

- Raters may arrive at different evaluations on the basis of what they deem important.
- If ratings are assigned to each item within the portfolio and then combined systematically, decisions must be made about levels of importance. If only selected items within a portfolio are rated, then a complete profile of the learner is not considered.
- The meaning of the assessment to students may be totally different than it is to the teacher.

Ward and Murray-Ward (1999) agree with McGinitie, as they observe that the scoring of portfolios, is not as reliable as first hoped and that the procedure used (averaged or global) can affect outcomes.

If portfolio assessment is problematic in terms of validity and reliability, why should teachers consider its use in the classroom? Portfolio assessments do provide a means of examining actual student performance on authentic tasks. In addition, the very process of assembling and developing the portfolio, contributes to student learning. Student learning continues as the student reflects and self evaluates his portfolio tasks.

Gillespie, Ford, Gillespie, and Leavell (1996) suggested that educators consider a new vision of assessment that includes traditional strategies (standardized tests) and authentic assessments (portfolios). They conclude, "By using a variety of forms of assessment, teachers will be able to create a better picture of student progress through assessments that encourage student thinking, as well as application of skills." (p. 490)

Tierney and Readence (2000) noted that the effectiveness of portfolio assessment is closely tied to how the process is implemented and the ability of students to self-analyze and trace their development. They caution that portfolio may mean different things in different settings.

Tierney and Readence (2000), cite Wile and Tierney (1994) who noted the following pitfalls with portfolio assessments:

- Imposed vs. emerging portfolios
- Overly rigid prescriptive guidelines

- Formalizing self-assessment
- Imposed and standardized criteria to guide student evaluations
- Viewing the portfolio as an end rather than the means of engaging students in the self-assessment process
- Teacher and district take-over of student portfolios
- Methods of evaluation that are not aligned with portfolio process
- Pre-packaged portfolios

Tierney and Readence (2000) observed that portfolios seem a natural extension of the various learning activities with which students are engaged. Portfolios appear to help teachers and students keep track of, reflect upon, and plan their extended reading and writing projects and activities such as conferencing, journals, and shared book experiences. They also provide an umbrella for the integration of learning. Students are apt to include in their portfolios material from across subject areas as well as activities related to their interests outside of school. (p. 485)

Given the current popularity of student portfolios, you may envision that standardized tests may be phased out as a means of assessment. Tierney and Readence (2000) reject to this idea for the following reasons:

- Scoring portfolios as outcome assessments would be very time consuming.
- Scoring would be unreliable unless the portfolio criteria was strictly specified (This would result in portfolios losing effectiveness as a instructional management tool.).
- The very nature of the portfolio development process, an on-going, active, self-reflective learning experience, suggests that portfolios will not replace standardized testing strategies. Rather, portfolios provide a means to enhance our profile of student learning achievement within the classroom.

Checklists and Inventories for Student Evaluation

One form of alternative assessment for student learning is the checklist. A checklist (sometimes called an inventory) is a listing that describes minimal acceptable criteria that students are expected to master. Some checklists include rating scales with categories such as "Usually", "Sometimes" and "Never." Checklists require that the person using the checklist, "check off" each criteria that has been achieved. Checklists are mainly used for evaluation purposes, however, they are also useful for instruction.

Lorber (1996) observes that teachers use checklists as both instructional and evaluation aids. When used for instructional purposes, checklists provide students with "a logical sequence of steps or points that, if followed or included, lead to the development of an acceptable product." (p. 273) When used for evaluation, checklists identify specific criteria being sought in a finished product. Consider the following example of how a teacher might use a checklist for instruction.

During the instructional presentation, students in social studies classes are asked to work in small groups to research information on the United States immigration between 1877-1920. The teacher distributes the following checklist to guide students with their group work.

Checklist: Topics to Include in Group Reports (Make sure you address all of the following topics.)

		Maximum Points	Grade	Comments
_____	Political influences	25		
_____	Social issues	25		
_____	Immigration trends	25		
_____	Reform movement	25		
	Total	100		

The checklist above serves as a guide for learning. While working on group reports, students can continuously refer to the checklist so that they will be sure to include each of the specified topics.

This same checklist can also be used for purposes of evaluating the final student report. The teacher can check off each topic that was included in the report. A comment can be assigned to each topic as well. Notice the teacher's assignment of the numerical value and comments in the Sample Checklist.

Checklist: Topics to Include in Group Reports (Make sure you address all of the following topics.)

		Possible Points	Grading	Comments
✓	Political influences	25	25	(An in-depth analysis of the issues)
✓	Social issues	25	15	(More discussion needed)
✓	Immigration trends	25	25	(Comprehensive and thorough report)
✓	Reform movement	25	0	(Not addressed in report)
	Total	100	65	

The checklist above identifies specific content that should be included in a student project. It also lists the earned points for each section of the report. As the teacher examines the final reports, the content is either present or not. If the content is present, it may or may not be developed fully. The teacher has the flexibility to assign partial credit for a less developed section of the report.

Some checklists can be problematic in assessing student learning. Glazer (1998) cautions about the use of checklists for reporting student academic achievement. Some of the dangers include:

- Descriptors can be interpreted in many ways.
- Some things are always (unintentionally) left out of skills lists.
- There is an assumption that all students must learn all the skills on the list.
- There is a need to continuously revise checklists to match curriculum content.
- Descriptions of student behavior may be limited.
- There is a tendency to view checklists as test scores.
- There is a tendency to create grade-level equivalents for mastery of each skill. (p.337)

In conclusion, while checklists or inventories are helpful in evaluating some types of student learning, they may not be appropriate for the many types of academic tasks that we commonly find in academic settings.

RUBRICS

The word <u>rubric</u> actually comes from the Latin word <u>ruber</u> for red (Popham, 1997). In reproducing sacred literature, Christian monks in the 15th century would begin each major section of the book with a big red letter, and the word rubric came to refer to the scarlet-enhanced headings. What this term actually has to do with assessment in education is questionable, but the term rubric is a lot catchier than a <u>scoring guide</u>, which is what the 21st century rubric really is. Stated succinctly, "A rubric is a device for organizing and interpreting data gathered from observations of student performance" (Rose, 1999, p. 30). A rubric is a scoring guide that distinguishes different levels of student performance on more complicated tasks. For example, portfolio assessment is a complex matter, and has been incorporated into only a few large-scale assessment programs (Koretz, 1998). The Kentucky Portfolio Assessment Program, one of the most clearly defined, uses a rubric. The original scoring system included three levels: Apprentice, Proficient, and Distinguished. A fourth category, Novice was established for students who failed to meet the Apprentice criteria. Each level has specific, measurable performance indicators that increase in sophistication up to the highest level.

Rubrics have been used in portfolio assessment (See sample rubric for Teaching Portfolio), writing performance, in evaluating district performances, and as advanced organizers because they let students know exactly what is expected of them (Pate, Homestead, & McGinnis, 1993). Rubrics have also been used in arts evaluation (Huffman, 1998), physical education (Lund, 1997), assessing discussion skills, an often overlooked area of learning (Frazier, 1997); and even assessing the assessments of student teachers (McConney & Ayres, 1998). Science teachers seem especially partial to rubrics because a rubric provides them with the means to evaluate students' mastery of the scientific method and application of concepts, as well as their expertise in demonstration (Jensen, 1995; Liu, 1995; Radford, Ramsey, & Deese, 1995; Shymansky, Enger, Chidsey & Yoreet, 1997).

A rubric has three basic features:

- Evaluative criteria are used to distinguish acceptable from unacceptable responses. The criteria vary depending on the skill involved. You can either weigh criteria equally or assign different weights to each.
- Quality definitions describe the way that qualitative differences in students' work will be judged. Each level has its own specified quality descriptors.
- Scoring strategy may be either holistic or analytic. Holistic strategy encompasses all the evaluative criteria and aggregates them to make a single overall quality assessment. With analytic strategy you score each criterion separately. The scores may or may not be aggregated into an overall score (Popham, 1997).

In a paradoxical twist, at the same time educators, were deploring the use of standardized testing procedures which do not accurately reflect students' mastery of skills, and which have been criticized for cultural bias, there has been a move toward state and national standards. The need for accountability in the realization that, the simplest methods for measurements, do not really measure what we need to know to help students succeed in the world, resulted in a quandary: how to demonstrate students' proficiency in a reliable manner. States one district consultant, "Rubrics help teachers clarify exactly what students need to achieve in content and performance standards" (Rose, 1999, p. 30).

Therefore, rubrics provide a clear-cut framework and fall under the umbrella of alternative assessment. In effect, rubrics offer a framework for grading performance-based tests, which measure students' expertise in authentic or real world situations (Pate et al., 1993; Popham, 1997).

Rubrics provide a clear-cut framework for the assessment of higher-order skills. Like any other assessment measures, they have strengths and weaknesses. The following is a list of pros and cons concerning rubrics:

Pros

- Clear expectations. Students refer to the rubric to ensure their work is on target. They can also assess another's work, sharing suggestions for meeting the criteria.
- Student motivation. Students see what they need to do to move to the next level of achievement. Involving students in the process of designing rubrics further enhances motivation.
- Student involvement. You can discuss the learning goals and expectations for a given project with your students, and work together to develop the rubric.
- Rubrics facilitate fairness. Students see that their work is compared to the rubric rather than to other students.

Cons

- Rubrics differ from other grading systems. For example, you may have to translate the levels of achievement on your rubric to the traditional letter grades or to numerical figures. The Kentucky Portfolio Assessment Program has devised a sophisticated method for converting rubric scores to numerical figures, but few other such programs exist (Koretz, 1998).
- Developing rubrics can be time-consuming. The more detail, the clearer the assessment but the more time it takes to design. You have to achieve a balance between a system that is too simplistic and one that is so complex that others may not understand it. Once you have created a few rubrics, you can make a template so they can be modified for various skills and curricula.
- Rubrics can be difficult to explain to parents. Parents are used to the standard multiple choice or true-or-false tests. Rubrics may seem more subjective, so the key is to make the criteria as clear as possible. On the plus side, using rubrics will make grading seem less subjective to parents in areas such as visual arts, composition, and oral presentation skills (Brudnak, 1998).

The Challenges of Using Rubrics

Some educators take a more skeptical view. Popham (1997) is not against rubrics per se but the way in which they are often implemented. According to this critic of rubrics, "Although they are receiving near-universal applause from educators, the vast majority of rubrics are instructionally fraudulent. They are masquerading as contributors to education when, in reality, they have no educational impact at all." (p. 73) Popham cites four major flaws that are common in both teacher-designed and commercially produced rubrics:

- Task-specific evaluation criteria. This is the most important element in a rubric. The problem is that the evaluative criteria may be linked only to the specific elements in a particular performance test. The author finds this flaw especially common in nationally standardized tests that call for constructed responses from students.
- Excessively general evaluation criteria. This is the opposite number to task-specific criteria. Despite the clamor for specificity, numerous rubrics have evaluation criteria that are actually very vague. In spite of their pretensions, many rubrics do not provide useful information about what is genuinely significant about a student's response.
- Dysfunction detail. While sketchy rubrics are useless, too detailed criteria are likely to go unread by most teachers. If you are willing to read through the technicalities, overly detailed rubrics do have good points, and you can abbreviate for yourself.
- Equating the test of the skill with the skill itself. This problem generally resides with the users of rubrics. A common misunderstanding is to get so caught up in the particulars of a given performance test that you begin to think of the test as the skill. The important thing is to instruct students toward the skill itself, not toward the test. If you instruct toward the

test, you will find yourself falling into the trap that created the need for alternative assessment in the first place.

On the positive side, Popham believes there is serious hope for rubrics, when they are designed in a way that will genuinely help teachers to judge students' performance as well as helping students acquire the skills needed for the performance:

- Start with three to five evaluation criteria.
- Be sure that each evaluation criteria represents a key attribute of the skill being assessed. In short, each evaluation criteria must be teachable.

To avoid mistakes in selecting your evaluation criteria, try this simple checklist:

- List the most important parts of a learning activity. Use this list to develop rubric sections, which include process, content, mechanics, presentation, source variety, neatness, etc.
- Develop a scale for each section showing expected criteria.
- Weigh the rubric sections. Determine what sections are most important or whether they are equally important.

Starting from Scratch

Many of the flaws described by Popham (1997) refer to commercially published rubrics, although given the newness of the venture, teacher-designed rubrics are unlikely to be exempt. Brudnak (1998) offers some tips for writing your own:

- Collaborate with a colleague. Don't go it alone until after you have mastered the art of creating the rubric.
- Choose one subject to start with and introduce rubrics gradually.
- Keep language simple. You want to be sure your students know what they are being asked. Also keep parents in mind.
- Choose a scale with an even number of levels. With an odd number, you're likely to score most of your students in the middle. The lowest level on some scales is one; on others it's zero.
- What to call your levels? The levels defined by the Kentucky Portfolio Assessment Program are one example. Common terms used to define performance levels include:
    - Exemplary, proficient, progressing, or not up to standard.
    - Distinguished, proficient, progressing, or novice.
    - Level four, level three, level two, or level one (this one is a bit too prosaic for our taste!)
    - Exemplary achievement, commendable achievement, limited achievement, minimal achievement, or no response.
    - Star, smiley face, or straight face (if you are feeling whimsical or teach very young children).
- Test it out. If you want to know if your rubric works, try it out! Use it to assess some of your students' papers. Ask yourself if the students seemed to understand what was expected. If not, go back to work on it until it is clear. But avoid those excessive details!

Making Students Part of the Process

Ownership and empowerment are two words that appear prominently in the literature on rubrics. At the most basic level they mean involving stakeholders in important decision-making. Creating and using rubrics for assessment empowers teachers and students alike. Many teachers are angry about national standards and national tests because of an implicit assumption that the focus on content or performance standards, as developed by test makers and policy makers, will help teachers gain professional expertise in curriculum development and assessment (Nathan, 1995). The only thing that will help you become a more accomplished professional is active participation. Teachers who are involved in the assessment of their own work, as well as the work of students, tend to have higher professional esteem and more of a sense of responsibility to the community. Schools that encourage this participation are also likely to be schools that foster a strong bond between teachers and students. There is a greater understanding between both groups, and teachers are better able to identify and build on the strengths of individual students.

Active involvement in developing assessment in the form of rubrics is important for students as well as teachers. As one teacher astutely observes, when students are given the opportunity to contribute to the content of a rubric, "then it is much easier to hold them to its standards" (Rose, 1999, p. 31). It is noteworthy that these are the words of a kindergarten teacher. Even the youngest children can be involved in the process! Enlisting the help of students can be a powerful motivational strategy, and for young children, it can help them to develop a sense of responsibility for their own learning and performance. A staunch enthusiast of rubrics, Rose believes that rubrics both improve and inform teachers' instruction while providing students with the feedback needed to learn and grow.

Rubrics By Discipline

While many educators have embraced assessment with rubrics, the acceptance of rubrics varies by discipline. Science teachers are particularly enthusiastic about having specific criteria for grading students on all components of the scientific process.

Science

Overall, science educators believe that because high quality science instruction is generally experiential, interactive, and constructive, activity-based assessment is simply a logical extension of the concept of student-centered learning (Shymansky et al., 1997). Rubrics facilitate the assessment of activity-based learning.

One experiment involving science educators in rubric design, asked three key questions:

- Is performance-based assessment doable within the framework of a large-scale testing program?
- Do responses to performance-based assessments reveal important information about learners not revealed through traditional multiple-choice assessments?
- How do students perform on performance-based tasks? (Shymansky et al., 1997).

As stated by Jensen (1995), "The purpose of authentic assessment lies in the student response. Analysis, problem solving, comparison, collaboration, and communication must come together." (p. 35) In science, students must be able to demonstrate that they can develop innovative approaches to solving the analytical problems of the task and the social problems within their lab group. They must also be able to compare the results with their expectations and communicate the ideas to a general or specific audience. The emphasis on collaboration is especially important, since in the real world, teams typically conduct scientific research. In fact, in many professions today, teamwork is an integral part of professional life. Team problem solving and communication of process and findings are an integral part of a comprehensive rubric.

Liu (1995) states that the way we define science in our science classes defines science not only for students but also for much of our society. Some questions a science teacher might ask are:

- How do we encourage and document critical thinking?
- Do students need science-specific vocabulary to communicate with others who are doing science?
- What laboratory skills will students need in the future?
- How will this be of value to students as they approach college or the workplace?

Collaboration among science teachers, and perhaps with teachers from other disciplines can help to answer these questions and translate the information into valid criteria to include in rubrics.

The study of Shymansky et al. (1997) found that the development of effective rubrics for science requires significant effort and resources to provide important information on student performance. However, science teachers seem to agree that it is well worth the effort. Performance-based assessment offers documentation of mastery of authentic tasks, that are valid examples of real science inquiry, provides valuable information that is not revealed by traditional assessment methods, and detects differences in quality science work. Liu (1995) concludes, "Additive rubrics allow students to assume responsibility for the quantity and quality of their work and see its value beyond the letter grade they receive." (p. 51)

Physical education

One discipline for which rubrics offer a perfect fit is physical education: observational performance assessment is integral to the perfection of physical skills (Lund, 1997). Lund provides the example of a lifeguard. Before a lifeguard is qualified for the job, the person typically did classroom work and reading as well as passing a written test. An additional test of competence is required to demonstrate the ability to rescue "victims" from the water using a variety of techniques depending upon the circumstances surrounding the "drowning." Although the scenario is constructed, the script gives the potential lifeguard the chance to demonstrate the required skills needed to save a real victim, should the need arise. Since a specific set of criteria is used, the test constitutes an example of authentic assessment. In essence, it provides a critical link between what is learned in the instructional setting and what will be carried out in the real world.

Integrated studies

Middle schools are turning increasingly to integrated studies formats that require careful planning in all aspects of implementation and assessment. Because integrated studies involve both individual and small group work, as well as transcending subject lines, traditional examination methods are grossly inadequate (Pate et al., 1993). Integrating subject areas grounds learning in a real world context. Therefore, authentic assessment such as the use of rubrics, is essentially the only way to accurately evaluate students' mastery of knowledge and skills.

Arts, Writing, and Discourse

Some writing teachers wax enthusiastic about the use of rubrics to evaluate writing skills. Wyngaard and Gehrke (1996) describe the Memoir Writing Project that utilized a twofold assessment system. The presentation of rubrics helped to: 1) generate an excellent class discussion about the role of audience in shaping text; and 2) led some students to the discovery that their visceral responses as readers were a perfect starting point for critically engaging a text. Ultimately, the discussion of rubrics helped to demystify the critiquing of a text because the audience had important credentials as critics: I am a member of the audience. The most important part of the project was the Peer Evaluation Workshop, which included a Peer Review Worksheet. Both peer-assessment and self-assessment were integral parts of the project. Overall, the Memoir Writing Project exemplifies a model that actively engages students in all phases of the evaluation process.

In sharp contrast, Mabry (1999) views using rubrics to assess student writing as a step backwards: rubrics impose rigid standards on a discipline meant to encourage creativity and originality. Ironically, the alternative assessment "makes direct writing assessments more like the multiple choice tests they were meant to improve upon." By standardizing scoring within a writing rubric, rubrics imply that good writing is the sum of the criteria on the writing rubric, and that writing that does not conform to the criteria is not good.

At the same time, however, Huffman (1998) celebrates rubrics as a way of assessing students in visual arts, historically a complex and subjective process. In the sample production rubric presented by the author, originality and aesthetics are embedded in the rubric itself. The rubric includes:

- Preparation
- Research
- Assignment goals
- Craftsmanship
- Originality
- Aesthetics
- Critique (i.e., insight)

The above criteria can be adapted for writing as well as visual arts (or multimedia). If rubrics are used to discourage creativity in writing, it exemplifies Popham's (1997) assertion that rubrics can be heavily flawed.

Assessing the Rubric

If we are to keep rubrics from undermining authentic assessment instead of enhancing it, then we may want to have a rubric for assessing rubrics. The following criteria are intended for assessing student teachers' assessments, but they provide a valuable framework for all teachers:

- Alignment with learning outcomes. Teaching is more effective when learning outcomes, teaching plans, assessments, and contextual considerations are carefully aligned.
- Clarity and understanding. Quality assessment demands that tasks be clear and understandable.
- Reliability. Assessment results must be reliable (i.e., consistent) across assessors and across time
- Feasibility. Good quality assessments are feasible from the perspective of students and teachers alike.
- Diversity of assessment strategies. Because not all students learn in the same way, multiple assessment strategies are needed to fairly evaluate students' knowledge skills.
- Developmental appropriateness. Assessments of student learning and skills must be consistent with students' developmental level.

At this point, assessments with rubrics are still in the rudimentary stage. The more teachers collaborate in the process, the more rubrics will be refined and the less they will undermine the purpose for which they are designed: authentic assessment.

Suggested Learning Activities:

- Create a student examination using ten true-false questions, matching column, fill in the blanks and multiple-choice questions. Administer the exam to a group of students and grade the tests.

- Create an essay exam for students. Administer the test and then grade the essay according to the guidelines provided in this section.

- Obtain a copy of a standardized test for elementary or high school students. Examine the test and evaluate it in terms of ease of use and appropriateness for your students.

- Videotape yourself teaching in the classroom. Analyze the tape and identify two or three areas of needed improvement. Create a plan to improve your teaching performance.

- Begin to gather materials for your own teaching portfolio. Purchase a large binder and begin to assemble your portfolio.

- Create a student evaluation worksheet. Ask your students to evaluate your lessons in a particular unit or subject area. Collect evaluation sheets and write a prescription for self-improvement.

- Keep a weekly journal on your teaching. Make a list of the teaching strategies that were particularly effective for student learning. Incorporate the effective strategies into future lesson plans.

- Prepare an instructional presentation and teach it in class. Evaluate your presentation using the self-evaluation checklist provided in this section.

REFERENCES

Airasian, P.W. and Gullickson, A.R. (1997). Teacher self-evaluation tool kit. Thousand Oaks, CA: Corwin Press, Inc.

Angelo, T.A. and Cross, K.P. (1993). Classroom assessment techniques: A handbook for college teachers. 2nd ed. San Francisco, CA: Jossey-Bass.

Borko, H., Michalec, P. and Timmons, M. (1997). Student teaching portfolios: A tool for promoting reflective practice. Journal of Teacher Education, 48, (5), 345-357.

Brudnak, K. A. (1998). Keeping current. Mailbox Teacher, 27, (1), 18-20.

Burniske, R.W. (1994). Creating dialogue: Teacher response to journal writing. English Journal, 83, (4), 84- 87.

Chandler, A. (1997). Is this for a grade? A personal look at journals. English Journal, 86, (1), 45-49.

Cutforth, N. and Parker, M. (1996). Promoting affective development in physical education: The value of journal writing. Journal of Physical Education, Recreation and Dance, 67, (7), 19-23.

DeFina, A.A. (1992). Portfolio assessment: Getting started. New York: Scholastic, Inc.

Dougherty, B.J. (1996). The write way:A look at journal writing in first-year algebra. The Mathematics Teacher, 89, (7), 556-560.

Edwards, M.A. (1995). Growth is the name of the game. Educational Leadership, 52, (6), 72-75.
Ernst, K. (1998). Looking back to move ahead. Teaching Pre K-8, 28, (8), 34-35.

Frazier, C. H. (2997). The development of an authentic assessment instrument: The scored discussion. English Journal, 86, 37-40.

Gillespie, C.S., Ford, K.L., Gillespie, R.D. and Leavell, A.G. (1996). Portfolio assessment: Some questions, some answers, some recommendations. Journal of Adolescent and Adult Literacy, 39, (6), 480-491.

Gronlund, N.E. (1985). Measurement and evaluation in teachingen. 5th ed. New York: Macmillan.

Holmes,V.L. and Moulton, M.R. (1997). Dialogue journals as an ESL learning strategy. Journal of Adolescent and Adult Literacy, 40, (8), 616-621.

Huffman, E. S. (1998). Authentic rubrics. Art Education, 51(1), 64-68.

Hurst, B., Wilson, C. and Cramer, G. (1998). Professional teaching portfolios. Phi Delta Kappan, 79, (8), 578-582.

Jensen, K. (1995). Effective rubric design. Science Teacher, 62(5), 34-37.

Johnson, A. J., Dupuis, V.L., Musial, D., Hall, G.E., and Gollnick, D.M. (1999). Introduction to the foundations of American education. Needham Heights, MA: Allyn and Bacon.

Koretz, D. (1998). Large-scale portfolio assessments in the US: Evidence pertaining to quality of measurement. Assessment in Education, 5, 309-334.

Lang, S.S. (1997). Student ratings soar when professor uses enthusiasm. Human Ecology Forum, 25, (4), 24.

Lapp, D., Flood, J. Farnan, N. (1996). Content area reading and learning: Instructional strategies 2nd ed. Needham Heights, MA: Allyn and Bacon.

Lee, E.P. (1997). The learning response log: An assessment tool. English Journal, 86, (1), 41-44.

Liu, K. (1995). Rubrics revisited: Allowing students to assume responsibility for the quality of their work. Science Teacher, 62, (7), 49-51.

Lorber M.A. (1996). Objectives, methods, and evaluation for secondary teaching. Needham Heights, MA: Allyn and Bacon.

Lund, J. (1997). Authentic assessment: Its development and applications. Journal of Physical Education, Recreation, & Dance, 68(7), 25-29.

Mabry, L. (1999). Writing to the rubric: Lingering effects of traditional standardized testing on direct writing assessment. Phi Delta Kappan, 80, 673-679.

MacGinitie, W. (1993). Some limits of assessment. Journal of Reading, 36, (7), 556-560.

Marshall, M. (1998). Using teacher evaluation to change school culture. National Association of Secondary School Principals. NASSP Bulletin, 82, (6), 117-119.

Mayo, R.W. (1997). Trends in teacher evaluation. The Clearing House, 70, (5), 269-270.

McConney, A. & Ayres, R. R. (1998). Assessing student teachers' assessments. Journal of Teacher Education, 49, 140-150.

Meyer, C., Schuman, S, and Angello, N. (1990). NWEA white paper in aggregating portfolio data. Lake Oswego, OR: Northwest Evaluation Association.

Nathan, L. (1995). Assessing assessment: Lessons of innovative practices in urban schools. Daedalus, 124(4), 63-68.

O'Rourke, R. (1998). The learning journal: From chaos to coherence. Assessment and Evaluation in Higher Education. 23, (4), 403-413.

Pate, P. E., Homestead, E., & McGinnis, K. (1993, November). Designing rubrics for authentic assessment. Middle School Journal, 25-27.

Popham, W. J. (1997). What's wrong--and what's right--with rubrics. Educational Leadership, 55(2), 72-75.

Radford, D. L., Ramsey, L. L., & Deese, W. C. (1995). Demonstration assessment: Measuring conceptual understanding and critical thinking with rubrics. Science Teacher, 62 (7), 52-55.

Root, C.H. (1996). Having art students use a journal. Teaching and Change, 3, (4), 331-355.

Rose, M. (1999). Make room for rubrics. Instructor, 108(6), 30-31.

Ross, C.L. (1998). Journaling across the curriculum. The Clearing House, 71, (3), 189-190.

Searfoss, L.W. and Enz, B.J. (1996). Can teacher evaluations reflect holistic instruction? Educational Leadership, 53, (6), 38-41.

Shymansky, J. A., Enger, S., Chidsey, J. L., & Yoreet, L. D. (1997). Performance assessment in science as a tool to enhance the picture of student learning. School Science and Mathematics, 97, 172-183.

Teven, J.J. and McCroskey, J.C. (1997). The relationship of perceived teacher caring with student learning and teacher evaluation. Communication Education, 46, (1), 1-9.

Tierney, R.J. and Readence, J.E. (2000). Reading strategies and practices: A compendium. Needham Heights, MA: Allyn and Bacon.

Ward, A. W. and Murray-Ward, M. (1999). Assessment in the classroom. Belmont, CA: Wadsworth Publishing Company.

Wolf, K. and Siu-Runyan,Y. (1996). Portfolio purposes and possibilities. Journal of Adolescent and Adult Literacy, 40, (1), 30-37.

Wyngaard, S. & Gehrke, R. (1996). Responding to audience using rubrics to teach and assess writing. English Journal, 85, 67-70.

Part II

Essay 1: REDUCING SPEECH ANXIETY
Edward A. Schmalz, Ed.D.

A common anxiety experienced by teachers and other professionals is speaking in front of groups. Even the most competent classroom teacher may experience anxiety when called upon to speak in front of peers or other adults. An elementary teacher, who is comfortable with younger children, may become unnerved speaking at a parent/teacher night or making a presentation in front of their colleagues. In this essay, you will learn some helpful strategies to address the problem of speech anxiety.

Surveys report that seventy-five percent of individuals have a fear of speaking in front of people (Cronin, Grice & Olsen, Jr., 1994). It is a fact that teachers will be called upon to speak in public at some point in their lives. Due to their anxiety surrounding public speaking, many people will avoid these opportunities and thus deny themselves the chance to share their knowledge. This is a loss to both the potential speaker and to the potential audience members. On the occasions when a nervous inexperienced speaker does agree to present his/her ideas, the anxiety associated with this process may result in a less effective and shorter speech. Nervousness on the part of a speaker can result in an embarrassing, disconcerting presentation which is excruciating for both the speaker and for the listeners. Teachers are particularly affected by this issue, for they are required to speak in front of a group on a daily basis. A teacher's reoccurring stage fright will seriously impede his/her ability to help his/her students learn the required material. Although a little nervousness is acceptable, especially on the first day of school, stage fright is not.

Often the most anxious moments for a speaker are those few minutes just before the presentation. To reduce speech anxiety, you can learn some simple techniques to become more relaxed. The best method of reducing anxiety is to be thoroughly prepared and to understand how you are going to communicate with your audience. Secondly, you can learn to control your excess nervous emotion. (Keep in mind that these emotions are communicated all too easily to an audience, especially to a group of students.) Several proven techniques are highly effective in controlling your emotions. The first is to use positive thinking. Our internal speaking is correlated to our speech anxiety (Hu et al., 1992). Negative thoughts prior to giving a public presentation result in higher anxiety about it, whereas positive thoughts lead to lower anxiety. In an experiment, students who were speech phobic were divided into three groups that used positive, negative, or neutral thinking just before giving a speech. In this experiment, subjects were not only asked about their subjective feelings about the process, but also had physiological responses monitored to determine if there were cardiovascular changes due to their internal thinking. Just as positive thinking reduced subjective and cardiovascular responses, negative thinking increased them. The researchers stated categorically that positive thinking is an effective means of reducing speech anxiety.

Associated with positive thinking is the use of visualization with your inner speech. Visualization is a form of concentration. When we are nervous about our presentation, we are focusing our energy on what might go wrong. Visualization helps us to concentrate on how it will go well: "Concentration is the focusing and harnessing of your inner thoughts. No thought is more powerful than a visual picture" (Wydro, 1981, p. 13). Wydro (1981) suggests the following steps to visualize:

- Slow the mind down, relax, and clear the mind.
- Consciously and deliberately let go of cares and worries. Clear the movie screen in your mind. This will allow positive images to appear.
- When your mind is blank, form a positive image of your presentation. Feel relaxed and purposeful about this image.

Wydro (1981) believes that in a given exchange where there is a mutual benefit for both speaker and listener, a conscious purpose is needed to help the speaker find the right words from a higher perspective. This involves taking the time to give yourself something specific to do and a definite goal to accomplish. By clarifying in your mind what you want to happen as a result of your speaking, you can create a specific image visualizing the accomplishment of that goal. Wydro suggests asking yourself the following questions:

- What effect do I want to have on this audience?
- What do I want the audience to do as a result of my word? (p. 33)

Putting the audience in your mental image helps you to handle the pressure and tension that can result from speaking to groups of people. Focusing on what you as the speaker can do for this group will allay the fear of criticism, concern, and self-doubt that plague so many speakers and diminish their presentations.

Another means of reducing speech anxiety is through the use of cognitive restructuring and interactive video instruction (IVI). Cognitive restructuring is similar to positive thinking in that the goal is to change irrational thoughts that people have about themselves, such as thoughts about communicating with others. People make certain assumptions about themselves that lead to self-defeating internal dialogues or self-statements that adversely affect behavior. Cognitive restructuring replaces negative self-statements with positive, coping statements. Interactive video instruction is a means of using a computer with a videotape, videodisc, film, slide, and graphic material to provide individualized, self-paced instruction. Subjects who used IVI and cognitive restructuring to reduce speech anxiety found it to be successful and effective (Cronin, Grice & Olsen, Jr., 1994).

Preparation of the speech or talk can reduce speech anxiety. One survey found a positive relationship between the time spent in preparation and the quality of the speech that followed (Menzel & Carrell, 1994). Preparation includes practice, but what kind of practice? Some experts believe the practice should be as realistic as possible. Speech anxiety may be due to the fact that a person feels his or her skills are deficient. By practicing, a person can increase his or her skills and change the belief that their speech-making skills are deficient. Practice can include silent and oral rehearsal and time spent cognitively processing the speech. Practicing out loud is thought to be helpful because it helps a person clarify his or her thoughts. Speaking in front of an audience is considered a realistic rehearsal and an effective means of working out difficulties that are not noticed when rehearsing solo. Although people are sometimes embarrassed about hearing the sound of their voice, an effective means of a rehearsal is to tape-record your presentation. Put it away for a day or two and then listen to it. This will help you to be more objective and hear where the speech needs improvement. Speech anxiety may be due to a lack of confidence, hyper-analysis, and fear of audience reaction. These traits result in poor performance. Preparation reduces the possibility of poor performance by decreasing anxiety and helping the speaker relax more.

Although most experts agree that following a text is not advisable, this is one strategy to reduce speech anxiety. The key is to use a prepared text effectively so that you do not appear to be reading line by line. The first step is to prepare the text in large print and in triple space. Larger print makes the material easier to read, you can absorb it more quickly, and you can make eye contact with the audience since your eyes are not focused on tiny print. Triple space helps you keep your place or avoid losing your place as you make eye contact with the audience. When people are anxious about oral communication, they often race through their presentation to get through it as quickly as possible. To avoid this common mistake, parenthetical directions should be put in the body of the presentation (e.g., [pause], [smile], [glance at the audience]) to remind yourself of these important nonverbal forms of communication. Speakers who rattle off their information in an uncaring, mechanical way lose their audience. The lack of spontaneity is almost inevitable in this type of presentation and should be used with caution (Gladis, 1989).

The memorized presentation has many drawbacks, although it is sometimes necessary when the speaker wants to communicate his or her thoughts exactly as planned. It requires a greater investment of time because it has to be memorized word for word. Again, it is difficult to maintain spontaneity and has the additional drawback of the possibility of forgetting a word or phrase which may result in the loss of one's composure. With a memorized speech, the speaker often becomes more concerned with remembering words than with sharing ideas with the audience. You should also note that memorized speeches are not particularly effective in classroom settings. It is generally not to your advantage to memorize your instructional plan format. Firstly, memorized class lectures, may discourage you from implementing the motivational, developmental and summary activities required by the Instructional Plan format. It may also prevent you from drawing upon active learning strategies. (See Essay 3, Part II, "The Importance of Active Learning.") Secondly, whether you are speaking to a group of 100 or a group of 15, chances are someone will ask a question, or wish to contribute a comment. If you have memorized your talk, a student interruption may disconcert you and prevent you from continuing. Your success as a speaker in this classroom setting often relies on your ability to integrate student participation with your presentation. Similar points might apply to the presentation that you might make on a parent-teacher night. The new audience, made up of potentially critical parents, may cause you considerable anxiety even if you are a teacher who is generally very comfortable in his/her classroom. Memorizing a speech for parents will also discourage discussion. Ultimately, by reducing the initial opportunity for exchange and contact, a memorized speech might prevent you from getting to know your students' families and vice versa. Furthermore, should a parent in the audience wish to interrupt your speech in order to ask a question, you may lose your train of thought and not be able to continue. Such an occurrence will only intensify your anxiety.

If the few minutes before a presentation are the most nerve-wracking, the first few minutes of a talk make or break the speaker. Audience members, whether they are students, parents, or fellow teachers, often make up their minds in those first few moments whether they like the speaker and whether they think it is worth paying attention to him or her. Nervousness reduces the opportunity to connect with the audience. To avoid this, you can write down the opening comments of your presentation and read them verbatim in a natural and controlled voice while making sure not to speak too quickly (Anholt, 1994). Using a personal introduction, a joke, a short story, quote, or a reflection appropriate to the talk conveys the feeling that your learner/audience is important to you. Simply telling them why you are happy to be here, why you think this group of people is special, or thanking your host for having you speak rarely fails as an introduction. Seeing a smiling audience with heads nodding in approval in front of you will also ease your nervousness.

The introduction to your presentation is also your first means of establishing your credibility with your audience. One technique that has proven effective is to find common ground with your audience. Sharing information about yourself that reflects a value system similar to the audience or including supporting material in your presentation that the audience can identify with enhances your credibility and rapport. Another means is to mention your special credentials or knowledge that makes you uniquely qualified to speak on this particular topic. This must be done without bragging and with sincerity.

In addition to preparing the talk, you must also prepare the room to be used. In a live performance, some situations are out of our control. A presentation offers many possibilities for things to go wrong or, at the least, not as planned. Flexibility is required for those moments when unforeseen situations occur. Delays such as not having the room adequately prepared, missing equipment, or poor sound systems are not atypical. Under these circumstances it is wise to remember that these occurrences reflect the host and the host institution, not the speaker. However, some events are within your control. A common occurrence is to leave one's prepared text on the podium until the time of the speech. The problem may be that someone will remove the text or replace the podium with another. A better option is to carry your text with you when you are introduced. How your text is physically constructed can be another challenge. Anxiety, associated with a public presentation, sometimes results in the speaker's hands shaking. If a podium is not available, a way to avoid paper trembling is to place the pages in individual plastic document folders, on a book, or on a piece of stiff cardboard. They stiffen the page even when your hands are still shaking. A text should never be stapled together. Clip it and remove each page to the left as you complete them. Amateurs will staple pages together, fold them over, and then under, much to the annoyance of the audience. Each page of text should be numbered and checked before the presentation to insure that they are in their proper order. The transition from one page to the next can be made smoother by looking up at the audience when the speaker shifts to the next page.

Other facets of a presentation that one can control are the use of visual aids in the presentation. Although it is beyond anyone's control when a light bulb goes out in a projector or the battery dies in your laser pointer, these distractions can interrupt the flow of your presentation. Flexibility means using a ruler or pen instead of the laser pointer or speaking louder when the sound system fails. In some cases, it may be better to wait until the problem is fixed. A good rule is for you to arrive early, check your room that you are presenting in and check all the equipment that you will be using to make sure it is in working order and it is what you need. Be sure to have a spare bulb for the projector. Check out the room to make sure that the temperature of the room is not too hot or too cold, the chairs are comfortable, and the room is laid out correctly. Although you as the speaker are not responsible for these situations, you must assume control of them. Do your best to remedy the situation by arriving early, inspecting the site, and then by consulting with members of the host institutions. You don't want members of the audience to be distracted from the subject matter of your talk by physical discomfort. They should be comfortable so that they can concentrate on listening to you, and not on their aches and pains. You don't want them to leave your talk or your class more concerned with their cold feet and/or aching backs than with the ideas you worked so hard to present to them.

Speech anxiety can manifest itself in many ways. It sometimes happens that during a presentation, the speaker "freezes" and develops a mental block. An important point to remember when this occurs is that the audience usually does not notice that this is happening. To regain your composure, pause and find your place in your notes. Read your material the way you have written it. This will help you to compose yourself and carry on without the audience being aware of what has taken place.

Gaining a knowledge of the audience is an effective means of reducing speech anxiety. By knowing whom you are addressing, you can tailor your presentation to the demographics of that group of people. A sound suggestion is to look upon your presentation as a dialogue with the audience, not a monologue (Anholt, 1994).

> Be sensitive to the needs and interests of your audience, and reflect on the questions: What do they expect to learn from my presentation? How can my presentation be useful to them? A presentation prepared with these questions in mind is more likely to succeed with the audience than a presentation intended from the outset solely to impress the listeners by glorifying the speaker's self-perceived accomplishments." (p. 12)

A false sense of superiority, especially when used to make up for a lack of knowledge about the topic, is quickly detected by an audience. Perhaps more important than any other advice is to simply be yourself. You are one person talking to another person. Be natural.

Another audience characteristic to take into account is the size of the group. A larger group may mean a more formal presentation and less likelihood of interacting directly with the audience. For example, if you are teaching a class composed of 100 students you will be more likely to lecture than if you are speaking to a class of 15 students. When you are speaking to a larger group, be it in a lecture hall or in an auditorium, it is more difficult to respond to feedback because it is harder to establish eye contact with members of the audience. With a smaller audience, you may be able to present more abstract material because you can detect any nonverbal feedback from the audience that indicates they are not following what you are saying.

Whether your audience will be familiar with your topic is another facet of the presentation to consider. Unfamiliarity with the topic means that a more elementary approach may be in order. Sometimes the speaker must face a hostile audience and the presentation is used as a means of diffusing a situation. In these situations, the presentation must be sensitive to the topic and address the issues at hand.

If possible, you should monitor the audience for signs that they are still with you. This is particularly important for classroom teachers. If their attention is beginning to drift, you can ask a question directly of the audience or focus attention on a member who is drifting as if you were talking to him or her directly. Signs of disinterest include slumping in chairs, folded arms, yawning, failure to take notes, or whispered conversations. Evidence of this behavior means that you have to take action immediately by involving those parties in the discussion.

Asking questions of the audience and having the audience ask you questions are effective in getting the audience involved. Once the ice has been broken and the audience feels comfortable interacting with the speaker, the challenge is to maintain control of the questions. You might want to consider setting up some ground rules in the beginning of the discussion to avoid potential problems. One method of motivating the audience is to repeat the correct reply in the exact words used by the member of the audience who answered the question. This is highly motivating and reinforces the behavior (Richards, 1988). If you cannot answer most of the questions asked of you, then you are talking about the wrong subject. When you know the answer to a question, provide that answer simply and clearly. Then ask the questioner if he or she is satisfied with the answer, and elaborate if necessary. If the questioner probes too deeply and wastes time, offer to discuss the subject after the presentation. Never make up an answer. If you are unsure of an answer, tell the questioner that you will research it later and get back to him.

To help reduce the focus on you as the speaker and to redirect it to your presentation, remember that the audience is interested in your message, not you the person. You are not the center of attention. Most people have been in the position of having to speak in front of a group of people they did not know and can empathize with the speaker's nervousness. Developing a positive attitude, "I have something interesting to tell people," will help to defuse some of the anxiety. It also helps you develop confidence that carries over to your audience and encourages their enthusiasm. Remember, the goal is to get the audience actively involved in your topic.

Many people are afraid of public speaking because they think they will forget what they want to say, the audience will reject them, or people will think they are stupid, undereducated or fraudulent. A thorough understanding of your subject matter, preparation of the room to be used, and knowledge of the audience is the best means of relieving anxiety when giving a presentation whether to your students, to their parents, or to fellow professionals at a national conference.

REFERENCES

Anholt,, R. R. H. (1994). Dazzle'em with style. New York: W. H. Freeman and Company.

Cronin, M. W., Grice, G. L., and Olsen, R. K. (1994). The effects of interactive video instruction in coping with speech fright. Communication Education, 43, 42-53.

Gladis, S. D. (March 1989). Public speaking from a prepared text. FBI/Law Enforcement Bulletin, 17-22.

Hu, S., Bostow, T. R., Lipman, D. A., Bell, S. K., and Klein, S. (1992). Positive thinking reduces heart rate and fear responses to speech-phobic imagery. Perceptual and Motor Skills, 75, 1067-1073.

Menzel, K. E. and Carrell, L. I (1994). The relationship between preparation and performance in public speaking. Communication Education, 43, 17-26.

Richards, I. (1988). How to give a successful presentation: A concise guide for every manager. London: Graham & Trotman.

Wydro, K. (1981). Think on your feet: The art of thinking and speaking under pressure. Englewood Cfiffs, NJ: Prentice-Hall, Inc.

Essay 2: ENHANCING PRESENTATIONS WITH GRAPHIC ORGANIZERS
Sister Margaret Egan, S.C., Ed.D.

INTRODUCTION

During their freshmen orientation classes, beginning college students often hear these "words of wisdom" which tend to set an emphatic tone in many classrooms, "When you were in high school, teachers were strongly concerned about your success. They guided you and monitored your class attendance, attention and performance. Now that you are in college you are on your own. You are responsible for your own note-taking and your own learning."

Be that as it may (or may not), any motivated college instructor does not, or should not, view his or her students as "on their own." Brookfield (1990) has written an insightful book designed to help all teachers, but especially college teachers, improve the vitality of their teaching performance. One of the major aims of the book was to "...rekindle the sense of the importance and purpose of college teaching..."(p. xiii) In the book Brookfield challenged the reader with what he labeled the simplest but perhaps most profound truth of all. The truth is that the (college) teacher should view herself as a "helper of learning." Brookfield notes that "anything you do that contributes to this purpose is skillful teaching no matter how much it may depart from your traditional expectations about how teachers are supposed to behave." (p. 209) Brookfield's crucial, poignant and necessary question is: Are my actions helping students learn? (p. 210) In this chapter we will ponder that question as we ask ourselves, "What can I do differently that may help me become a better teacher and help my students become more enthusiastic, involved learners?" In response to this question, I suggest that you may use "graphic organizers (GOs)" in planning for and teaching your classes. This chapter offers suggestions for use of GOs. It also includes a review of a case-study analysis of classroom use of GOs and concludes with helpful guidelines that will prove useful in the implementation of GOs for instruction.

SUGGESTION 1–USE OF GRAPHIC ORGANIZERS (GOs)

Good college instructors constantly search for ways to enhance their presentations. They use varied forms of technology, role-playing, simulation, cooperative learning and other strategies among a host of alternatives. In this chapter we shall discuss the graphic organizer (written as GO) as a viable classroom teaching aid, one that the instructor can use to focus his or her own thinking as well as that of the students.

Generally, one defines a GO as a visual representation of knowledge, a way of structuring information, and of arranging essential aspects of an idea or topic into a pattern using labels (Bromley, Irwin-DeVitis & Modlo, 1995). Others (Flood and Lapp, 1998) use the term *mapping* to describe similar instructional activities. (Jones, Pierce & Hunter, 1998) refer to the term *graphic representations* and define them as visual illustrations of verbal statements. Clark (1991) describes GOs as *visual organizers* which he defines as visual representations of different kinds of thinking processes. Clark notes the clear advantage of visual organizer use in teaching. He maintains that visual organizers can help reflect patterns of lower and higher order thinking. With visual organizers teachers can help students attend to thinking skills while maintaining focus on the content area material. This makes learning meaningful. Other terms such as webbing, mindmapping, mindscaping and clustering have become more familiar, particularly in elementary and secondary schools, during the last thirty years.

GOs are widely accepted as a beneficial way to help students organize and clarify their thinking at all developmental levels of learning (Alvermann, 1986; Bromley, Irwin-DeVitis, & Modlo, 1995; Friend & Bursuck, 1999; Heimlich & Pittleman, 1986; Murray & McGlone, 1997; Pearson & Spiro, 1982). GOs stimulate productive thinking because their non-linear, visual style and manipulative features encourage associative recall and add clarity to the comparison of and/or generation of ideas.

In recent years there has been extensive research on the brain and its role in the learning process. We are called to listen carefully to what researchers are telling us--information that is, perhaps, familiar or unfamiliar to us.   In her research summary, Sprenger (1999) defines five memory lanes of learning in the brain that are used to access and store information for long-term memory. These lanes or paths of learning are semantic, episodic, procedural, automatic and emotional. Semantic memory, the brain path most traveled in learning, holds information learned from words. It is most heavily relied upon in classroom situations that include extensive use of learning from textbooks and lectures and other forms of learning associated with words. Semantic memory requires repetitive reinforcement and association and/or comparative stimulation in order for it to cause permanent learning. So, from this viewpoint of cognitive theory, the GO imitates the semantic memory structures of the mind. This is often the principle utilized by teachers who implement the age-old strategy of encouraging memorization through the use of associative recall. For example, *Every Good Boy Does Fine* brings to mind the names of the five lines on a musical staff--*EGBDF*. Accordingly, in today's classroom each instructional delivery needs to be conducted in an organized, meaningful way or else it should not be taught (or, to say the least, it should not be *taught* by an unorganized instructor). One of the ways a college teacher can support students as they use their semantic memories to process information is through the effective use of a GO.

As is true of all teaching tools, GOs are effective only if they are used in a timely and appropriate fashion (Egan, 1999). Traditionally, teachers, particularly those in elementary, middle and secondary schools, have used GOs to teach students to chart their predictive, organizational or summative thinking patterns. These are fine instructional activities which, for the most part, involve the interaction of the learner and the written text. However, as teachers we need to look beyond this limited use of the GO. We need to explore ways in which the GO can be used to improve listening and notetaking skills for students and, equally important, organizational and delivery skills for teachers. Moore and Readence (1984) conducted an extensive qualitative and quantitative review of GO use in the classroom. One noteworthy outcome of their study was their report that teachers involved in the studies felt that they were better prepared to teach their lessons after having constructed GOs during their preparation. In their summary comment, the authors suggested that GOs seem to "help teachers clarify their instructional goals by providing a map of the upcoming concepts to be taught." (p.17)

SUGGESTION 2--USE OF THE GO IN PLANNING AND TEACHING

All students appreciate a clear, well-organized lecture or presentation. Let's admit it--at times, for one reason or another, our classroom presentations may be less organized than desirable. Here enters--the GO. Ask yourself the following question, "How do I want to organize this presentation? How do I want my students to perceive the material? Are my instructional deliveries such that my students will be able to develop clear, well-ordered outlines or summaries?"

Any teacher having difficulty responding to one or more of these questions may want to consider using the GO in planning and presenting information. This can be done in many ways using one or several GO models. Perhaps it would be helpful to consider appropriate organizer structures to use in preparation and presentation. First, however, you need to consider your content and determine which concepts are primary, reflecting essential ideas and which concepts are secondary but, nontheless, important. After that, you need to organize the material and then begin to "plot" representative key words on whichever GO framework seems suitable to your instructional purposes.

Regardless of which representation is used, Jones, Pierce & Hunter (1988) suggest a basic but crucial question that must guide teachers' use of the selected GO. They ask, "Will the frames or sets of questions or organizational categories represent the schematic essence of the text?" In other words, "Will the pattern of the graphic truly mirror the structure of the text it reflects? Which graphic pattern best represents the information I wish to convey?" For our purposes we will broaden that definition to include the schematic essence of the nonprint text--the lecture, panel discussion or film, whichever medium the teacher uses to present the class material. As teacher, you must be clear about the goals, objectives and organizational schema of the presentation in order to reflect that clarity in the GO.

Smith & Tompkins (1988) recommend that teachers model a developmental approach in their use of the GO. Proceed from what is more simple and obvious, to that which is more abstract and less familiar. Hence, in ongoing instruction, one might use a descriptive graphic (if appropriate) and "advance" to cause-effect, problem-solution, problem-solution-result, comparison-contrast, and then more complex semantic webs or matrix formats.

Jones, Piece & Hunter (1988), suggest a sampling of questions that teachers may use in selecting appropriate instructional patterns to represent their class presentation objectives.

1   Are the concepts presented in a hierarchy?
2.   Does the material suggest a timeline of events or information?
3.   Does the content intend to compare and contrast two or more ideas?
4.   Is the presentation a detailed account of something?

These questions and similar ones will help you to clarify your own thinking processes and class objectives as you explore your planned instructional framework.

With slight variation there are widely accepted definitions of the types of expository writing that usually convey information. Smith & Tompkins (1988) suggest seven structures most commonly used in expository text. A listing of these seven structures as well as informational purposes and possible GO representations are illustrated in Table 1 and Figure 1.

Table 1

EXPOSITORY TEXT	PURPOSE	SUGGESTED GO
1. Description	1. to list the features of a concept or event.	1. Simple Description
2. Time order	2. to list a sequence of events or steps of a process.	2. Time-order Frame
3. Cause-Effect	3. to show relationship(s) between cause and effect.	3. Hierarchical or Sequential Frame
4. Problem-Solution	4. to suggest outcomes for an issue.	4. Problem-Solution
5. Problem-Solution-Result	5. to suggest outcomes and effects of outcomes.	5. Problem-Solution-Outcomes
6. Comparison/Contrast	6. to list similarities and differences of a concept.	6. Comparison-Contrast Matrix
7. Definition/Example	7. to present verbal or textual attributes concretely.	7. Definition/Example Web

Figure 1

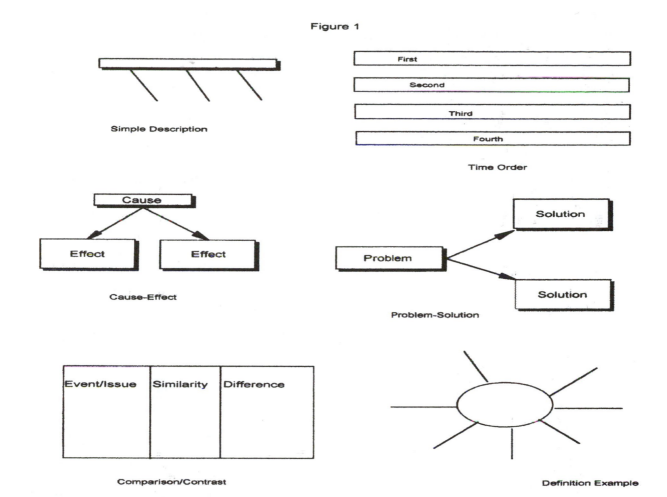

Simple Description

Time Order

Cause-Effect

Problem-Solution

Comparison/Contrast

Definition Example

IMPLEMENTATION

Perhaps the best way to illustrate the GO approach is through a case study of an actual classroom presentation for students enrolled in a foundation course in teacher education. One three-hour session was devoted to the study of the history of education in the United States. Specifically the topic was *American Education: Influences and Trends*. This subject matter is vast indeed and my task of trying to organize my material, engage students and teach effectively in this limited time period was a challenge indeed.

My *goal* in teaching this class was to present a holistic, but obviously limited, view of the history of education in the United States. Essentially, I wanted students to be able to see that in some ways, "...there is nothing new under the sun." I wanted to help students realize that many of the educational principles and practices that were advocated by ancient Greek and Roman educators as well as those of the 17th and 18th Centuries are cited as "best practices" in educational literature in contemporary United States. Also, I wanted students to be able to see that there was much more to United States education than the traditional study of curriculum and methodology that occurred in the New England, Middle Atlantic, and Southern colonies. I wanted students to be aware of the fact that there were non-European groups of people in the United States (Native Americans, African-Americans, Asian Americans, Mexican Americans) who did not experience the educational benefits given to European Americans. *For my behavioral objective*, I wanted students to be able to discuss these Greek/Roman and European influences. Also, I wanted them to be able to describe relationships between one of the historical issues studied and contemporary education in the United States.

How did I begin? I prepared my outline using a simple hierarchical GO developed on an Inspiration software package (Inspiration, 1997). (Figure 2) As I reviewed and revised my notes, I referred to and modified the GO according to my perceptions of how best to organize and present the content. Conversely, I used the GO as a framework to help me visualize the content and see the relationships among my ideas. As I was readying the completed GO for duplication for class use, it occurred to me, that there was more than one way to format the layout to encourage student participation. I could distribute the GO as completed (*Plan A*) (Figure 2) or I could distribute it with major topics only, *American Education: Influences and Trends* and invite students to complete the graphic outline throughout the session (*Plan B*) (Figure 3). Since I was teaching this topic to two different class sections, I chose to use *Plan A* with Section A and *Plan B* with Section B. With both sections I could still model organized instructional delivery.

As I introduced the class session and topic, I explained the purpose of the organizer and suggested that students might want to use the GO to help them follow the class presentation. It is important to note that it was a suggestion, not a requirement, that students use the GO. (I also advised the students that they might want to use the GO to keep a check on how organized I was as a teacher.)

Figure 2.   **Figure 3.**

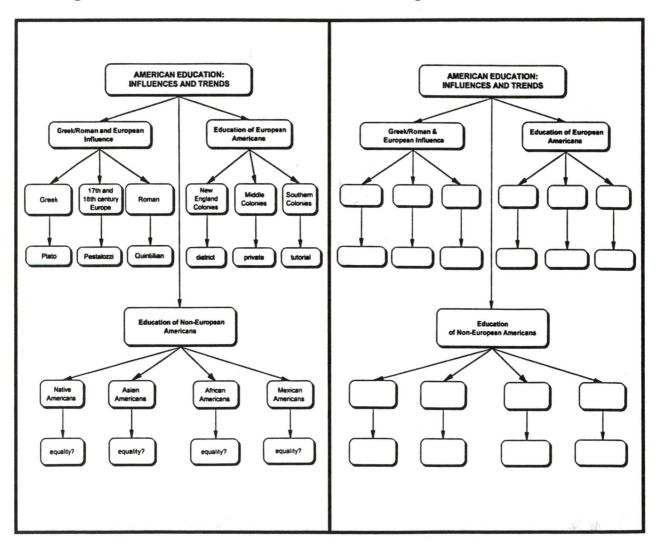

SUGGESTION 3--SOLICIT FEEDBACK FROM STUDENTS

The former mayor of New York City, Edward Koch often asked his constituents, "How am I doing?" He asked the question throughout his time as mayor, not just when he had completed his term of office. Reflecting on that practice, I asked myself, "How often do I pose that question to students throughout the semester?' So often, I wait until the semester concludes before obtaining course effectiveness feedback. It is too late then, at least too late to implement immediate change. So, in working with these GOs during those two class sessions, Section A and Section B, I developed a set of questions designed to obtain brief but immediate feedback on students' responses to my use of the GO in each class section. In addition, I presented each section with an overhead transparency view of the GO used in the other section. Also, in my assessment I did not want to overlook those students who may be more comfortable with a linear approach to thinking and note taking--using the more traditional outline approach. So, at the conclusion of both class sections, I also asked students to comment on the helpfulness of the traditional outline (Figure 4) which I displayed as a transparency. My questions were presented accordingly:

FOR SECTION *A*--How did my use of this GO (Figure 2) help (or not help you) learn? Explain whether or not you would have preferred a GO with only the major topics included and the rest left blank for you to complete during class (as indicated on the displayed transparency (Figure 3). Explain whether or not you would have preferred an outline format. (as indicated on the displayed transparency) (Figure 4).

FOR SECTION B--How did my use of this GO (Figure 3), help (or not help you) learn? Explain whether or not you would have preferred a GO with all major topics and subtopics included (as indicated on the displayed transparency (Figure 2). Explain whether or not you would have preferred an outline format (as indicated on the displayed transparency) (Figure 4).

Figure 4.
AMERICAN EDUCATION: INFLUENCES AND TRENDS

    I. Greek/Roman and European Influence
        A. Greek
            1. Plato
        B. Roman
            1. Quintillian
        C. 17th and 18th century Europe
            1. Pestalozzi
    II. Education of European Americans
        A. New England Colonies
            1. district
        B. Middle Colonies
            1. private
        C. Southern
            1. tutorial
    III. Education of Non-European Americans
        A. Native Americans
            1. equality?
        B. Asian Americans
            1. equality?
        C. African Americans
            1. equality?
        D. Mexican Americans
            1. equality?

OUTCOMES

The results of this informal analysis indicated that there was not an overwhelming student response to my use of the GO in either class. (See Table 2). As the instructor, I found the GO most helpful in my preparation and delivery and I was somewhat perplexed by students' less-than-enthusiastic response. However, after requesting students' input regarding my use of the GO, realization came quickly. Students' responses can be combined with my reflections and offered as *guidelines to consider* before using GOs to plan presentations with the ultimate goal of helping students follow and organize their class note taking activities. Table 2, a matrix GO, summarizes student responses to my request for input.

Table 2.

QUESTION	SECTION A	SECTION B (Larger class)
How did the use of a GO help or not help you learn?	Most students agreed that the organizer helped them follow the presentation. A few stated there was not enough room to write their notes.	Most students were "OK" about the use of the organizer. Many stated there was not enough room to write their notes
Explain whether or not you would have preferred a GO without subtopics included (Section A) or with subtopics included (Section B)	All preferred the organizer with topics included.	All preferred the organizer with topics included.
Explain whether or not you would have preferred an outline (linear) format.	About 10-15 % preferred an outline format because it provided more space on which to write.	Almost 10-15% preferred an outline format because it provided more space on which to write. Some commented that the format was more familiar.

It was interesting that the students almost unanimously indicated a preference for a GO with all topics included. Based on these preferences, I could probably assume that students like working with completed GOs because the key information is displayed for them. Most likely, their notes would be more accurate and less risk would be involved in learning. Also, for most students it is, no doubt, easier that way. It is probably safe to assume that as teachers we prefer a more challenging GO with subtopics not included. We would see this as more conducive to active student engagement. I would predict (and hope) that with more frequent exposure to and use of GOs, students' preference would change, reflecting their desire to become more engaged in attending to and organizing the teacher's presentations.

GUIDELINES FOR IMPLEMENTATION (STRONGLY OFFERED)

Many college students have been exposed to GOs throughout their educational careers, in their use of elementary and secondary texts and other instructional materials. Nevertheless, a large number of them are not familiar with the use of GOs in their own college course work, much less with their college teachers' use of them. They are not "tuned in" to this visual mode of note taking. Therefore, the following considerations should assist you if you decide that you want to utilize the GO in planning for and teaching your classes:

1. SIMPLIFY INITIAL PRESENTATIONS. The GOs used in Figures 2 and 3 were probably overly dense for first-time use for many students. A more simplified graphic representing less content (such as that in Figure 5 or the Venn-type diagram in Figure 6) would have given the students greater ease as well as space in following the presentation. For example, the graphic representation in Figure 5 is focused more on one issue, thus differing from those in Figures 3 and 4. In this case, the graphic could even be larger and students would have more room to add their own expanded notes or details. The Venn diagram in Figure 6 would also depict less content; however, it would help students see the differences and similarities pertaining to the topic under discussion

Figure 5.

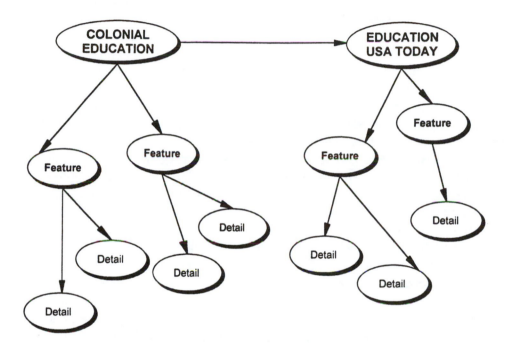

Figure 6.

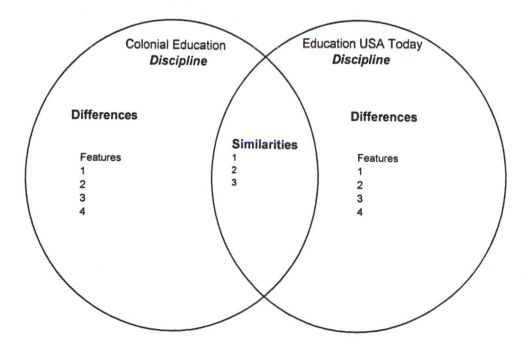

2. MAKE NO ASSUMPTIONS. Effective use of the GO can help you organize and present your information. However, in the beginning stages of use, I strongly advise that you guide students' visual observations of the GO either by writing in each subtopic on transparency as you introduce it, or by pointing to each already printed subtopic as you refer to it in your presentation.

3. UTILIZE THE GRAPHIC. After you use an organizer in presenting, continue to refer to it. Use it for review and to help students visually associate important ideas and relationships that might otherwise go undetected. Use it to help students summarize the presentation or a portion of it in their own questions and class discussions.

4. "TEST RUN" THE ORGANIZER. As subject matter specialists in college teaching, we can develop a certain "tunnel vision" about our content and how we present it in the classroom. In offering advice to secondary school teachers who use GOs, Tierney and Readence (2000) suggest a self-assessment whereby the teacher asks a student or colleague, preferably of another discipline, to comment on the clarity of the developed organizer. Likewise, college teachers can benefit from the same advice. After sharing the GO you designed, you can ask questions that will indicate whether the student or colleague understands the organization sequence and accurately interprets the relationships among the items in the organizer. It is amazing how a simple evaluative procedure can provide valuable feedback that can give you more teaching confidence and make your organizer more helpful for you and for students.

5. REVISE, REVISE, REVISE. This is what good teachers often do. We must consistently re-examine our course material and notes so we can fulfill our professional obligation to keep ourselves current and relevant. Once you develop a GO for class use, continue to assess its effectiveness and modify it whenever you believe it is not sufficiently fulfilling your intended class objectives.

6. BE FLEXIBLE. This advice applies to all good teaching. With GOs it is especially applicable. If we encourage students to use GOs in their note-taking and studying, or even reporting, we may find that things do not turn out as intended. As well-prepared teachers, we know our organizational sequence and our intended emphasis. However, students often do not graphically see things as we see them; yet their perceptions are on target. As long as students' graphic interpretations of your presentations are accurate, coherent and explainable, they should be accepted and deemed as appropriate as your own.

7. DON'T PUSH IT. In this section I discuss using the GO not as an end in itself but as a "means to the end" of more focused planning and instructional delivery by teachers. Also, I suggest that you may wish to have your students use GOs in their own note-taking or studying after you have modeled this practice in class. Nevertheless, there is the possibility that some students may resist this visual tool especially if imposed too consistently or rigidly. If you perceive that some students resist or see little value in the GOs, then let it be. This does not prevent you from taking full advantage of GO use in your own planning and teaching.

SUMMARY AND CONCLUDING THOUGHTS. In this section we considered the feasibility of using GOs in planning and presenting content material in the college classroom. Then, looking briefly at the research we found support for GO use on all levels of instruction from elementary to college. Examples of different organizers were illustrated. A specific case study, reported on GO use in foundation of education courses. Finally, suggestions for GO implementation in college classrooms were offered.

Some of the GO examples used in this chapter illustrate their use specifically in the study of history. However, their use is relevant in all content areas. (Black & Black, 1990; Vacca, 1999; Braselton & Decker, 1994; Bromley, Irwin-DeVitis & Modlo, 1994). While most of the literature refers to instruction at the elementary and secondary levels, application of GO use for organizational and problem-solving processes in all subject areas may be applied successfully at the college level with the creative mindset and skill of a motivated college instructor.

A word of caution accompanies the use of GOs. Hyerle (1996) in his excellent text *Visual Tools for Constructing Knowledge* exhorts teachers to come to a full understanding of the different types of GOs or *visual tools* as he prefers to calls them. He cautions that the term *organizer* as used with *graphic* could be limiting in that it implies organizing and storing information perhaps in a latent or passive manner. This could cause students to "fall prey" to becoming static receivers of information. His definition of *visual tool* more accurately transmits the broader use of a GO which is, not only to organize receptive inflow of information, but to stimulate creative, divergent thinking as well. Hyerle would have students use GOs to brainstorm, organize ideas, seek open-ended associations and engage in meta-cognitive conversations. This writer could not agree more strongly with Hylerle. Yet, the purpose of this chapter is to help teachers *first* use the tools to organize and present their own instructional material. Once teachers and students have become accustomed to basic use of GOs, there is limitless possibility to their creative, divergent use in all types of teaching-learning situations.

REFERENCES

Alvermann, D. (1986). Graphic organizers: Cueing devices for comprehending and remembering main ideas. In J.F. Baumann (Ed.), Teaching main idea comprehension (210-226). Newark, DE: International Reading Association.

Black H. & Black, S. (1990). Organizing thinking, book 2. Pacific Grove, CA: Midwest Publications Critical Thinking Press and Software.

Braselton, S. & Decker, B.C. (1994). Using graphic organizers to improve the teaching of mathematics. The Reading Teacher. 48, 276-281.

Bromley, K. Irwin-DeVitis, L.& Modlo, M. (1995).Graphic Organizers. New York, NY: Scholastic Press.

Brookfield, S.D. (1990). The Skillful Teacher. San Francisco, CA: Jossey-Bass.

Clarke, J.H. (1991). Using visual organizers to focus on thinking. Journal of Reading. 37, 526-534.

Egan, M. (1999). Reflections on effective use of graphic organizers. Journal of Adolescent and Adult Literacy. 42, 641-645.

Flood, J. & Lapp, D. (1988). Conceptual mapping strategies for understanding information texts. The Reading Teacher. 41, 780-783.

Friend, M. & Bursuck, W. (1999). Including students with special needs: A practical guide for classroom teachers. Boston: Allyn & Bacon.

Heimlich, J.E., & Pittelman, S.D. (1986). Semantic mapping: Classroom applications. Newark, DE: International Reading Association.

Hyerle, D. (1996). Visual tools for constructing knowledge. Alexandra, VA: Association for Supervision and Curriculum Development.

Inspiration 5 K-12 (1997). Inspiration software. Portland, OR: Inspiration.

Jones, B.F., Pierce, J. & Hunter, B. (1988-89). Teaching students to construct graphic representations. Educational Leadership. 46, 20-25.

Moore, D.W. & Readence, J.E. (1984). A qualitative and quantitative review of graphic organizer research. Journal of Educational Research. 78: 11-17.

Murrray, J. & McGlone, C. (1997). Topic overview and the processing of topic structure. Journal of Educational Psychology, 89 (2), 251-261.

Pearson, P.D. & Spiro, R. (1982). The new buzz word: Schema. Instructor, 91 (9), 46-48.

Smith, P.L. & Tompkins, G.E. (1988). Structured note-taking: A new strategy for content area readers. Journal of Reading. 32, 46-53.

Tierney, R.J. & Readence, J.E. (2000). Reading strategies and practices: A compendium (5th ed.). Boston, MA: Allyn & Bacon.

Sprenger, M. (1999). <u>Learning and memory: The brain in action</u>. Alexandria, VA: Association for Supervision and Curriculum Development.

Vacca, R.T. (1999). <u>Content area reading literacy and learning across the curriculum</u> (6th ed.). Menlow Park, CA: Addison Wesley.

INTERNET RESOURCES

www.graphic.org/
(Comprehensive web site which contains powerful strategies for employment of graphic organizers in all curriculum areas.)
www.inspiration.com/
(Contains download demos, feature lists, lesson plans, case studies and testimonials on the use of Inspiration in classrooms.)

Essay 3: ACTIVE LEARNING
Kathleen Schmalz, Ed.D., RN, CHES

Reading makes a full person; writing a ready person.
Francis Bacon

Even at the earliest grade levels, no subject stands isolated. Children read about the three little pigs and they learn how to count. They learn about the American Revolution and they wonder what it might have been like to live in a world that had lots of candles but no computers. They learn about their peers in other countries, and in our diverse society, they often interact with them face-to-face within and outside of the classroom. With access to the Internet, many children establish friendships in distant parts of the world. Difference and distance lose their importance. With asynchronous learning, time counts for nothing at all.

Innovative teachers make use of these opportunities, and many others, to form links across disciplines, to build on students' interests, and to keep knowledge grounded in real world experience. Going higher in grade and age, the links become more complex. Simple content areas like math and reading and social studies pale before the array of disciplines these basic subjects spawn by the time students reach college. Even more complex are the students themselves. Engaging older students can be a real challenge. Active learning has to go far beyond joining in a group song about the day's lesson (although that strategy can get an immediate response from adults; just be wise in your choice of song).

Take the subject of human sexuality as it is taught at the college level. The subject of human sexuality is inherently multidimensional (Schmalz, 1999). Classes for young adults include instruction of the biology and physiology of human sexuality and reproduction as the core component, but it is impossible not to limit the field and not include topics and issues encompassing sociology, psychology, cultural anthropology, history, and of no small importance, ethics. With ongoing research in the scientific fields, even objective data is subject to change and inevitably, subject to debate.

A curriculum in human sexuality may not seem the ideal example for explaining the way knowledge is interrelated because it is intrinsically personal with an interpersonal orientation. It cannot be removed from the social context. That, however, is exactly the point. The problem with the traditional approach to learning lies in the attempt to isolate subjects from one another and from the social context. In the end, the most isolated and alienated subject has been the student.

WRITING ACROSS THE CURRICULUM

Writing across the curriculum developed as a way to promote linkages across content areas as well as developing writing skills. In effect, writing is linked with everything. With fourth graders having to demonstrate their skills in writing essays to meet the rigorous new standards, it becomes obvious that writing is essential to all academic areas. Beyond the learning environment, the ability to write coherent business reports, research articles, and even e-mail is gaining critical importance. Employers want job applicants who can demonstrate writing skills and interpersonal skills. Active learning strategies help to develop both.

Writing across the curriculum is one of the most important curricular developments of the past two decades. Stated succinctly, *"The productive use of language, and especially writing, is a valuable tool for learning for all students in all subjects at all ages"* (Mayher, Lester, & Pradl, 1983). At its broadest, writing involves any situation in which the mind is involved in choosing words to be put on paper (or screen). It runs the gamut from scribbling a shopping list to creating a literary work. Writing involves the choice of words and it involves critical thinking.

Writing across the curriculum has been approached from a number of perspectives, two of which can be broadly defined in terms of expressivism and social construction (Bean, 1996). Expressivism has been especially influential. A "neo- Platonic pedagogy that has its roots in the language-across-the-curriculum movement in British secondary schools" (p. 47), expressivism exalts the value of students' individual voices and of their cultures. In other words, it is the antithesis of the objective, fact-laden style of prose traditionally taught in American academia. At the heart of expressivism is the value it places on the experience of the individual. The writer is freed from the constraints of objectivity to express her or his own voice.

From the social construction perspective, academic disciplines are constructed by their discourse (Bean, 1996). One of the tasks of writing across the curriculum is to initiate students into the discourse style of a particular academic community. In the scientific community, for example, students learn how to pose questions, collect and weigh evidence, and construct arguments as members of a scientific discipline.

Social constructivists raise concerns about the personal, social, ethical, and political costs of being socialized in an academic community. The proliferation of lawyer jokes gives some confirmation to that concern. (Q: What's the difference between a lawyer and a vampire bat? A: One is a blood-sucking parasite and the other is a mouse-like creature with wings.) At the same time, neither the Harvard Law Review nor the New England Journal of Medicine has much interest in "voice," unless it is backed by hard, solid fact and embedded within a cogent argument.

Writing is a broad enough field to encompass both subjective and objective approaches. There is plenty of room for the voice of the philosopher and the artist, the lawyer, the biologist, and the CEO, and all their respective communities.

In today's classrooms, whether students would like to commune in the woods like Thoreau or head straight for Silicon Valley upon graduation is only a small part of the diversity that encompasses language, culture, socioeconomic status, and other classifications that give rise to voice. With motivation a key issue, educators wonder what they can do to motivate so many diverse learners.

One way in which some sources in business as well as education tackle the issue is by way of indicators like the Myer-Briggs Type Indicator (MBTI), which was derived from Jung's theory of personality (Bean, 1996). The MBTI classifies personality types according to preferences on four different continua: extroversion (E) or introversion (I); sensing (S) or intuition (N); thinking (T) or feeling (F); and judging (J) or perceiving (P). In all, there are 16 personality types, for example: ESFJ or INTP.

In brief, extroverts are inspired by people and events while introverts draw inspiration from the inner world of thoughts and ideas. Sensing types collect facts through their senses and like writing assignments with clear-cut instructions and organization. Intuitive types tend to reach beyond the everyday world of the senses for future possibilities; they rebel at having to follow prescribed guidelines. Thinking types make decisions based on impersonal data and logical deductions of cause and effect; their writing is logical and concise. Feeling types prefer self-expression; the concept of voice was made for them! Judging types tend to like short-term plans and see them through to a quick closure, while perceivers prefer to remain open to new possibilities - sometimes seemingly endless possibilities.

The MBTI is used a lot in team building. The goal is not to create a homogenous team but to get a good complementary mix - which is exactly what you will find in the classroom. The only way to stimulate 16 potential personality types is to use a variety of strategies for engaging students and include writing assignments of different types. You may be surprised what you find, too. Encouraging students to work in other than their preferred mode helps them to expand the ways in which they interact with the world around them, including the way they process information and select the words to put down in writing.

Here are some basic principles to help motivate all students to write:
- Most students, especially in lower decision courses, prefer a series of short assignments to one long one (Introverts and intuitive types may disagree.)
- Long assignments (e.g., research papers, term papers) will be more successful if you break them down into stages.
- Sharpen your own creative skills. Use a mixture of different types of assignments: journals, learning logs, and freewrites; formal academic assignments; and reflective or creative pieces that emphasize personal voice.

- Provide frequent opportunities for group work and experiential learning.
- Sequence assignment to promote a gradual increase in the level of challenge. Early successes will promote ongoing engagement.
- Clearly explain the purpose of each assignment.
- Provide frequent and timely feedback. Be sure to deliver it in a way that promotes improvement and decreases anxiety (Bean, 1996).

Journal writing has become a favorite technique for writing across the curriculum. Journals range from totally open-ended to highly structured (Bean, 1996). Among the most popular types of journals are:

- Open-ended journals. These are sometimes called "learning logs." Students are free to write about the course in any way they choose, summarize lectures, expressing ideas, posing questions, etc. The journal provides a record of the student's intellectual journey through the course.
- Semi-structured journals. This type of journal offers a framework for expression in writing while allowing students almost as much freedom as an open-ended journal. For example, the teacher may provide a set of questions; students respond to one or more questions of choice.
- Guided journals. In a guided journal, students respond to content-specific questions created by the teacher. The questions are designed to promote critical thinking skills and deductive reasoning.
- Dialogue journals. Also called a "double-entry notebook" or "dialectical notebook," this very popular type of journal requires students to first reflect on course material and then reflect on their reflections.

WRITING ACROSS GRADE LEVELS

Entering a college writing course in which they are met with phrases like "find your voice," many students feel like they have been let out of a cage. Describing their high school writing experience, students report things like "the teacher controlled the topic" or "you had to write about what the teacher wanted which was usually about a book we had read" or "something you didn't know much about." Even the topics about the book were "very regimented" (McAndrew, 1999).

In this scenario, old habits may be very easy to unlearn. Students want to be creative, not constrained in their writing. Two themes emerge from students whose high school experience with writing was less than positive:

- They had little or no choice in content or form or both.
- There was no interaction among students. Rarely did students read and respond to each other's writing.

Both of these deficits can be remedied by creating an engaging, interactive learning environment. To create your learning environment you can:

- Begin the class with a mental imagery exercise. This will help students to get into a reflective mode.
- Begin with a group discussion about your topic. If the topics are self-selected, use that for your discussion. By sharing ideas with others, students can get new ideas about their own topics.
- Ask students to share their writing with each other. For students who never had the opportunity, especially, sharing their work can be exhilarating! (Silberman, 1996)

Teachers of first-year college students have to help students transcend their prior experiences with writing, not try to forget them. After all, the power of voice is that it comes from one's experience. Many students share the same experience, and shared experience is a way to interact with others and gain insight into oneself. The following questions can be used as a starting point for the college writing class.

- What did you read and write about in high school? Did your experience encourage creativity or stifle it?
- Did you ever have two writing teachers with very different approaches? Tell stories about the two classes.
- Do you think the writer rules in a writing class? That is, do you think that writing should be done for the writer's purpose? Should the writer choose the topic? Elaborate on your position.
- Have you ever shared your work with peers before? How did it work? How can you make the experience really successful?
- What influences do you feel when you are writing?
- Try writing two descriptive scenarios. In scene one you are alone; in scene two you are with others. How do you feel in each one? Which scene is more conducive to writing?
- How do you feel in the writing classroom? Shy? Confused? Right at home? If you are shy or confused, how can you feel more at ease? If you feel right at home, how can you help others who are shy or confused?
- Now you are a full-fledged class member and writer. Explain what you contribute to the class (McAndrew, 1999).

The above questions do not assume that students' previous experience with writing is negative. Teachers at all grade levels can promote students' exploration of writing, beginning with the self-exploration that is essential to the development of voice.

Middle school students like to try out their wings. But they are not yet ready to solo. They need clear-cut objectives embedded in flexible guidelines. Self-selection of topics may leave younger students with more confusion than freedom. A good way to engage students in the writing process is to use props. That way they have something concrete to build on. And they can apply their imagination to how they use their prop as a an inspiration for writing. For example:

- Collect a variety of hats. Ask each student to choose a hat and become the character who would wear it. Students can:
  - Write a short-first person narrative from your character's viewpoint
  - Write a study of your character describing physical as well as personality traits.
  - Write a short list of quotations from your character or a dialogue between your character and another person.
- Use an object instead of a hat. Ask students to:
  - Imagine a situation or event of which your object has a key role.
  - Write a brief, creative short story scene that includes your object.
  - Imagine you are a newspaper reporter and put your object on the front page.
- Have your students write a haiku. The classic Japanese 17 syllable poem is short and intriguing - two keynotes for middle school years. The format consists of three lines containing five, seven, and five syllables:
  See the red berries
  Fallen like little footprints
  On the garden snow
     -- Shiki, 1866-1902

The haiku is also good for middle school students because it contains concrete elements. The four concrete elements are: event, time, place, and nature.
- Draw upon students' age experience and feelings. Ideas include:
  - When will my parents let me grow up?
  - It's not fair! You may find you have some budding protest song writers.
  - Topics from current or community events.

- Two-legged, four-legged, flying, and swimming friends. (National Council of Teachers of English [NCTE], 1996)

High school students may feel a bit silly walking into a classroom and choosing from hats, rocks, or glittering objects. They are mastering abstract reasoning and they like interacting with peers. A 10-minute preclass discussion is a perfect way to engage students and help them select topics to write about. Have a different student lead the discussion each day (NCTE, 1995). Have the leader choose a topic from school, community, national, or global events. For example:

- How would you feel if you were a refugee in Kosovo?
- What do you think of Vice President Gore's and the EPA's plans for testing toxic chemicals on animals?

On a less serious note, have students describe a family meal in detail. Or describe how they would spend a $10,000,000 prize. Or create a pilot for a new science fiction show.

High school students are ready to embark on the process of self-exploration that will not only help them find their own voice but will draw them away from a myopic view of the world to a perspective based on greater appreciation and understanding of others.

WRITING WITHIN THE DISCIPLINE

Writing within the discipline refers to the construction of basic prose within a fairly standardized format. The classic example is the major research paper. When students apply critical thinking skills, the research paper can be a highly valuable assignment. It is up to teachers to ensure that within a standard framework, students present their own ideas and logically and coherently defend them.

The skills required for critical, coherent thinking should be an integral part of all writing classes (indeed, of all classes). Presumably, students have been learning and sharpening these skills throughout all activities. However, the research paper poses some specific problems. Handouts can be a useful strategy, for example illustrating the way to present quantitative data and include charts and graphs. Techniques for taking the pain out of research writing in general can be synthesized into handouts. Here are some basic suggestions:

- Emphasize the asking of research questions. Help students think of their research topics in the form of a question or problem. It helps ensure focus.
- Require a prospectus in advance of the due date. This will help students to think out the process instead of turning in a rush job. Typical questions in the prospectus include:
  - What research problem do you intend to address?
  - What is the significance of the problem?
  - How far along are you on the project? Are you ready to formulate a thesis statement? If so what is it?
  - Attach a working bibliography of the sources you have already used.
  - Write a brief annotation of each one.
- Teach the prototypical introduction: Problem, Thesis, Overview. Provide examples to illustrate this format.
- Teach students how to read and write academic titles. The most common types of titles are: a) the *question* ("How Effective is TQM?"); b) the *summary of thesis or purpose* ("The Relationship Between Peer Tutoring and Self-Esteem in Sixth Graders"); and c) the *two-part title with a colon* ("The Y2K Bug: Real or Myth"). The last one seems to be the most popular title of all. Some researchers have found a connection between colons and being published!
- Provide models. Develop a file of model research papers from your previous classes. Attach to each one an explanation of why the paper succeeds. Models are especially

useful for scientific reports, providing a clear example of how to display quantitative data, summarize and focus these data verbally, and how to analyze and evaluate these data in discussion.

- <u>Develop a strategy for teaching research skills</u>. Once called "library skills," searches can now be conducted at home by surfing the Web. In fact, some students may be students may be so adept at this mode, they can pass on their skills to the rest of the class. For library and other outsources, try designing experiential projects in which students go out hunting in small groups to locate resources (Bean, 1996).

For the best results on the research project - or on any ambitious projects - break the task into stages. Just be sure that in breaking it down you do not neglect the critical element: synthesizing material. Draw on the critical thinking skills that enable students to make connections between seemingly diverse elements and to dissect seemingly similar ones. Think of the way research reports differ across disciplines. For example, how would a report written by a biologist sound different from a report written by a sociologist?

WRITING TO LEARN (WTL)

The concept of writing to learn (WTL) is rooted in the premise that writing is an act of discovery (Schmalz, 1999). In contrast to the traditional "product" model of writing, WTL uses a "process" approach. The entirety of the writing process constitutes a learning experience, from the first inkling of an idea to the fully revised and polished final draft.

All the above examples of classroom techniques make use of WTL. All have a pre-writing component. WTL has four basic overlapping stages:

- Pre-writing to gather and organize ideas.
- Drafting to translate ideas into written form.
- Revising to clarify and polish the draft.
- Editing to find any problem with grammar and usage.

Group Writing to Learn

Critical feedback is an integral part of the process. Incorporating group interaction at the start of the writing process sets the stage for giving and receiving and receiving feedback.
In fact, structuring the class into small learning groups is an excellent way to facilitate the entire writing process. A growing body of research confirms that group learning produces learning and social outcomes that are superior to those yielded in the traditional teacher-led classroom (Schmalz, 1999). Through active involvement in learning groups, students acquire more factual knowledge, sharpen their reasoning and analytical skills; and enhance their social skills and by extension, their self-esteem. The small group environment facilitates trust and collaboration with peers.

Critical thinking is central to the development of writing proficiency, and small groups can be used to advantage to foster critical thinking skills. John Bean (1996) states succinctly, "A good small group task, like a good writing assignment, needs to be carefully designed." (p. 151) Good tasks feature open-ended critical thinking problems that require solutions justified with well-founded supporting arguments. Reaching consensus may be the group goal but this is often difficult to achieve. In fact, it is not always desirable. Going for consensus all the time can lead to groupthink - the opposite of the critical thinking the group is formed to accomplish. Instead, the group can "agree to disagree." Like Supreme Court decisions, the final report will contain majority and minority views with each side clarifying the causes of disagreement.

As a strategy to enhance writing, small group tasks can be used conjointly with a formal writing assignment. Within the group, students brainstorm ideas for their upcoming essay or story, discover and rehearse arguments, or critique rough drafts.

The best size for groups tends to be about five or six members (Bean, 1996). In corporate settings, groups are often structured to obtain the optimal mix of personality styles that will foster dynamic interaction in growth. Few teachers have the option to organize groups in this way, but teachers can ensure the growth of all members by pointing out different ways in which people interact. For example, an introvert may prefer to think things out before making a point. The teacher can point out that quiet members frequently have a lot to contribute - it just has to be done in their own way. Alternately, some quiet members may need to be drawn into the group discussion by their more extroverted peers.

A well-structured group component has several steps:

- <u>Assigning the task</u>. Ideally, the task should be given to students in a handout or overhead projector. The assignment and its objectives should be clearly stated, including a specified time limit.
- <u>Completing the task.</u> Once the students are clear about the task, they are left to work on it independently. Some teachers believe that leaving the room entirely is the best way to promote autonomy, while others prefer to minimize their presence but remain in the room.
- <u>Group reporting.</u> When the allotted time is up, a designated reporter from each group reports the group's solution to the class as a whole. The reports are not summaries, but perspective papers. Always rotate the group reporter. The reporter gets to practice public speaking skills and with responsibility for being a group representative, often acts as a facilitator, keeping the group on task.
- <u>Group critiquing and discussion</u>. As groups report, the teacher becomes more active in the discussion. The arguments of the various groups and subgroups generates further discussion, and the teacher's role is to help the class synthesize group reports by pointing out strengths and weaknesses in the arguments, and validating diverse perspectives. The students are typically eager to hear the teachers solutions, but empowered by their active participation in the group, are not afraid to challenge their audience (including the teacher).
- <u>Relating the task to the learning sequence.</u> The best small group tasks are tied into a clearly stated ongoing objective. Frequently, that objective is a formal writing project.

LEARNING TO WRITE

Unless the writing project itself is collaborative, for example, a screenplay, writing is a solitary activity. Even extroverts who draw inspiration from having things going on all around them are inherently alone with the pen, pencil, or computer keys. Mayher et al. (1983) describe a seven-stage process for independent WTL:

- Choose a problem from your journal, your work, or your daily life that you would like to explore through writing. Consider your audience. Write a first draft, and feel free to experiment.
- Reflect on and write down the steps you went through in writing your draft.
- Take an idea that interests you and write a short paragraph. Monitor the stream of thoughts that went through your head as you wrote and try to distinguish a pattern.
- Brainstorm a list of activities targeted to promoting writing among your students. Next to each activity, write a brief description of what kind of writing it could generate and a short explanation of why.
- Revise the writing you did for either Task 1 or Task 3. List the revisions you made and the reasons for the revisions. What kind of feedback did you get? Did the ideas for the revisions come from you or your audience? What were the cues?
- Edit the piece of writing you just revised. What were the most common problems? How did you solve them?
- What were the steps you took in creating your final product? What did you do to create meaning? Did you go back to earlier parts of the paper before writing more? When did you go back?

The above method is an exercise for the teacher that illustrates the way in which writing is taught to the class.   The model favored by most academic writers begins with a fledgling idea and progresses through six stages:

- Starting point or perception of problem. There is always something that elicits raised eyebrows and quizzical looks. Translate the idea into writing.
- Exploration. Think of all the ways you can gather data - library, experience, online, memory, introspection, laboratory, field research. Probe every corner you can think of for information.
- Incubation. Take some time off and reflect. You may find your original perception of the problem has changed.
- Writing the first draft. Try to get your ideas down in preliminary form. Some writers like outlines. Others do not. There are many options for creating a rough draft to suit individual learning styles.
- Reformulation or revision. Take another look at the problem. Do some more thinking. What may happen is that as you think you are going to scrap your original outline, draft, or idea, the "Eureka!" experience will show that the right idea is embedded in a seemingly obscure sentence. Make several drafts. Experiment.
- Editing. This is where form links with content. Check for unity, coherence, format, and structure. Never neglect the basic spelling and punctuation. In the final draft, every detail counts. You may want to retrace your steps at this stage. Writing is not meant to proceed in exact sequences - that's why the process approach is the one that works!

The Dynamic Writing Assignment

Here is a sample writing assignment submitted by Dr. Barbara Smith that utilizes feminist theory. The topic is "Women's Lives and Voices." Select a specific title, focusing on the following assignment:

- Compare and contrast the character of Olenka in the film "The Darling" to that of Antonia in "Antonia's Line." Use the following points: identity formation, effect of main character on those around her, and your explanation of that effect.
- What do you see as the main point of the film? In what ways is the main point connected to the theme "Women's Lives and Voices?"
- Describe at least three of Antonia's personality traits. Do you like her? Admire her? Why or why not?

To add diversity to the assignment, students can formulate different answers from the perspective of different disciplines. For example, psychology, sociology, film-making, acting. Each model should adhere to the points for writing discussed throughout this chapter.

REFERENCES

Bean, J. C. (1996). Engaging ideas: The professor's guide to integrating writing, critical thinking, and active learning in the classroom. San Francisco: Jossey-Bass.

Mayher, J. S., Lester, N., & Pradl, G. M. (1983). Learning to write/writing to learn. Portsmouth, NH: Boynton/Cook.

McAndrew, D. A. (1999). That isn't what we did in high school: Big changes in the teaching of writing. In W. Bishop (Ed.), The subject is writing (2nd ed.) (91-98). Portsmouth, NH: Boynton/Cook.

National Council of Teachers of English (1995). Teaching the writing process in high school. Urbana, IL: Author.

National Council of Teachers of English (1996). Motivating writing in middle school. Urbana, IL: Author.

Schmalz, K. (1999). Informing our values and sexual behavior through the use of writing communities. In A. Roberson & B. Smith (Eds.), Teaching in the 21st century: Adapting writing pedagogies to the college curriculum. Garland Press.

Silberman, M. (1996). Active learning: 101 strategies to teach any subject. Boston: Allyn and Bacon.

Essay 4: Teaching Writing Process to Enhance Learning
Barbara Smith, Ph.D.

When professors outside of college English departments hear that I teach writing, most complain about the writing skills of their students, their lack of motivation, their general carelessness, laziness, and ignorance of grammatical rules. Many ask what they can do about the poor papers they receive, but refer only to grammar and sentence construction errors. Some suggest that the English Department provide a course in grammar that will make student writing "correct." The reality is that learning to write well is a long process for a lot of students, a process that must be understood and utilized by teachers of all disciplines if we are to address effectively the reciprocal concepts of learning to write and writing to learn. These concepts are reciprocal because doing more assigned writing not only helps the student write better, it also helps students learn the course content. Writing promotes thinking, and thinking, of course, promotes learning. Addressing either of these ideas (writing to learn or learning to write) in isolation—from each other and from the discipline's content—will lead to unsatisfying results in both writing and learning.

Objective testing provides the instructor with knowledge regarding which students read the material and memorized or internalized at least that portion of the material included on the exam. Grading is relatively quick and straightforward; a numerical grade is easily assigned. Objective testing has its place in many disciplines, but objective testing alone can't get a handle on what the students are thinking, how the students apply their knowledge to larger situations, make connections, or see new knowledge as a logical result of prior learning. Additionally, they will not learn the necessary conventions of writing in the context—joining the "conversation"—of a particular discipline. Providing support, for a psychology paper is different from assessing the causes and results of an historical event. Analyzing a chemical reaction is different from analyzing a literary text. No one course (certainly not one focused on grammar!) can sufficiently address these differences. Even essay exams which allow students to show evidence of critical thinking and their ability to synthesize information and ideas do not provide students with the benefits of writing process. To that end, writing in the disciplines programs have been implemented, some curricula including a writing course for each discipline, taught by faculty from that discipline's department. Unfortunately, not all instructors feel confident or eager to teach such courses. This was not their expectation upon leaving graduate school, and some who understand the need for pedagogical flexibility given the reality of changing demographics in the college population, acknowledge the need for writing instruction in their discipline, but have not been trained to provide it, and so are reluctant and unsure of how to go about it. Many were taught the "think, then write" method (Elbow, 1998) in which writers simply record their thoughts. There, the writer begins with a topic, moves onto a thesis, outlines, writers a draft, then edits. The problem is that little room is left for discovery and clarification during the writing process, since the thesis and outline dictates—at the outset—the content of the paper. In actuality, most good (even professional) writers respond to an issue, question, or problem first by exploring it, then arriving at a working thesis which they further explore through research, and/or feedback, then re-think, and revise. What I want to suggest is a process that is now taught in most writing classes that is mindful of the thought process, and that can be used in all disciplines. It is intended to be of service both to new teachers of writing as well as to faculty in other disciplines. The process is time consuming; however the reward is not only better essay exams and papers, but also better learning of the course content. The teaching of grammar should not be ignored, especially by writing teachers, and some suggestions are included here in the discussion of stage three of the writing process.

Background

In 1977 Mina Shaughnessy, upon her analysis of the placement exams of four thousand students over a period of five years concluded that basic writers are simply beginning writers who learn by making mistakes. A poor grade accompanied by advice to proofread underscores students' incompetence while denying them an effective way to gain competence. It is not enough, she says, to understand what is "missing or awry" in students' writing; we must also understand "why this is so." (Shaughnessy, 1977, p. 5). That is, we have to learn to look at the process of students' writing, and intervene at certain moments in order to effect change. Types of intervention will be discussed in a separate section of this essay.

Since 1977 research has shown that the writing process is messy. Few writers produce good writing in a single draft; ideas develop *during* the writing process. Writing helps students learn and explore and develop new ideas that emerge while writing. An audience is needed—again *during* the writing process—because writing is a struggle during which student writers need helpful feedback and encouragement rather than notations in the margin identifying grammatical errors after the final paper is submitted.

There are several recent resources for teachers interested in writing to learn/learning to write which help teachers design assignments and set up classroom procedures to promote active, engaged learning. I have included some of the sources in the recommended readings at the end of this essay. My focus here is to provide access to the writing process as it may be applied to most essay writing—in English classes and many other disciplines: thesis based writing. Since short or extensive term papers and portfolios (which may or may not include research) are still, in conjunction with tests, the most widely used assessment tools, it is to that writing process that I would like to turn my attention.

Thesis-Based Writing and Writing Process

I tell my freshmen writing students that there are only two major concepts they'll need to learn in my course: 1. the idea of thesis and support and 2. writing process as it applies to the composing of essays. This is a semester-long challenge that must be reinforced several times throughout the students' four years—in classes in most disciplines—if we are to graduate students with writing proficiency. Like most other skills, writing ability diminishes if not practiced. Freshman composition, where students learn the basics of college writing, is only a start.

Most confused ("bad') writing is the product of confused thinking. An adequate working thesis statement clarifies thinking for the writer and sets up the expectations of the reader. Students all too often come to my course with a misguided notion of what a thesis statement is and when it should be formulated. They will state a fact, declare their purpose, praise an author in vague terms, present a problem, or claim to "prove" something that is unprovable. As a result, they don't see a clear writing path ahead of them. ("Where do I go from here?") With a clear thesis statement, the path is clear: support it. The writer's job—no matter what the discipline—is to convince the reader that the thesis is valid. Because the thesis statement serves as the basis for the paper, it cannot arise out of thin air, but rather must be the product of thinking, exploratory writing, discussion, and perhaps research.

A good thesis is the one controlling idea of the paper. It is focused and specific so that the writer can discuss it intelligently and support it effectively within the length limitation of the assignment. It states a point of view, position, or attitude. But these are not usually known before the writer begins to write. An effective way to get students to formulate thesis statements is to have them freewrite (Note: Freewriting is writing that is spontaneous and free-flowing; writers are free to write their thoughts knowing that no one will see this writing [it is private], and they write for a prescribed amount of time. Focused freewriting, the kind suggested above, is freewriting on a particular topic. Public freewriting is freewriting that will be shared. The writer should know this ahead of time. For more on freewriting, see Elbow.) for ten minutes about their perception of a problem (usually in response to a prompt such as assigned reading, a controversial class discussion, or a problem posed by the instructor). They may focus their freewriting on what they will try to do in relation to that problem and what the purpose of the writing is. (Note: laGuardia and Guth [1977] provide examples of purposes: sharing information; writing to explain; investigating a trend; correcting a misunderstanding; writing to define; arguing a point; writing to persuade.) The instructor may then ask the students to explore the nature of the problem through research (library and/or field); journal entries; and conversations. After the explorations are over, ask the students to re-think the issue, then to come up with a working thesis statement for that topic. "Working" means that the thesis at this stage is really more like a hypothesis. In the next class, divide the class into small groups of three or four, and distribute a checklist of set of guidelines for good thesis statements. Ask the group to evaluate each member's thesis statement on the basis of a checklist, and ask each to include suggestions for a better thesis statement if not all criteria are met.

A checklist might look like this:

- The thesis has only one controlling idea.
- The thesis is focused enough to be thoroughly discussed in ___ pages.
- The thesis statement makes the writer's point of view, position, or attitude clear rather than just declaring what the topic will be.
- The thesis is supportable.
- An intelligent person might well take an opposing view.
- The thesis statement is interesting.

When students have revised their thesis statements, either in class or at home, the instructor should review them to be sure that they are adequate and that the writing path is clear. The next step is to ask the students how they intend to support their thesis. Adequate support depends on the nature of the discipline. If research is involved, the student should provide a list of sources for the instructor's approval. (Many students have not learned to distinguish between legitimate sources and "pop" magazine articles or undocumented information on the Internet, for example.) If research is not involved, the instructor should make clear what comprises support: personal experience? anecdotes? informal surveys? logic? the writer's ideas based on common knowledge? Once it is clear that the student has an adequate thesis statement and means to support it, the student may move onto the next stage of the writing process.

Writing Process

Given the reality of the difficulty some instructors have in their struggle to cover adequately the topics on their syllabi in a fourteen-week semester, I am not suggesting that every stage of the writing process be done as groupwork for every written assignment. That is unrealistic, and the process would soon become tedious. I suggest that the process be done in its entirety for one short paper early in the semester. (Longer papers will require too much class time, and students will have too much material to review effectively in a group setting.) This way the writing process will have been modeled in a memorable way, and students can be expected to know how to apply it to their own work at home. Subsequent written assignments should be the product of individual revision based on the three stages of revision and their questions, supplemented perhaps by visits to the writing center, if your institution has one (writers should bring the revision questions with them), or perhaps by class sessions that focus on only one stage of revision, e.g., stage one for the next assignment; stage two for the third; stage three for the fourth).

The outline below is not meant to suggest that the writing process is linear. Thesis statements are changeable. We cannot know what we will think or write until we write it. If research is involved, we cannot know what it will yield until we have analyzed it. It is not cheating to revise the thesis statement to reflect the thoughts and learning that further inquiry has provided. Earlier passages including the one containing the thesis statement may need rethinking or reseeing (re-vision!) throughout the writing process. The writing process is recursive.

I.   Pre-writing

Pre-writing consists of any technique that will get the writer started such as freewriting, brainstorming, clustering (or branching), reading, discussing, or outlining. (Note: For detailed descriptions of freewriting, brainstorming, and branching, see Eppley and Eppley, 1997, 51-54.) Pre-writing should then be used to give the writers a preliminary idea of what they already know, what they need to find out, what they want to include, what they have to say on the topic, why they hold the position they do, what opponents of their view might argue, how they would refute their opponents' arguments. It is a time for exploring ideas. The prewriting should not be graded, but should be included—along with drafts—with the submission of the final paper. Instructors may want to collect the pre-writing in order to make suggestions or provide guidelines, but if students sense that the pre-writing will be evaluated, the writing will be hampered and stilted, defeating the purpose of the technique which is simply to get the student started. (Many professional writers claim that getting started is the hardest step [some say discarding passages is] in the writing process.) When the instructor and the students feel confident that the line of inquiry is clear and do-able, it is time to move on to stage two, composing or drafting.

II.   Composing or Drafting

Students who are unfamiliar with writing process (most if not all of them) are under the false impression that this stage means getting it right the first time. Most of them are products of classes in which this was the norm. If they harbor this misguided notion, their energies will be divided among the tasks of referring to their pre-writing, integrating research, finding the perfect words and phrases, trying to be all-inclusive, organizing, providing details and examples, and checking for spelling punctuation, and grammatical and structural errors. They will become "paralyzed" during this stage. Where can they fit in the most crucial component of all—thinking?

Trying to get it right the first time is self-defeating. It is juggling too many balls at once; all will come crashing down. Writing, like other aspects of life, can be overwhelming and must be divided into manageable increments. (A draft is exactly that—a draft.) The student should take heart that in the next stage, revision, there will be ample time for reorganization, improving word choice and style, supplying additional details and support, and focusing on issues of correctness. It is in the composing (or drafting) stage that the writer formulates a tentative thesis statement.

The question then becomes: what do we do with drafts? collect them? grade them? simply check to see if they are done? provide comments? The answer depends on your time constraints and students. I prefer not to collect and grade drafts at this stage because peer feedback often provides many of the comments I would make as well as other benefits (discussed below). However, some students may not take a draft seriously enough if they know it will not be graded. Others do, knowing that their peers will see and scrutinize it (in a highly structured setting), and that it will be submitted along with the final paper. Perhaps trial and error will determine the best policy for a particular class. The instructor should be cautioned, though, about a significant problematic aspect of grading drafts: if the paper will undergo two or three revisions, a draft with a grade of B or C will, theoretically, improve with each revision, resulting in not much latitude for a final grade. Unfortunately, not even after several revisions will all papers earn an A or B. Instead of grading drafts at this stage, a more effective intervention may be to "workshop" them in highly structured settings. Once the initial draft is completed and "workshopping" or collaborative peer reviewing begins, we enter stage three, the longest stage and most comprehensive stage in the writing process.

III.   Revision

It helps to explain the entire writing process to students at the outset. When they know that they will not have to worry about issues of correctness during the composing stage, they will be more fluid writers. If they can see that the issues that concern them during the composing stage will indeed be addressed at a later stage—with no penalties for the time being—they can write and think more clearly. There are three steps to the revision stage. The questions below are specific to each stage of revision. They must be specific for the collaborative process to work, otherwise students may wander off the task, provide simplistic praise, or engage in insensitive, counterproductive negative criticism. However, these questions should be modified if necessary to fit the assignment.

Step 1: Quantity

The writer should make enough copies of the essay so that each group member has one. The writer should read the paper out loud, slowly. Here the focus is on putting it all down on paper. The questions are designed to add information to the draft based on the readers' needs. The other group members function as an audience, not as teachers. The writer should be provided with a response sheet including a list of questions which he or she asks the group.

Questions for Step 1 of the Revision Process

a.   What have I left out? What do you as a reader need or want to know that isn't there?

b.   Do I have a working thesis statement? Where is it?

c.   Do I have enough details, examples, data, description, explanations, reasons?

d.   Which paragraphs could be more fully developed?

e.   Do I include opposing viewpoints? Where? Can you think of additional opposing viewpoints?

f.   Do I convincingly refute those opposing viewpoints? Where? What needs to be added to make my refutation more convincing?

g.   Do I have a conclusion that provides closure to the piece? Does it relate to the thesis statement? In what way?

h.   What else do I need to add for you to be convinced that my thesis statement is valid?

The writer takes notes on peer responses, then revises accordingly. The group may then go on if time permits, to workshop the papers of the second and perhaps the third person in the group, depending on the length of the session, but only stage one should be the focus of this class. It might be good to include a word to the wise here. Students should be cautioned that in the end, the writer, and only the writer, is responsible for deciding what the final paper looks like. Feedback is enormously valuable, but since writing is a series of decisions, the writer must decide which suggestions to take and which to veto. This not only gives the writer authority, it prevents later excuses to the instructor such as, "I was going to do what you've suggested, but my group told me not to" or "I had it right, but my group changed it." After the revision is done, it is time to move on to step 2.

Step 2: Quality and Style

When the writers have addressed the issue of completeness by adding necessary information, description, examples, or other details, and are convinced that nothing is missing from their essays, they can turn their full attention to their means of expression. How can they say what they've said more effectively? The following response sheet may help writers to get the audience reaction they need in order to clarify and make their writing more accessible to their audience. It may be helpful to remind students that their readers are not expected to be more knowledgeable about the topic or about writing. Their purpose is to enable writers to learn the effect of their words and sentences on an audience. What is clear to the writer may well be confusing to a reader who sees only the written words, and who has no access to the thoughts that dwell only in the writer's mind.

Questions for Step 2 of the Revision Process

a.   Where is the writing most interesting? Why?

b.   Which sentences need to be made shorter? Longer?

c.   Which words could be made more specific?

d.   Which sections could be more concise?

e.   Where is the paper confusing? What do you need to know to be clear about what I mean?

f.   Do you see any logical organizational principle at work? (chronology, sequence of subjects, simple to complex, etc.) How can I reorganize so that there is a more logical reason for the sequence of sections?

g.   Where would a transitional sentence be helpful to get you from one paragraph or idea to the next?

h.   Where do I get repetitious? vague? dull?

i.   Which paragraphs do not relate to my thesis statement?

The instructor should be circulating from group to group throughout feedback sessions in order to be sure that all students are on task and that they are clear about what the questions mean. Readers as well as writers should benefit from these sessions as they enter into a conversation about writing and consider the topic under review. While no question is designed to elicit a simple "yes" or "no" response, some readers may need a push to say something other than "It looks fine to me." Spending five or ten minutes with each group helps all participants to become more engaged, thoughtful responders.

After all students have finished stage two, they revise again, at home, then submit this draft (the second) to you. Again, you will need to decide whether or not to assign a grade. What is most helpful, however, are questions and comments to the writers (not more than four or five) that will keep them focused on the requirements of the assignment, and that you—as a reader—need addressed for a thorough understanding of the thesis and to become more convinced of the writer's position. Questions posing opposing viewpoints are also helpful. It is appropriate, especially at this stage, to suggest (or require) a one-on-one conference with the student to help him address your comments. It may not be necessary to confer with all students, but for those who are confused or whose papers invite much response from you, a brief discussion can make all the difference to a writer whose path is obscured by what she perceives as puzzling, sometimes overwhelming commentary.

If we want to emphasize that correcting grammatical, spelling, and structural errors is confined to stage three, instructors should refrain from making such corrections on the students' drafts at this point. This is hard! But your comments will be enough for them to contend with here, and soon enough there will be an entire stage devoted to correctness.

Step 3: Proofreading - Correcting errors in grammar, mechanics, punctuation, and spelling

It is this step that most people—students and teachers alike—mistake for the entire revision process, and that some attempt as they write their first draft. Now is the time to consider the grammatical, mechanical, and structural issues that were deferred during the first two stages of the writing process. The focus here is on grammar, punctuation, spelling, and sentence construction. Students will need a good dictionary and handbook, brought to class for use at this time. Studies have shown that even students who have been taught grammar and who do well on grammar drills have difficulty with grammatical concepts out of the context of the drill (Braddock, Lloyd-Jones, and Shoer, 1963 and Hartwell, 1985). Students have higher motivation when approaching issues of grammar in structure in their own writing. Sometimes simply reading their work out loud brings errors to students' attention (Bartholomae, 1980). They hear what they cannot see. Often students miss errors in their own writing because they have looked at it for so long that the errors look right. And sometimes the student senses that something doesn't look or sound right, but doesn't know how to fix it. Here is another point in the writing process where intervention is indicated. There are several good strategies that may be implemented here:

1. After becoming familiar with the types of errors the student frequently makes, require him to work on those (two or three types of errors, one at a time) with a writing center tutor who will explain the grammatical or structural principle at work, and practice overcoming them in future assignments. The instructor should designate which error is to be the focus of the tutorial session, e.g., agreement, fragments, comma splices. Instructor, writing center, and student should own the same handbook so that the student can be shown the pages to study at home. Often students cannot name the error they consistently make;

therefore, they cannot look it up in the index of the handbook on their own. Of course one-on-one conferences focused on one grammatical, structural or mechanical error at a time would also be helpful, but given that most instructors teach seventy-five to one hundred students a semester, time and energy constraints may preclude this. Writing center instruction is crucial.

2. In small groups (three students) in class, ask each student to read aloud the most recent draft (of which others members of the group have copies). As the student reads, she is to correct all the errors she hears; if she cannot correct them immediately, she may circle them and come back to them later. The group should do the same on their copies, then discuss the error, consult the handbook if necessary, correct the error, and provide their rationale for the correction. If an error seems apparent, but cannot be named or corrected, the group should signal the instructor who will join the group and direct it to the appropriate page in the handbook.

3. Students may exchange copies of papers (retaining the original) and work on each other's errors for homework. Readers should write the name of the error and state the reason for the correction in the margin. A discussion of the changes made or suggested may be the focus of the groupwork in the following class. With this method, only one or two class periods are taken up with grammatical and structural issues. Any remaining questions may be addressed by the instructor during that class period or by a tutor at the writing center soon after class. Too many red marks pointing out grammatical and structural errors not only discourages students, but are cognitively overwhelming. In any one session on grammar, in addition to the "simple" errors (those made carelessly and picked up quickly when the paper is read aloud) only two or three types of grammar or sentence-construction errors should be addressed and attended to in revision. (All errors of those types should be corrected.)

After the completion of this stage, papers are submitted to the instructor. In writing classes, the students should expect to revise one more time on the basis of the instructor's comments. Revision instructions should be framed within the context of writing process language, that is, the student needs to spend more time on stage one, having left out pertinent issues or data; or stage two, having too many vague terms or organizational problems; or stage three, too many fragments. This paper may be graded with the understanding that if the paper is revised substantially, the revision will likely result in a higher grade. Or the paper may simply receive a checkmark indicating its adequacy except for indicated errors, which must be corrected in the next (final) draft, which is to be graded.

In non-writing classes, the instructor may grade the paper, indicating areas to be worked on for the next written assignment. Instructors should take note of those areas for each student in order to enable themselves (instructors) to see if indeed the student has done this for the next assignment. The issues indicated may not be grammatical; they may well be specific to the discipline (insufficient data or analysis; areas of inquiry left unaddressed or inadequately addressed; hasty conclusions).

Like any newly learned procedure, writing process will be most time-consuming the first time it is attempted. It is imperative to remember though, that the two weeks or so spent on producing the first paper not only helps students to write better by concretizing the process—in the discipline and in general—but perhaps even more importantly from the perspective of the instructor, fosters discussion, learning, and reinforcement of the discipline's content—the topic of the essay as well as the "real world" idea that much knowledge, while based on accepted fundamental principles, is socially constructed.

Socially-Constructed Knowledge

According to Kenneth Bruffee, whose work is informed by Thomas Kuhn, L. I. Vygotsky, Jean Piaget, M.L.J. Abercrombie, and Richard Rorty, knowledge relies on social relations rather than on attempts to mirror reality (Bruffee, 1982). What separates collaborative learning from other forms of group work is that collaboration involves intellectual negotiation. Therefore, the tasks of the group members must be highly structured and written down, such as on response sheets. Students must be given enough time to discuss their responses and try to come to a consensus so that the feedback given is based on more than personal preference. The answers to questions posed in collaborative learning projects should not be predetermined. The learning here occurs in the ways students negotiate and support their consensual answer. The instructor may need to intervene to facilitate consensus or, if necessary, to resolve the issue by agreeing to disagree. Depending on the discipline, a further step may be needed which compares the consensus with differing opinions (of either other groups or relevant texts). The goal here is not to establish right and wrong (except in cases that are rule-based such as grammar and sentence construction), but to understand, analyze, and evaluate how a different approach or answer was constructed. The purpose is to see knowledge as socially constructed, not simply for the process to *appear* more social by the new placement of desks and new emphasis on student interaction. The objectives here are different from those of the lecture format, Socratic dialogue, or group work designed to solve a problem with a correct answer or to reinforce the internalization of factual material. I don't believe that using lecture (an expedient way to provide information) and Socratic dialogue is inconsistent with collaborative learning. Some knowledge is already out there, and need not be rediscovered. But much—more than we think, I'd venture—is yet to be determined and would crystallize or reveal its complexity better under collaborative scrutiny. Additionally, students will see themselves as integral to and to a large degree responsible for their own learning of course content and of their means of expressing this learning. They may see themselves as part of a community of learners; they may be more motivated to think, study, and do research, since their *informed* ideas are valued by and integrated into that community. And when students have something to say and believe their thoughts to be worthwhile, they may be happily surprised by their new motivation to be understood—in writing.

References

Bartholomae, D. (1980). The study of error. College Composition and Communication, 31, (3), 153-269.

Braddock, R., Lloyd-Jones, R. & Shoer, L. (1963). Research in written composition. Urbana: National Council of Teachers of English.

Bruffee, K. (1982). Liberal education and the social justification of belief. Liberal education, 68, 95-114.

Elbow, P. (1998). Writing without teachers. (2nd ed.). New York: Oxford University Press.

Eppley, G. & Eppley, A. (1997). Building bridges to academic writing. Mountain View: Mayfield Publishing Co.

Hartwell, P. (1985). Grammar, grammars, and the teaching of grammar. College English, 47, (2), 105-127.

laGuardia, D. & Guth, H. (1977). Issues across the curriculum. Mountain View: Mayfield Publishing Co.

Shaughnessy, M. (1977). *Errors and expectations*. New York: Oxford University Press.

Recommended Readings

Anson, C., Graham, J., Jolliffe, D., Shapiro, N., & Smith, C. (1993). Scenarios for Teaching Writing. Urbana: National Council of Teachers of English.

Bazerman, C. & Russel, D. (1994). Landmark essays on writing across the curriculum. Davis: Hermagoras Press.

Bean, J. (1996). Engaging ideas: the professor's guide to integrating writing, critical thinking, and active learning in the classroom. San Francisco: Jossey-Bass Publishers.

Bond, L. & Magistrale, A. (1987). Writer's guide: psychology. Lexington: D.C. Heath & Co. (part of the Heath Writing Across the Curriculum Series edited by A. Biddle which includes *Writers Guides* in history, life sciences, and political science as well as psychology).

Elbow, P. (1998). Writing with power (2nd ed.). New York: Oxford University Press.

Elbow, P. (1998). Writing without teachers (2nd ed.). New York: Oxford University Press

Eppley G. & Eppley, A. (1997). <u>Building bridges to academic writing</u>. Mountain View: Mayfield Publishing Co.

Hult, C. (1996). <u>Researching and writing across the curriculum</u>. Needham Heights: Allyn & Bacon.

Hult, C. (1996). <u>Researching and writing in the humanities and arts</u>. Needham Heights: Allyn & Bacon.

Hult, C. (1996). <u>Researching and writing in the social sciences</u>. Needham Heights: Allyn & Bacon.

laGuardia, D. & Guth, H. (1997). <u>Issues across the curriculum: reading writing, research</u>. Mountain View: Mayfield Publishing Co.

Langer, J. & Applebee, A. (1987). <u>How writing shapes thinking</u>. Urbana: National Council of Teachers of English.

Murray, D. (1998). <u>The craft of revision</u> (3rd ed.). Fort Worth: Harcourt Brace College Publishers.

Murray, D. (1996). <u>Write to learn</u> (5th ed.). Fort Worth: Harcourt Brace College Publishers.

Murray, D. (1989). <u>Learning by teaching</u> (2nd ed.). Fort Worth: Harcourt Brace College Publishers.

Noguchi, R. (1991). <u>Grammar and the teaching of writing</u>. Urbana: National Council of Teachers of English.

Robertson, A. & Smith, B. (1999). <u>Teaching in the 21st century: adapting writing pedagogies to the college curriculum</u>. New York: Falmer Press.

Shaughnessey, M. (1977). <u>Errors and expectations</u>. New York: Oxford University Press.

Tate, G., Corbett, E., & Meyers, N. (1994) <u>The writing teacher's sourcebook</u> (3rd ed.). New York: Oxford University Press.

Zinsser, W. (1988). <u>Writing to learn</u>. New York: Harper & Row.

Essay 5: Effective Use of the Library
Stephen Feyl, MLS

Introduction

As we look at the development of libraries over the past 10 years, we see dramatic changes in the approach to library research. Innovations in technology have caused the slow extinction of traditional methods of accessing information. The days of the card catalog and of print indexes are, alas, numbered.

The driving influence in replacing these traditional access methods is the development of the Internet as an effective research tool. Online book catalogs and online indexes permit the researcher to access information beyond what the traditional methods allowed. The researcher can now access information simultaneously from multiple access points through keywords in addition to the traditional search categories: author, title, and subject.

The Internet has also revolutionized library research in freeing the research process from the constraints of the library building. The library no longer needs to physically own the information on site in order to access it. Libraries now have the ability to access information globally from a single workstation in the library.

While the Internet has drastically changed the way in which we do library research, the fundamentals of researching, remain true. Research involves skills and values that have not changed with the technology. Having a sound, rational, and logical approach to doing research is still as important in today's modem library as it was in a traditional library setting.

The challenge to teachers and students today is to embrace the technological improvements in the library while not abandoning the tenets lying behind sound research. By establishing a proactive and cooperative relationship between librarians, teachers and students, this bridge can effectively be crossed. Cooperatively developing sound research strategies and basic research skills will provide the students with the backbone for their research. This backbone combined with modern library technology will provide the student and teacher with a well balanced and effectively approached library research project.

Establishing the Librarian/Teacher/Student Relationship

As a librarian I have encountered a myriad of reasons why students do not use the library. Many students find the library to be a very intimidating environment where they feel ashamed of not knowing how to properly use the library's resources. Not knowing how to do seemingly simple tasks such as finding a book on the shelf or checking out a book from the library can cause students to stay away from the library. Researchers call this behavior "library anxiety." In a study done by Sharon Bostick (1992), she identifies five characteristics which cause students with "library anxiety" to stay away from the library. These five characteristics are "barriers with the staff," "affective barriers," "comfort with the library," "knowledge of the library," and "mechanical barriers." (Quoted in Jiao & Onwuegbuzie, 1997). I believe that by properly engendering a librarian/teacher/student relationship, all of these factors of "library anxiety" can be alleviated. By fostering this relationship, students and teachers will feel comfortable using the library, which is the first key element in fostering effective library usage.

Teacher-Librarian Relationship

Before the students even enter the library for research, the librarian and teacher first need to meet and talk about the library as it relates to the class. These first meetings are important because not only do the students suffer from "library anxiety," but teachers also. Because the technology of researching has changed so rapidly over the past few years, many teachers feel that they have been left behind and no longer feel connected to the research process. The librarian can allay some of this anxiety by spending time with the teachers and taking them through the process, through which their students will be taken.

Besides beginning to foster a personal relationship between the teacher and librarian, these initial meetings should also be used to begin developing the library research assignment. It is important to make sure that the assignment is appropriate and can be supported by the library. In an article by Kathryn Johnston (1999), she notices common errors that teachers often make when coming up with library classroom assignments. Teachers often design "inappropriate assignments" such as outdated library "treasure hunts," which provides obscure challenges for reference librarians rather than assignments in which students learn how to better use the library. (p. 100)   Typical library orientation assignments that are designed to teach students about the library are not very effective. Students need a personal connection to their research in order to effectively learn how to use the library. Assignments that correspond to classroom topics cause students to have more of an interest in what they research. As noted by Khami-Stein and Stein (1999), "library instruction should be relevant to the student's academic needs." (p. 174)   These assignments have more of a personal connection with the student and their interests than handing out a fill-in the blank form to the students and telling them to find the answers in the library. By collaboratively working with librarians, ineffective assignments can be avoided.

Another common problem that can be avoided in meetings between the teacher and librarian is to make sure that the library can support the assignment that the students will be researching. All library collections have subject strengths and weaknesses. These areas tend to run along the lines of areas that the school emphasizes in its curriculum. By coming up with assignments cooperatively, both teacher and librarian can be assured that the assignment can be researched properly from that library location.

By the end of the initial meetings between the librarian and teacher, three goals should be accomplished:

- An open relationship between the librarian and teacher should have begun
- Any misconceptions or feelings of "library anxiety" between the librarian and the teacher should be presented and cleared
- An assignment that is both useful and appropriate for the library should be developed

A comfortable, open, cooperative relationship between the librarian and the teacher will act as the basis for establishing a similar relationship with the students in the class.

Librarian- Student Relationship

The key relationship to establish in order to alleviate student "library anxiety" is the relationship between the librarian and the student. If the student feels comfortable working with the librarian, then almost all areas of "library anxiety" can be overcome. Carle and Krest (1998) note how important students find "seeing a familiar face when they came, into the library" was to "overcome their fear of asking questions." (p. 342)   If they feel comfortable with the librarian, it follows that the students will feel comfortable working in the library and with the technology found in the library (at least inasmuch as there is someone that they can turn to if they have a question).

So much can be accomplished through effort on the part of the librarian. When students come into the library with a question, they are looking for someone who will put effort into answering that question. Many students are alienated from the library because they have been belittled or trivialized in the past by library staff. By demonstrating to the student that they have put honest effort and thought into answering the question, students will most often leave the library on good terms for that effort shown. Many times students will come back to that librarian on the basis of that person showing effort in attempting to help them.

Body language can also make a big difference in bridging the gap between the librarian and the student. A simple smile when a student approaches the desk to show that they are not an interruption or a bother can go a long way. Also when students are seated at a terminal or a desk, getting down to speak with them at eye level is important. This helps break the feeling that the librarian is there to bequeath information upon the student. It promotes a feeling of working cooperatively to solve their problem.

Having an informal relationship with the students also works well with many librarians. The goal for each encounter with a student should be to make that student a library "regular." The librarian should make sure that students know their name and where their office is located. Just as in restaurants and other social gathering places, people will come back to a place where they are known and feel welcomed. Follow-up is also an important way for students to feel welcomed. A simple "So how did you do on your paper?" will lead that student to come back again for help. I try to prove to students that just as it is important in life to know a good mechanic, doctor, and lawyer, so it is also important to get to know and be friends with a librarian. In the long run in their studies, it will prove beneficial to them and their work.

Teacher/Librarian/Student Relationship

The librarian, teacher, and student need to work together as a unit. In order to promote this unity, there needs to be a mutual respect between each group for another.

It is important to treat the student as a fellow scholar. Mary Ann Ramey (1996) notes the importance of recognizing the skills which students possess and have the potential to possess. Working collaboratively with the students in learning "convey such respect for student ability, knowledge, and judgement." (p. 247) This does not mean that mistakes will not be made, but it is important not to belittle or trivialize them when they occur.

Having a responsive relationship is also key for unity. The relationship between the three groups must go beyond the teacher handing out an assignment on a piece of paper and leaving it at that. Responding to inquiries and showing interest in students' research all demonstrate that the librarian is working with them and not against them. Teachers need to clarify unclear points that arise from the assignment. Librarians need to make themselves available to make sure that the students are properly approaching their research and using the appropriate tools. Students need to be open and honest in conveying their concerns to the teacher or librarian. In the end, the ultimate goal for both teacher and librarian as it relates to the library is to create a self-sufficient researcher out of the student.

The two key qualities that need to be established between the librarian, teacher, and student are cooperation and openness. Carle and Krest (1998) note that "to be effective and productive, such an undertaking requires close collaboration between the librarian and the teacher, specific integration of library research and writing assignments, and open channels of communication among the librarian, the teacher, and the students." (p. 342)

In Developing Research Skills

Before students can begin to use the library effectively, they need to understand certain concepts associated with researching in a modern library setting. These skills are important in order for them to take their assignment seriously and begin to think of that assignment in library terms.

The common element central to all of these skills is the proper use of words. A key component of library research is the use of a controlled vocabulary system. Davis (1996) observes that "controlled vocabulary is the connecting cord that binds together the component parts of the research process." (p. 206) Students need to appropriately use words in their library research in order for their search to be effective. The following techniques are important in developing skill on how to use words properly for library research.

Keywording

The most important skill for students to master for their library research is to be able to turn their description of a topic into a series of keywords. Students often believe they can go into a library database and type in a search as it appears on their assignment sheet and expect to find information. Keywording involves taking the description of a topic and keeping only the most important words from that description as a basis for searches. Common words and phrases are eliminated to reveal only the essence of the research topic.

Once these words are flushed out, alternatives for those words must also be discerned. Students not only need to think of how they would describe their topic, but they also need to think of how someone else might describe their topic as well. I describe this process as thinking of the topic in parallel thoughts-describing the same topic but in multiple ways. Many online indexes include thesauri that help students translate their topic into the controlled vocabulary of that particular index (see section on Subject Headings). Regular thesauri can also be useful tools in keywording. The librarian, teacher, and fellow students are also important resources in helping to come up with alternative keywords to describe topics. In going through this process, the student also needs to think of their topic in narrower and broader terms. The purpose of keywording is to come up with as many variations as possible to describe the topic. Students need to understand that the computer does not know what they are looking for. It searches for words that are typed in and then matches occurrences of those words with the citations in its contents. By using only one set of keywords, students may not be retrieving all relevant documents that may be helpful to their research. Davis (1996) uses a fishing analogy to help describe this idea to students. She describes using various sets of keywords as similar to using different types of baits when fishing. Not all fish are attracted to the same bait and therefore it is imperative that multiple baits and lures be used to catch all the fish possible. The different lures and baits, represent the various keywords that students use to describe their topic. The fish represent the sought information. This metaphor describes in a very concrete and understandable way the importance of keywording.

Keeping track of the keywords used is also very important to make sure that all options and variations of those words are used in searching. Making lists of possible keyword combinations and the databases those combinations have been used in is a good way of keeping track of searches so that they don't get too confusing for students. Davis (1996) advocates the use of a search matrix to keep track of possible searches. (p. 209) In any situation, the student needs to keep track of how and where they searched for resources.

EXAMPLE

Topic: The psychological effects of television violence on children

Keywords: Television, violence, children (Note: The words "psychological" and "effects" are possible keywords but are not integral to the topic. The words may be used in more peripheral ways in searching. For example, the word "psychological" gives us a key to possible types of databases to search. In this case, psychological databases such as PsycINFO.

Alternative keywords:

Television: TV, media, news

Violence: Violent, anger

Children: Adolescents, teenagers, young

Possible combinations:
1. Television, violence, children
2. TV, violence, children
3. Media, violence, children
4. News, violence, children
5. Television, violence, adolescents
6. TV, violence, adolescents
7. Media, violence, adolescents
8. News, violence, adolescents
9. Etc.

From this example we see how many combinations of keywords are possible. This is why keeping track of possible combinations is so important and why Davis' search matrix is a nice way of facilitating and controlling these numerous combinations.

Boolean operators

Now that the keywords for the topic have been established, there is the issue of how to put those words together when searching. If words are just typed into a search box, the computer will most often search for those words as a phrase and not as combinations of independent thoughts. In the library world there are tools called "Boolean operators." These operators are words that are used to combine independent topics into the same search. The three main operators are the words "and," "or," and "not." More advanced search tools may also allow words such as "near" or "within."

When introducing this idea to students, I limit the introduction to the words "and" and "or." These two operators cover all the necessary functions which students will need at the basic level of researching without confusing them with advanced search jargon.

The word "and" is the most common connecting word used when searching. It tells the computer that you are searching for all the words to occur in the record/citation but not necessarily together. The word "or" is used to tell the computer that you are searching for either word to occur in the citation. This is a good way of searching for multiple variations of a word at the same time. Marydee Ojala (1991) states in simple terms that if the student wants less records, add a word to the search using the "and" operator. If the student wants more records to appear, they should add a word using the "or" operator. (p. 8) Combining different boolean operators into the same search is difficult as it requires the student to use parentheses.

For this reason, introducing them to only one operator per search is best so as not to confuse the student.

EXAMPLES:

Search #1:	Television and violence and children
Results:	Will retrieve records that contain all the words "television," "violence," "children" in the same record but not necessarily together.
Search #2:	Television violence and children
Results:	Will retrieve records that have both the phrase "television violence" and the word "children" in the same citation. The word "Children" does not have to appear next to the phrase however.
Search #3:	Televison or TV
Results:	Will retrieve records that have occurrences of either the word "television" or "TV"

Subject headings

The ultimate example of the use of controlled vocabulary in the library is the use of subject headings. Subject headings are set words and expressions that are used to describe topics. These set expressions are assigned to articles and books by indexers. These people look at the content of articles and books and then assign these set expressions based on the content of the article or book. The purpose of doing this is so that it limits the number of words that are used to describe the same topic. The utility of this for researchers is that if they can find out those set expression(s) which are used to describe their subject, they can drastically reduce the number of searches they will need to perform in order to retrieve all of the articles/books on their topic. The problem is that subject headings assigned to articles and books vary from database to database so that a subject heading used in an online book catalog may not match the subject headings used in a periodical index.

So we are presented with a situation where we have a tool that can be very useful for researching, but loses utility in that it is not uniform. There are two main methods we can use to access this tool. The first is to use an online thesaurus that is specific to the database if one is available. The researcher can type a topic into this thesaurus and it will give them possible subject headings used to describe the topic. The other way to utilize subject headings is that the student can use keywords to bring up a citation to a book or periodical that matches what they are looking for. They can then use the subject headings used to describe that record to find others like it. This process identifies the distinct concepts used in their search. (Bates p. 55) Once these concepts are identified, the student can use these expression(s) in a new search to find similar articles.

EXAMPLE:

Keyword search: Television and violence and children

Subject headings used: Television programs, violence, television violence, children and youth, television and children

Reading citations

Another important skill which many students need assistance on is how to properly read citations. Citations for books will include call numbers that may be unfamiliar to students. Citations for journal articles will include journal titles, volume numbers, issue numbers, page numbers all in specific formats which the student will look at as an encrypted code rather than a legible key to finding information. It is also important for students to learn to read citations in order that they can properly cite the information they find in their own works cited.

EXAMPLES:

Periodical citation:

Davis, M.A. (1996). Tackle box strategy: Using a matrix to facilitate library research strategy. Research Strategies, 14 (4), 205-213.

Means:

This article is written by an author with the last name of Davis. The article was published in 1996 in the journal Research Strategies. The article can be found in volume 14 issue number 4. The article is on pages 205-213.

Book citation:

Gibbs, J.T., & Huang, L.N. (Eds.). (1991). Children of Color: Psychological interventions with minority youth. San Francisco: Jossey-Bass.

Means:

This book was edited by two people with the last names of Gibbs and Huang. It was published in 1991 and has the title Children of Color. It was published by the publisher Jossey-Bass in San Francisco.

Depending on the situation, citations may appear slightly different and may contain other various types of information to decipher. Periodical indexes may split citation information up to make it easier to read. They may also include abstracts as well as different fields of information that are only useful to the most advanced researcher. These all act as distractions to the student and make it very difficult for them to physically locate the information even though they have the location information right in the citation. Another difficulty students may have in reading citations is specific to finding books. Citations in online book catalogs will include call numbers of where to find the book in the library. Many students are unfamiliar with classification schemes of libraries. This is further exacerbated by the multiple classification methods used in libraries. Many students may finally be familiar with the Dewey Decimal System by the time they reach college only to find in college that they must now learn a whole new system called the Library of Congress (LC) System.

In order to avoid confusion, librarians need to give students examples of call numbers that they will find in their library. Students need to understand that classification systems may look different physically, but their purpose is the same.

Classification systems are an orderly way of putting books on the shelf so that books on the same general subject matter are located in the same area. In learning how to find books on the shelf, however, there is no substitute for having students physically locate a book on the shelf for themselves.

EXAMPLES:

Subject: Nursing theory
Dewey Decimal call number: 610.73

Meaning: Books on technology are put in the 600-699 section. Medicine, considered a subset of technology, is given numbers between 610-619. Nursing, a subset of medicine, is given numbers beginning with 610-610.9. This is further subdivided into more specific subjects until you get 610.73 where other books on nursing theory are located.

Library of Congress call number: RT 84.5

Meaning: Books on medicine are shelved with letters beginning with R. Books on nursing are a subset of medicine and are given the letters RT. Books on nursing theory, a further subset of nursing, are thus assigned numbers that correspond to other books on nursing theory.

Teachers and librarians need to recognize the difficulty involved in doing seemingly simple tasks in the library. Students who are unfamiliar with reading citations or library classification systems may find their research quickly bogged down in a world of numbers and jargon. Patience is the key in getting students accustomed to issues involved library navigation. Taking the student to the shelf instead of merely pointing them in the direction of the book or periodical will alleviate these confusing location issues.

Sound Research Strategy

When students enter the library, they usually have no planned approach to their research. Deborah Fink (1989) remarks that students come into the library with no clear search strategy in mind and no idea of the types of information or the tools needed to access that information. They, in the end, find resources only by sheer serendipity. (p. 73) It is important to impart to the student the need to have a particular strategy in mind when approaching library research. Having a search strategy in mind has several purposes.

A.   It focuses the student on exactly what they are researching
B.   It shows the student what kinds of information they will be retrieving
C.   It gives them a time frame to work with in order to retrieve that information
D.   It gives a logical framework to their research so that they aren't approaching it through "serendipity."

The teacher may wish to have the student hand in their work as it corresponds to the steps in the research process. This will act as insurance that the student is working on their project, and it will help instill the importance of having and using a research strategy.

The following is an example of a possible research strategy with resources and goals for each of the stages.

Stage 1:   Deciding on a research topic
Resources: Brainstorming, browsing current periodicals, class notes, discussion with the teacher
Goal: To have a general idea of the focus of the research
Stage 2:   Turning that topic into library terminology
Resources: Keywording, thesauri, subject headings, discussion with the librarian

Goal:	To have as many search combinations to describe the research topic as possible
Stage 3:	Identifying potential resources
Resources:	Library web page, discussion with teacher and librarian
Goal:	To identify the databases that will be useful to conduct searches in and to identify any alternate sources of information
Stage 4:	Gathering information
Resources:	Online book catalogs, print and online periodical indexes, Internet, alternate resources
Goal:	To locate and then retrieve information. Information that needs more time to be retrieved should be addressed early in this stage while saving the items, which are more quickly gathered for later.
Stage 5:	Absorbing information
Resource:	Time
Goal:	To read and absorb the information that has been gathered so that it can be used in the writing process
Stage 6:	Writing
Resources:	Writing centers, style manuals, consultation with teacher
Goal:	To begin the writing process

Sources

Now that the skills and a strategy have been established in approaching the research, there are specific issues that need to be addressed with the different types of library resources.

Book Sources

In searching for book sources, the students will be consulting an online book catalog. When doing searches in the online book catalog, the student cannot be as specific in their searches as they might be when looking for periodicals. The reason for this is that the citations for books are generally shorter than for periodicals. Citations for books in a book catalog tend to include, title, author, subject heading, and sometimes chapter titles. The key ingredient missing is an abstract. Without an abstract, the students must think of their topic in more general terms when searching for books. For book resources, there is no true substitute for actually going to look at the physical book and see if it contains information which may be useful for research. The goal for the students must be to identify potential books and then go to the shelf and look at the table of contents and the index to see if it meets their research needs.

The students do not have to limit their search to local book holdings however. If Interlibrary Loan service is available or another local library is accessible, other catalogs can also be searched for books. Interlibrary Loan is a service that many libraries offer to their students and teachers. If they need a book or article that is not available in their library, the librarian will find out where that book or article is available and have it sent to the library so that the student or teacher can use it in their research. The library sometimes administers fees in order to cover costs of retrieving these materials. Administering fees is sometimes dependent upon how quick the items will be retrieved. Some services, which offer electronic delivery of journal articles, may deliver the article in a matter of hours but the articles will cost a fee upwards of $15 for each article. Other Interlibrary Loan service for books that are free, except for shipping costs may take 2-3 weeks to deliver to the library. As a rule, students and teachers should expect to incorporate into their research strategy a time span of two weeks in order to retrieve any items through Interlibrary Loan. This is another reason to stress to the students the importance of doing their research ahead of time. Judgements also need to be made as to how far students should be allowed to go in order to obtain resources. One factor associated with this judgement is the level of research being conducted. In my opinion, someone in a freshman English class should be limited to only local library holdings while a senior seminar student should be given much more leeway in obtaining remote resources. Another factor that affects this judgement is time limitations.   A student with an assignment due in a week cannot expect to access anything beyond what is held locally while a student with a project due at the end of a semester has more resources available to them. When a judgement is made on this situation, the student, librarian, and the teacher will determine collectively at what level the student may wish to access books. The expanding levels of access for books are:

- Local library holdings--These libraries include the home library that the student is using, as well as, any other local public libraries that the student may access conveniently.

- Consortium holdings--Many libraries (especially colleges and universities) belong to a loose collection of libraries called a consortium. Based upon the extent of the cooperation that exists in the consortium, students will be able to use or access the resources available in the other libraries. Some consortiums may only share a common book catalog, whereas others may permit onsite access to library resources to consortium members. Depending on the level of cooperation in the consortium, it will prove the usefulness of this resource.

- State Library--At this level of searching, the student is no longer looking to actually go to the library to retrieve the book, but rather to identify possible books that they may be able to request via Interlibrary Loan. Each state has a library whose collections are accessible fairly easily through Interlibrary Loan. The large collections in these libraries, in combination with the relative ease of getting Interlibrary Loans, make this a good place to start to search for Interlibrary Loan materials.

- Other large university/public systems--If the state library does not prove to be helpful, move onto searching for books in other large universities or public library systems. If the librarian or student knows of a specific library that has a collection strength in the area the student is researching, those libraries should be accessed first.

- Library of Congress--At the final level of searching is the Library of Congress in Washington, D.C. It is the library that is the national depository of information of American thought, as well as, worldwide human knowledge. The Library of Congress contains, in its collection, over 12 million items. Only the most serious and in depth projects should reach this level of searching.

Each of these resources should be accessible from any workstation with access to the Internet. It is in this process of accessing different catalogs that the student truly begins to realize the benefits of researching in the modem library.

Periodicals

Searching for periodicals allows more flexibility for the searcher than does searching for books. Because abstracts are often included in the citations of most periodical databases, there are many more words for the searcher to work with when locating periodicals. This allows the searcher to be more specific when typing in their searches.

Periodicals also are different from books in the issue of currency. Because periodicals are published more frequently than editions of books, the material contained tend to be more up to date than the material found in books. For this reason, students need to decide which will be more helpful to their research when collecting information. Some topics tend to be covered better in periodicals than in books due to this issue of currency. While this process may lead the student's research to lean more toward periodicals, having a balance of books and periodicals is still important.

There are two main types of periodical databases which researchers use to find periodical articles: the full-text database and the citation index. A full-text database is a database where the full-text of journal articles appears on the computer without having to go to the print version of that journal. These databases are good for finding quick information without a hassle. Full-text periodical databases are most useful when narrowing down or choosing a research topic as they allow for quick retrieval of information. No time is wasted on searching the print periodical collection for articles that may not end up being useful.

The second category of index used for finding periodical articles is the citation index. This type of index includes both online indexes as well as print indexes. These indexes do not have the full-text included, but have abstracts about the article included so that the student can make a judgement whether the article will be helpful to their research. After citations are found in one of these indexes, the student must find out whether the journal that the article is found is owned or accessible from the library location. For ones that are not available at the library, the student may use Interlibrary Loan services if available for the most important articles they need to retrieve. This process of collecting articles can be time consuming, but is necessary to properly do research for periodical articles. Many core indexes to specific fields are not available in full-text format. Indexes such as ERIC, which is the core index to the teacher education field, or CINAHL, which is the core index in nursing, are not available in a substantial full-text database. It is therefore impossible to do research in fields such as these without consulting citation indexes.

Another important method of gathering periodical articles is a method I call "following the yellow-brick road." This process involves taking the best articles that the student has retrieved and using the works cited as miniature indexes. I tell students that if they find an article that is exactly what they are looking for, it makes sense that the articles which that author used to write the article would also be useful for their research. It's a matter of following a road that is already paved out for them. All they need to do is to follow it. By looking at the works cited section of an article, students have a focused list of material relevant to their research. Students need to be taught how to maximize the resources available to them in the library. This method of identifying resources often remains unknown to students yet it is one of the most helpful and easy ways to find resources relevant to their research.

An issue that also needs to be mentioned to students is the difference between a popular source and an academic journal. Students often do not know the difference between these types of information. Depending on the subject being covered, this can make a big difference in the quality of the student's research. Popular sources are magazines and newspapers that tend to be written for the general public. They tend to be easier to read than academic journals, but the quality of the information may not be as reliable. Information in popular sources tends to be more anecdotal whereas academic journal articles are based more on research and experimentation. When students approach their research, they need to understand that there is a difference between these types of information. Students should consult their teacher and the librarians in helping to identify which sources are popular versus those which are from academic journals.

EXAMPLE:

Topic:	Sudden Infant Death Syndrome (SIDS)
Results:	Doing a search on this topic will bring up different levels of information depending upon the source. A popular magazine such as *Parents Magazine* or *American Baby* may approach this topic from a more preventative aspect such as offering parents tips on preventing SIDS. They may also offer personal narratives on dealing with the death of a child. It is unlikely however that a researcher will find an original research study published in either of these journals. In order to find this information they will need to access academic journals such as *JAMA* or *Pediatrics* in order to find research-based articles.

Depending on the nature of the research project, this should be an issue addressed by the student and teacher. The librarian and teacher should emphasize the difference between the types of periodicals and the information contained in each and guiding students in using appropriate types of resources for the project.

Internet Sources

The resource most often associated with the modern library environment is the Internet. This touted resource is the center of debate as to its true research significance. This debate is centered on the duality of the Internet. The Internet in its vastness has an incredible amount of information. This wealth of information is tempered heavily by the amount of incorrect and misleading information that can also be found there. The student must be imparted with the role of sifting through this information and evaluating its research value. It is the role of the librarian and teacher to equip the student with the tools and knowledge they need in order to effectively accomplish this task.

The first step in educating the student as to the research value of the Internet is to educate the students about what it is not. The Internet is not a be all, end-all research resource. Kathryn Johnston (1999) states that the Internet does not satisfy all information needs and that many subjects still need to be addressed through traditional resources such as books and periodicals. (p. 102) Students are drawn to the Internet for its ease and convenience of use. They are enchanted with the idea of going to an Internet search engine, typing in their search, and instantly retrieving everything they will need for their research. This approach noticeably affects student's research. David Rothenberg (1998) in his article "How the Web Destroys Student Research Papers" states that the Internet is "latest easy way of writing a paper." (p. 59) The research done over the Internet "promises instant access-but actually offers only a pale, two-dimensional version of a real library." (p. 61)   Students need to understand that the Internet has limitations. Two limitations include:

Free vs. subscription

Not all information on the Internet is freely accessible to all. Because most research is done in the library, a false illusion is created that the same research could be conducted at home with the same results. Most databases accessible in the library are subscription databases. This means that the library pays money to access the information in those databases. Almost all periodical databases (full-text and indexes) are accessed by subscription. (Notable exceptions include MEDLINE and ERIC which are produced by the government.) Just as libraries subscribe to print journals and print indexes, they now pay for to access to that information through electronic databases. The information found in these databases is essential to a student's research paper.

This does not mean that students cannot find material that is relevant to their research paper freely accessible on the Internet. There is still is a lot of information that can be incorporated into a research paper. The advice that I give to students is to use information that they find openly on the Internet to augment their research but not as a basis for their research. At a base level, quality research should be based upon scholarly writing. Students will not find an appreciable amount scholarly writing freely accessible on the Internet. All of this information is either contained in subscription databases or in print journals/books collected in libraries. David Rothenberg (1998) characterizes the information that students retrieve from the Internet as mere shells of true information. Small snippets, commentaries, and summaries of information that are found on the Internet are not the in-depth research that should comprise a student's paper. All these things are not information, but "advertising for information." (p. 60)

The Internet is still a very important research tool, although the Internet may lack freely accessible scholarly writing.   Just as individual libraries have their subject strengths and weaknesses, so too the Internet has its own strengths and weaknesses. Some of the strengths that I find the Internet to possess include:

- Primary resources
- Corporate information
- Visual information
- Directory information
- Information published by the government

Copyright

Another major limitation to the information that is found on the Internet is copyright. Many people do not have a clear understanding of what copyright is and how it affects their research. Students believe that once an article is published, it is free to use and reproduce at will. Copyright and intellectual property laws dictate that this is not true and actually unlawful. With the advent and development of the Internet, copyright laws now protect an author from having their work reproduced and placed on the Internet without their permission and/or compensation made to them. This is the main reason why scholarly writing is minimally available freely on the Internet and why it is so prevalent in subscription databases. With subscription databases, companies can negotiate with authors and journals to get copyright permission to digitize and place their articles on online databases. The subscription costs then go back in part to pay for that copyright permission. Copyright also plays a big part in the currency of information that can be found on the Internet. Whereas a contemporary author's work may not be accessible on the Internet, classic authors will be found in abundance on the Internet because copyright no longer exists on their work. A student researching Aristotle, Plato, or Darwin, they will find a vast amount of information due to the expiration of copyright than will someone researching Stephen Hawkings whose works are still under copyright When a librarian or a teacher explains the Internet to students, they need to explain to some extent how copyright and intellectual property laws operate. This explanation will help students understand why the Internet has limitations and why those limitations are in place.

The Internet is a vast amount of unbridled and jumbled information. Students use Internet search engines in order create some order from this chaos of information. Search engines allow students to type in a search and retrieve information that may or may not be useful to their research. Just as with searching for books and periodicals, Boolean searching rules still apply when using a search engine. The biggest difference is the scale on which the student is now searching. Whereas in an index or book database, a student may be searching a couple hundred thousand records, they are now searching several million Web pages when they are using a search engine. David Rothenberg (1998) notes that searching the Internet is more akin to a slot machine than it is to a library card catalog. (p. 60) The vastness of the information received can engulf a student's research. It is common to retrieve 200,000 hits when searching the Internet with a search engine. Many students would find this a great dilemma to have. The problem is that only a very small portion, of those web pages, may have any significance to their research. The key method in trying to reduce this problem irrelevancy is to learn how to use one search engine very well. Each search engine has advanced searching techniques that can be used to cut down on irrelevant returns when searching the Internet. By learning these advanced techniques, a student can significantly cut down the time they spend sifting through irrelevant search returns.

EXAMPLE:

Search engine:	Altavista (altavista. digital. com)
Search:	Television and children and violence
Results:	2,916,750 matches
New Search:	+television and +violence and +children
Results:	10,408 matches (the plus sign makes the word mandatory to appear in the match)

Once the student has found a relevant Web site, he/she needs to consider another important idea. This concept is that "to search is not necessarily to evaluate." (Scott, 1996, par. 9) When a student finds a Web site, he/she needs to be extremely critical of that site and to put it through tests to insure that the information contained, is correct and not misinformed. These methods are documented in many sources such as Scott (1996), Hartman and Ackermann (1999), and Gardner, Benham, and Newell (1999). Some of these evaluation techniques are:

- Is there an author stated? If the article is signed, what are the credentials of that person?
- What is the affiliation of that person? This can be established by looking at the URL (Uniform Resource Locator) and seeing what the ending of the first part of the address is. Some common endings include .edu for an educational institution, .gov for a government sources, .com for a commercial source, .org for a non-profit source, and .mil for a military

source. Also, is there a "~" (tilde) in the address? This will usually indicate that the person may be associated with the source but not in an official capacity (i.e., a student at a university who has been given space to put up their own home page).

- How well is the site constructed and maintained? Are there links that don't work? Are there pictures that don't load properly or error messages that come up when the site is loaded?
- Is the information outdated or contradictory to previous knowledge?
- Is there bias presented in the information? Are they trying to persuade you on some issue or trying to sell you something? Is the argument supported by other credible sources?

It is essential that the student take a critical look at the sources that they take from the Internet. There is no publication or editorial process that needs to be adhered to as with a print journal or book. People are free to publish things on the Internet without proper knowledge or perspective on a topic. Students need to be aware of this so that they are able to (and prepared to) examine critically the quality of their Internet research. Students should understand that they should discard information from inferior sources.

In the end, we are still left with debate over the value of the Internet in research. I believe that the Internet has proven its value as a tool, but not as a freely available resource. It allows students to access information that is available in print sources in an online format. This online format is easier to use and more versatile to search. These sources, though, are still limited by the fact that a library must subscribe to them in order for students to access the information. The Internet has not proven its worth beyond a support role in terms of its free access to information. The amount of misinformation and outdated information causes the Internet to be relegated to that supporting role in a student's research paper.

Other Sources

Students must also be encouraged to go beyond the normal resources in researching. Students feel satisfied with finding books and journal articles and leaving their research at that. Librarians and teachers need to point out that there are other more "nontraditional" sources that can be very important to researching certain topics.

Interviews are often an overlooked research source. Students can set up interviews with local people who might have specific knowledge of the field that they are researching. This can add a very personal touch to a student's research.

Another type of overlooked resource is the primary resource. Students often rely upon other people's interpretations of a topic without going back to the original source for themselves. Using primary sources encourages the student not to rely on others' impressions of a subject, but to interpret topics for themselves as well.

Taking trips to local sites is another way for students to gather valuable information for their research. These resources may include local museums, science centers, historical re-creations, and special events. These types of resources allow students an opportunity to experience a topic firsthand instead of just reading about it.

Summary

As research technology develops and changes the nature of library research, the research process must be modified to meet this changing technology. New library skills associated with technology are important to impart to educators and students in order for them not to feel alienated from the library.

Where research technology has changed drastically, the basic tenets of research still remain valid. Rational, logical, and creative thought are all still integral parts of the research process. These ideals must not be replaced by library technology. Teachers, librarians, and students need to work together to embrace new technology while retaining the values lying behind quality research.

Learning Activities

Skeleton Research

One activity to practice the skills associated with library research is to conduct a skeleton research project. The essence of this project is to have the student conduct the research involved in an assignment but not to go beyond that. This will open the student to all areas involved in the research process but does not require the time associated with doing a full research project.

- Assign a specific research topic.
- Have the student keyword that topic and come up with alternate words that they could use to describe that topic.
- Create different search expressions that could be used to search for that topic. Have them use Boolean operators to create those expressions.
- Have them identify the different databases (see the Appendix at the end of this essay) that would be useful in performing those searches in available in the library. Using an online thesaurus, have them identify subject headings that are used in identifying the topic in each of those databases.
- Have the student print out the following information for sources relevant to their topic:
  - Two citations for books available in the library
  - Two full-text articles. Have one article be from an academic source and the other from a popular source.
  - Two citations for articles from a citation index which are available in the library. Have them photocopy the first page of those articles.
  - Two citations for articles that are not available in the library. Have the students fill out Interlibrary Loan forms for those articles.
  - Two Internet sites pertinent to the topic.
  - Identify possible alternate sources for information on the topic.
  - Create a reference sheet using APA format of the resources gathered.

Evaluating Internet Resources

Choose three different Internet sites pertinent to a topic being covered in the class. Try and find a variety of academic and commercial sites. Try and make sure one has complete and credible information while another has questionable or incomplete information. Give the student the web addresses to those sites and have them evaluate them based on material covered in the class. This assignment will give the students a more critical perspective of information they retrieve from the Internet.

References

Bates, M.J. (1988). How to use controlled vocabularies more effectively in online searching. Online 12(6), 45-56. Retrieved November 11, 1999 from Bell and Howell database (ProQuest Direct) on the World Wide Web: http://proquest.umi.com

Carle, D.O. & Krest, M. (1998). Facilitating research between the library and the science writing classroom. Journal of College Science Teaching, 27(5), 339-342. Retrieved October 10, 1999 from Bell and Howell database (ProQuest Direct) on the World Wide Web: http://proquest.umi.com

Davis, M.A. (1996). Tackle box strategy: Using a matrix to facilitate library research strategy. Research Strategies, 14(4), 205-213.

Gardner, S.A-, Benham, H.H., & Newell, B.M. (1999). Oh, what a tangled Web we've woven! Helping students evaluate sources. English Journal 89(l), 39-44.

Hartman, K. & Ackermann, E. (1999). Finding quality information on the Internet: Tips and guidelines. Syllabus 13(l), 52-53.

Jiao, Q.G., & Onwuegbuzie, A.J. (1997). Antecedants of library anxiety. Library Quarterly 67 (4), 372-390. Retrieved October 21, 1999 from Gale Group database (Health Reference Center Academic) on the World Wide Web: http://infotrac.galegroup.com

Johnson, K. A. (1999). A librarian's perspective on research. English Journal, 89(l), 99-106.

Kamhi-Stein, L.D., & Stein, A.P. (1999). Teaching information competency as a third language: A new model for library instruction. Reference & User Service Quarterly, 38(2), 173-179. Retrieved October 21, 1999 from Bell and Howell database (ProQuest Direct) on the World Wide Web: http://proquest.umi.com

Ojala, M. (1991). Knowing your 'ands' from your 'ors.' Link-Up. 8(6), 8-9. Retrieved November 4, 1999 from Bell and Howell database (ProQuest Direct) on the World Wide Web: http://proquest.umi.com

Ramey, M.A. (1996). Student choice: A modular approach to library instruction. Research Strategies, 14 (4), 246-251.

Rothenberg, D. (1998). How the web destroys student research papers. The Education Digest, 63(6), 59-6 1. Retrieved October 21, 1999 from Bell and Howell database (ProQuest Direct) on the World Wide Web: http://proquest.umi.com

Scott, B.D. (1996). Evaluating information on the Internet. Computers in Libraries, 16(5), 44+. Retrieved October 21, 1999 from Bell and Howell database (ProQuest Direct) on the World Wide Web: http://proquest.umi.com

Appendix: Subject Specific Periodical Indexes

Index Name:	Subject Area:
ABLINFORM	Business
ALTA Religion Index	Religion
America: History and Life	American History
Art Abstracts	Art/Art History
BIOSIS	Biology
CINAHL (Cumulative Index to Nursing and Allied Health)	Nursing
Communication Abstracts	Communications
Criminal Justice Abstracts	Criminal Justice
ERIC (Educational Resources Information Center)	Teacher Education
General Science Index	Sciences
Historical Abstracts	World History
Health Reference Center	Health/Nursing
MEDLINE	Medicine
MLA (Modem Language Association) Bibliography	Language/Literature
PAIS (Public Affairs Information Service)	Public Affairs
Philosophers Index	Philosophy
PsycINFO	Psychology
Social Work Abstracts	Social Work
Sociological Abstracts	Sociology

Note: Many of above indexes have variations that include full-text articles.

Essay 6: Teaching as an Inherently Ethical Profession?
Kathleen Schmalz, Ed.D., RN, CHES

It has been surmised that, "Teacher education may have neglected ethics because most people attracted to teaching bring strong character and high standards of personal morality" (Ungaretti, Dorsey, Freeman, & Bologna, 1997, p. 273). In other words, teachers do not feel that they have to discuss or forge a standard of professional ethics; they presume that the very nature of their profession assures the higher ethical standards of its members. No doubt this is an identity which teachers at all levels proudly embrace. In addition, we as a society, would like to believe that the members of a professional group entrusted with the development of our children and the dissemination of knowledge possess strong characters and high standards of morality! However encouraging (or flattering) this description is, Ungaretti and colleagues concede that:

> Individuals' morals are instinctive and idiosyncratic, however, and are unreliable to create a unified understanding of what it means to <u>teach well</u>. Professional ethics are public and specific, not intuitive. A code of professional ethics acknowledges that practitioners have responsibilities to their clients, the public, employing institutions, and fellow professionals. (p. 273)

Perhaps paradoxically, the fact that teachers tend to have strong personal moral codes makes it even more important to have a professional code of ethics. Studies show that teachers are consistently faced with difficult moral dilemmas in which their moral codes may clash with those of their students. For example, Kidder and Born (1999) cite the case of a fourth-grade teacher faced with a student who is bright but lacking in social skills. Cooperative learning is a keynote in the contemporary classroom. How does a teacher with limited resources deal with a student who won't cooperate? True, the girl was making some progress in getting along in a group, but the teacher could not help but notice that the members of whatever group she was in seemed to lose their cohesive focus. Does the teacher support the rights of the individual or the group?

Does this scenario sound familiar? The literature is replete with stories of teachers who want to help students who are having problems...but the students are disruptive and the classes suffer as a result. Or perhaps there is a student who has racked up his third lateness in a class with a "three strikes and you're out" for the session policy...just as he is beginning to make some academic progress. Does a teacher escort him out of the class, or does s/he make allowances and risk being unfair to the other members of the class who have managed to be punctual?

Without the supportive framework that comes from having a code of professional ethics, teachers can be left with the prospect of making ad hoc decisions. And reports from teachers confirm that dealing with such issues is universally an unpleasant prospect!

Take the example of a multicultural school within a relatively homogenous school district. In this school, the faculty and administration are attempting to resolve the ethic of care, as delineated by Carol Gilligan (1982) with the ethic of justice of Lawrence Kohlberg. The two concepts are not reconcilable; in fact, research shows that children tend to incorporate both concepts into their moral decision-making process (Smetana, Killen, & Turiel, 1991). However, young children are not in the process of running a school where grades are low, dropout rates high, and truancy is a major problem. The unfortunate fact for the high school described by Enomoto (1997) is that while well-meaning faculty and administrators attempted to reconcile ethics and justice, this translated into a school staff who "appeared to negotiate their roles, responsibilities, and relationships, handling problems individually as they thought fit." Inevitably, "the lack of consistent action and shared vision delivered neither care nor justice for those at the school. (p. 369)

Enomoto (1997) believes an examination of the fundamental differences between the two ethics, and consideration of the goal of caregiving linked with operationalizing an ethical school might lead to the reconciliation of the two ethics rather than haphazard efforts to negotiate care and justice. The examination of different concepts of ethics, along with the operationalizing of a professional code of ethics can be very valuable for teachers who are struggling to come to terms with the moral dilemmas we, as teachers, face every day in the classroom.

This section will be divided into two parts. The first part addresses the issue of ethics for the teacher. The second part addresses an issue which is gaining increasing attention: teaching ethics to our students.

Ethics for the Teacher

Professional ethics can be defined as "a shared process of critical reflection upon our obligations as professionals" (Feeney & Kipness, cited in Ungaretti et al., 1997, p. 272). Ethical codes convey a profession's distinctive responsibilities and relationships, both within the profession and between the members of the professional group and society as a whole. Ethical dilemmas involve a conflict between two or more basic values. Inevitably, they involve the sacrifice of one value for another. Ethical dilemmas can test the resolve and commitment of professionals who seek to maintain ideal standards of practice.

Professional Codes of Ethics

The National Education Association (NEA) adopted its standard of ethics in 1975. Although the code of ethics has been criticized for being overly general and perfunctory, it offers guidelines for determining additional steps for addressing ethical issues (Ungaretti et al., 1997). Since the adoption of the NEA code, more specific standards have been developed by organizations such as the Council for Exceptional Children and the National Association for the Education of Young Children (NAEYC), which has developed a Code of Ethical Conduct.

Inherent in the NAEYC code is respect for the uniqueness of all children, a basic principle of child-centered learning. As delineated in the NAEYC code, early childhood educators have committed themselves to:

- Appreciating childhood as a unique and valuable stage of the human life cycle.
- Basing our work with children on knowledge of child development.
- Appreciating and supporting the close ties between the child and family.
- Recognizing that children are best understood in the context of family, culture, and society.
- Respecting the dignity, worth, and uniqueness of each individual (child, family members, and colleagues).
- Helping children and adults achieve their full potential in the context of relationships that are based on trust, respect, and positive regard.

Ungaretti et al. (1997) emphasize that this code validates the caring and communitarian philosophies such as those of Gilligan (1982). However, in emphasizing the uniqueness of the individual, the code indirectly confirms the rights of the individual. The code provides an exemplary guideline for ethical standards, but like the NEA code, it does not provide a strong framework for making practical, everyday moral decisions.

Compared to the defined codes of ethics of healing professionals such as nurses and doctors, health educators, like most teachers, have been slow to develop a formal code of ethics. The Society for Public Health Education (SOPHE) published its first code of ethics in 1976, roughly the same time as the NEA code appeared. Bloom (1999), raises three questions in conjunction with social changes that generated new concerns for the health education profession:

- To <u>whom</u> are professionals in the area of health promotion accountable? The employer, the profession, the clients, or themselves?
- For <u>what</u> are professionals accountable? Results or how they were attained?

- What are the practical and ethical implications of the present emphasis in health promotion on individual behavior change strategies?

With respect to a professional code of ethics in teaching, these three questions can be adapted to the situation of all educators as well as to that of health educators in the schools. The import of the first question is obvious. Accountability has become a critical issue for teachers, and teachers are now accountable to all stakeholders in education. As to the second question, many educators are asking for what are teachers accountable -- for the performance of children on standardized tests or the new statewide evaluations, or for the process of learning itself? The third question returns us to the conflict between the individual and the group. Are students responsible for their own learning and their own classroom behavior? Or is it the responsibility of all stakeholders, including teachers, administrators, parents, and community, to ensure that children are taught in a safe and pleasant learning environment?

The SOPHE code of ethics defines the responsibilities of health educators to society and to the profession. With some modification, both aspects of the ethical code can be adapted to professionals in all areas of education.

SOPHE: Responsibilities to Society.

Health educators:

- Affirm an egalitarian ethic, believing that health [or knowledge] is a basic human right for all.
- Provide people with all relevant and accurate information and resources to make their choices freely and intelligently.
- Support change by freedom of choice and self-determination, as long as these decisions pose no threat to the health of others.
- Advocate for healthful change and legislation, and speak out on issues deleterious to public health [or the development and well-being of children].
- Are candid and truthful in dealings with the public [i.e., families, community], never misrepresenting or exaggerating the potential benefits of services or programs.
- Avoid and take appropriate action against unethical practices and conflict of interest situations.
- Respect the privacy, dignity, and culture of the individual and the community, and use skills consistent with these values.

SOPHE: Responsibilities to the Profession.

Health educators:

- Share their skills, experience, and visions with their students and colleagues.
- Observe principles of informed consent and confidentiality of individuals.
- Maintain the highest levels of competence through continued study, training and research [professional development].
- Accurately represent their capabilities, education, training and experience, and act within the boundaries of their professional competence [teach within their respective disciplines].
- Ensure that no exclusionary practices are enacted against individuals on the basis of gender, marital status, age, social class, religion, sexual preference, or ethnic or cultural background [respect diversity in the classroom].

Concepts of Moral Reasoning

The traditional standard of moral development was developed by Kohlberg, who sought to extend Piaget's line of inquiry into the cognitive processes underlying children's moral reasoning (Hayes, 1994). Most of Kohlberg's writings on moral development and moral education were related to teaching. In addition, although he initially trained as a clinical psychologist, Kohlberg also addressed the counseling profession. Kohlberg believed that counseling was important to the development of professional and client alike. He placed this belief within the context of moral development because he believed that listening requires the type of empathy and role-taking that is important for moral and psychological growth.

Interestingly, the focus on "empathy" and "role-taking" should seem to place Kohlberg's concept of moral development closer to Gilligan's (1982). Instead these two perspectives are frequently portrayed as opposing ideologies. Actually, Kohlberg believed that self-development is essentially the reality that people construct through the interaction of their own personal characteristics and experience. Counselors-- or teachers--who adopt this perspective attempt to understand how clients (or colleagues, students, or parents) make sense of personal experience. From this perspective, Kohlberg is hardly the antithesis to Gilligan's multicultural empathy, compassion, and understanding.

Kohlberg's standard of moral reasoning is the one that has come under fire in the past two decades, notably from feminists who believe that Kohlberg's focus on individual rights and justice neglects a personal ethics of care. Gilligan (1982) contested Kohlberg's model on the grounds that it evolved from a justice theory reflecting the public sphere that has traditionally been the domain of males. In contrast, theories of care exalt the values of the private realm which has traditionally been the female domain. Care ethics emphasize moral responsibilities and relationship to others rather than individual rights.

Many scholars, however, maintain that both the ethics of care and of justice need to be incorporated when making moral decisions and building ethical school communities (Enomoto, 1997). In effect, there can be no care (i.e., concern for others) in the absence of justice (i.e., respect for human rights and consistent treatment). Similarly, there can be no justice in an abstraction bereft of human concern.

In a Greek study using Kohlberg's moral reasoning scale, more than half of nearly 100 teachers scored on the post-conventional level of Stage 5 in their judgments (Tirri, 1999). While lauding this finding, Tirri cautions that responsible judgments in educational settings require more than justice-oriented solutions. The fact is that the real world dilemmas faced by teachers are very different from the hypothetical dilemmas formulated by Kohlberg.

It is noteworthy that the need to reconcile the ethic of care with the ethic of justice is maintained by an author addressing the administration of a multicultural school (Enomoto, 1997). Speaking as a black feminist, Thompson (1998) argues that Gilligan's (1982) care ethic is derived from the experience of white, female socialization; rather than providing an ethic of genuine caring for others, it reflects a state of self-doubt in which the self is degraded. Rather than encouraging a caring for others, an ethic rooted in the perception and approval of others acts as a barrier or threat to authentic relations. Many white feminists share this perspective. With respect to ethical classroom behavior, the acceptance of a dichotomy between a "male" ethic and a "female" ethic can actually undermine ethical decision making by reinforcing cultural stereotypes.

Thompson (1998) embraces the "womanist" ethic of care, a black cultural model in which the strength of the individual is related to the strength of the community. She notes that the public/private dichotomy which is a fundamental difference between the two ethical concepts has never extended to the black community. Caring within the black community has never been relegated solely to the family, but shared by the community at large. Furthermore, women have always played an important role in community networks.

Thompson (1998) proposes a model for classroom ethics that synthesizes justice and caring and encompasses respect and appreciation for diversity. In this model:

- Teachers need to show their respect for their students by knowing and understanding the students' situations. In effect, to provide students with guidance and support, teachers must get to know the whole child.
- Teachers need to help students develop strategies for survival. For students of all racial and ethnic identities, this means exploring the way in which social values are historically and politically contingent.
- The classroom must be a place where multicultural perspectives are treated with respect.
- Teachers and students need to become versed in a variety of cultural narratives and cultural contexts.

- Teachers and students need to embrace an inquiring stance that supports inquiry, along with the exploration and consideration of new and alternative views.

Dealing with Moral Dilemmas

A Finnish study identified four key categories of moral dilemmas commonly faced by teachers:

- Matters related to teachers' work. This was the biggest category, and included such situations as the appropriate way to deal with students' disruptive behavior, issues of confidentiality, how to deal with a colleague's unprofessional behavior.
- Morality of students' behavior regarding school and work. Included in this category are situations in which teachers perceive a dichotomy between the school's values and the values of the student at home, and students' engaging in physically and/or psychologically harassing behavior.
- The rights of minority groups. Needless to say, multicultural issues are far more complex in our own society than in the relatively homogenous Finnish society.
- Common rules in school. This category includes a discrepancy between prescribed and actual behavior, and the question of students' freedom in decision making.

All of the above categories can be conceptualized as moral dilemmas because they involve a conflict of basic values. In working with more than 5,000 participants in intensive decision making seminars run by the Institute for Global Ethics, Kidder and Born (1999) have identified four core dilemmas commonly faced by adults:

- Individual versus community. This situation is exemplified in the opening anecdote.
- Truth versus loyalty. Personal integrity is at odds with responsibility and promise keeping. Issues regarding confidentiality fall into this category.
- Short-term versus long-term. Real and important requirements of the present conflict with foresight, stewardship, and deferred gratification.
- Justice versus mercy. In this type of dilemma the ethic of care conflicts with the ethic of justice.

The reason that these decisions are all so difficult is that they are all grounded in core moral values. What are common core moral values? According to Kidder and Born (1999), the values most frequently cited can be reduced to five key terms:

- Compassion
- Honesty
- Fairness
- Responsibility
- Respect

The authors observe that, "These five ideas appear to be at the heart of humanity's search for its shared values." (p. 39) They emphasize that educators need to identify core values as part of the process of developing a successful character education program. An agreement on core ethical values precludes the imposition of values, as Thompson (1998) cautions, and can work to:

- Help build a common language.
- Help define a common purpose.
- Develop and maintain trust.
- Influence school climate to enhance teaching and learning goals.
- Provide the foundation for nurturing the spirit, extending the inspirational and holistic vectors, and creating a deeper sense of meaning (Kidder & Born, 1999).

Teaching Ethics to Students

Campbell (1997) states succinctly, "Teachers as moral agents transmit values both by formal instruction of the virtues or admonition and by becoming moral exemplars and viewing moral education as a way of life that informs their classroom behavior." (p. 256) Admonitions are simple: *Don't cheat on tests. Don't hit classmates. Don't steal each other's belongings.* Serving as moral examples is somewhat more complicated because it involves an awareness of the way in which conscious and unconscious behaviors influence students. However, certain qualities help make teachers valuable moral examples. These include: *humility, courage, impartiality, empathy, open-mindedness, enthusiasm, judgement, imagination.* Other related qualities such as *honesty, sense of justice,* and *care* also characterize the teacher's role as moral agent and role model, and should be reflected in professional practice. Campbell emphasizes the importance of reflection for preservice teachers, and this advice should extend to inservice teachers as well. Reflection and introspection should enhance teachers' awareness of the ethical dimensions of their roles, which includes modeling exemplary behavior for students.

Teaching and Modeling Moral Behavior

Wiest (1999) asks, "Should teachers keep their desks neat, wait in the cafeteria line with students, and refrain from talking with colleagues during class time?" Her answer is that in most cases, teachers should adhere to the rules they expect students to follow. Sometimes, however, this is neither practical nor possible.

There is no question that teachers are largely responsible for creating a classroom culture. As in a corporate culture, the values participants are expected to follow are both implicit and explicit within the culture. Wiest (1999) cites a survey in which 86% of teachers and 87% of principals agreed that teachers should abide by rules or expectations established for student behavior. The overwhelming reason: Teachers are role models! For the most part, the teachers surveyed began class on time, came to class well prepared, and kept school material organized. In these aspects, they provided exemplary models for students.

In other respects, however, there were some glaring discrepancies between the teachers' behavior and their expectations for students. Two key areas deal with classroom interaction. Although students are discouraged from talking socially during class, teachers reported talking socially with students in class (or study hall) fairly often. The standard for justification tends to be "when appropriate." Wiest (1999) proposes that teacher-student socializing is appropriate only when the answer to the three following questions is "no":

- Does the conversation occur when other students require monitoring, academic help, or intellectual challenge?
- Is the amount of time spent excessive?
- Do the conversations tend to take place more often with certain "pet" students than with others?

A second important discrepancy appears with regard to interrupting conversations. While students are expected to be attentive and not interrupt conversations, many teachers surveyed reported they interrupt students when they are talking. Teachers justify their interruptions by saying they interrupt to redirect or admonish the speaker or other students. In effect, they perceive interrupting as something of a "necessary evil" for maintaining classroom order and on-task behavior.

One teacher, however, disagreed strongly, declaring that interrupting in general is poor practice because of the importance in modeling listening skills (Wiest, 1999). Yet there are times when it is necessary to interrupt to maintain classroom order or keep a discussion on track, and there are times when adhering to the standards of behavior set for students would undermine teachers' effectiveness instead of promoting it.

Judgment is an essential component of ethics, and using proper judgment is critical in deciding when showing authority is more important than worry about being a good role model. In fact, modeling professional behavior will help students understand the type of behavior that will be expected of them in the workplace.

Wiest (1999) believes that the guideline for teachers to follow is one that involves mutual respect. For the most part this means adhering to one standard of rules governing classroom behavior. Creating an environment based upon mutual respect and conveying that respect to all students appears prominently in the literature on ethics. High school students especially, appreciate being treated by adults with fairness and respect.

Hansen (1993) cites the example of a Catholic high school teacher, Father Maran, who "treats his students with special respect, even deference." (p. 659) The older students are allowed to leave the room to go to the library or their lockers, and they have extra class time for independent work. Does this result in a mass exodus from class or in students valiantly feigning the appearance of work? On the contrary, the teacher's respect for his students is rewarded with respect for the teacher and the classroom climate he has created.

And what is one simple aspect of classroom behavior by which Father Maran conveys respect for his class? Nothing more complicated than hand raising. Father Maran takes the "moral philosophy" of hand raising a bit farther than most teachers (Hansen, 1993). During one lesson, three or four senior students raise their hands to offer comments on a Latin translation. As one student was chosen, the others dropped their hands. But instead of raising them again when the student was finished, they waited as Father Maran turned to each student for his respective opinion. He invariably remembered which students had been waiting to respond. And students invariably feel valued when a teacher shows them such respect.

Hansen (1993) views this prosaic classroom behavior as a benchmark for ethical behavior and presents a convincing case. Actually, many teachers see hand raising as a standard for moral behavior. Hand raising has been characterized as an important means of establishing order and turn-taking. It acts as a symbol of the rules governing social behavior. Hand raising involves issues of fairness. The way in which teachers respond to the raised hands illustrates their own sense of fairness. There are more than a few observational reports of teachers whose responses to hand raising are based on gender, race, or ethnicity. The way in which teachers call on students provides an arena where students can assess whether they actually follow the principles of fairness and respect for diversity they may verbally espouse.

In Hansen's (1993) view, as in the viewpoint of many educators, teachers' portray their values implicitly through their actions. Thompson (1998) cites the example of white teachers who take the "heroes and holidays" approach to creating a multicultural classroom environment. In one case, a 12 year old African American girl told her teacher, "that I wanted to learn a little more about my history and that everyone else should learn as much about black history as we do about white history." She was told by the teacher "that she had taught black history last year and this year she wanted to teach something else." However, the young girl astutely noted, "We talk about white history all the time non-stop."

Some teachers claim, "I don't care if my students are purple, green, or polka dotted! I care about them as individuals." These teachers may feel they are expressing an ethic of justice while they are actually avoiding confronting the realities of our society. To Thompson (1998), the teachers in both examples are simply suppressing lines of inquiry that have the potential to demythologize race relations.

Suh and Traiger (1999) view social studies and literature as content areas where values can be addressed. In Thompson's viewpoint, by including alternative histories and personal narratives, commonly called giving voice to traditionally silenced groups, teachers create an ethical climate that incorporates justice and caring. To Suh and Thompson, well-chosen materials from the social studies curriculum and children's literature offer teachers extensive opportunities for teaching moral behavior. The authors recommend four basic approaches:

- Inculcation: teaching values and providing consistent reinforcement for desired behaviors.
- Clarification: helping students become aware of their own values.
- Moral reasoning: helping students develop ethical principles for guiding their actions.
- Values analysis: helping students develop careful, discriminating analysis to examine values questions.

At Dowling College, aspiring elementary school teachers are taught to develop unit plans that actively engage students in the learning process. To this aim they use techniques that are commonly used in settings such as multicultural workshops: simulations, case studies, role playing, and small group techniques. In primary grades, students are asked to role play the view of the Native Americans in "A Different View of Thanksgiving." Students are asked to compared the past with the present view of Thanksgiving, and compare the Native American and European American views of this harvest celebration. In the upper elementary grades, students compare the concentration camps of Japanese Americans with Nazi concentration camps and research similarities and differences. Where possible, students interview survivors. If not, students read first hand accounts. Then they write up and discuss their findings.

The social studies curriculum is the ideal place to explore racism and the problems of learning to live cooperatively in a multicultural society. Students learn that all ethnic groups have contributed to make our country great. Suh and Traiger (1999) emphasize, "The young child must be taught this as soon as possible."

Children's literature provides an excellent means to teach ethical behaviors to students. The literature can be divided into 10 categories: picture books, poetry, folklore, fantasy, science fiction, realistic fiction, historical fiction, biography, nonfiction, and culturally diverse. In each of these categories are books that reflect desirable values, often incorporating a moral lesson into the story. Ironically, science fiction, which is sometimes dismissed by adults, typically involves a moral lesson. The fact that the lesson is often conveyed by the actions of whimsical alien species may make it palatable for older children, who may be skeptical of stories intended to teach a lesson. The fact that the lesson is often taught by "humanoids" who may indeed be purple or polka dot can serve as a springboard for discussing diversity or indirectly promote respect for difference.

Reflection is a technique used to promote ethical awareness in prospective and preservice teachers (Campbell, 1997). Reflection can also be stimulated in young learners by means of techniques such as journal writing, reading and writing stories with a moral or lesson, and perhaps most of all, through autobiographical essay writing (Suh & Traiger, 1999). The authors state categorically that, "Reading and writing are fundamental elements of social studies learning."

Beyond Teaching

In Education for Character: How Our Schools Can Teach Respect and Responsibilities, author Thomas Lickona offers teachers guidelines for helping children develop ethical values:
- Act as a care-giver, model, and mentor.
- Create a moral community.
- Practice moral discipline.
- Create a democratic classroom.
- Teach values through the curriculum.
- Use cooperative learning.
- Develop "conscience of craft."
- Encourage moral reflection.
- Teach conflict resolution.
- Foster caring beyond the classroom.
- Create a positive moral culture in the school.
- Create partnerships with parents.

In order to achieve the above objectives, teachers have to look beyond subject matter and pedagogical knowledge. Drawing upon research on the ethical and epistemological dimensions of teaching, Lyons (1990) sees several implications for portraying ethics in the classroom.
- Teachers cannot conceptualize their work primarily in terms of subject matter knowledge or define it solely by content and pedagogical knowledge.

- Teachers explicitly or implicitly, aware or unaware, interpret and assess students as knowers. Therefore it is essential that teachers understand and encourage students unique learning approaches.
- Teachers and students are interdependent as learners and knowers. This reflects the importance of mutual respect in the learning environment.
- Teachers are likely to be faced with ethical dilemmas, which they must be able to identify and reflect upon.
- Teaching involves several interrelated elements: self, craft, relationships, values, and ways of knowing.
- Teachers may want to be made aware of their own views about knowing, characterizing them and exploring how they fit into their goals and teaching strategies and materials.

Teaching ethics in the classroom involves unconscious expression as well as intentional modeling and instructions. Overall, teachers who are aware of their own values – including their own biases – and are willing to explore their feelings and engage in reflection and introspection are most likely to become moral exemplars, and to encourage similar reflection and exploration in their students.

REFERENCES

Bloom, F. K. (1999). The Society for Public Health Education: Its development and contributions 1976-1996. Unpublished dissertation. Teachers College, Columbia University.

Campbell, E. (1997). Connecting the ethics of teaching and moral education. Journal of Teacher Education, 48, 255-263.

Enomoto, E. K. (1997). Negotiating the ethics of care and justice. Educational Administration Quarterly, 33, 351-370.

Gilligan, C. (1982). In a different voice. Cambridge, MA: Harvard University Press.

Hanson, D. T. (1993). From role to person: The moral layeredness of classroom teaching. American Educational Research Journal,30, 651-674.

Hayes, R. L. (1994). The legacy of Lawrence Kohlberg: Implications for counseling and human development. Journal of Counseling & Development, 72, 261-263.

Kidder, R. M. & Born, P. L. (1999). Resolving ethical dilemmas in the classroom. Educational Leadership, 56(4), 38-41.

Lyons, N. (1990). Dilemmas of knowing: Ethical and epistemological dimensions of teachers' work and development. Harvard Educational Review, 60, 159-180.

Smetana, J. G., Killen, M., & Turiel, E. (1991). Children's reasoning about interpersonal and moral conflicts. Child Development, 62, 629-644.

Suh, B. K. & Traiger, J. (1999). Teaching values through elementary social studies and literature curricula. Education, 119, 723-727.

Thompson, A. (1998). Not for the color purple: Black feminist lessons for educational caring. Harvard Educational Review, 68, 522-554.

Tirri, K. (1999). Teachers' perceptions of moral dilemmas at school. Journal of Moral Education, 28, 31-47.

Ungaretti, T., Dorsey, A. G., Freeman, N. K., & Bologna, T. M. (1997). A teacher education ethics initiative: A collaborative response to a professional need. Journal of Teacher Education, 48, 271-279.

Wiest, L. R. (1999). Practicing what they teach: Should teachers "do as they say"? Clearing House, 52, 264-268.

Essay 7:   STRATEGIES AND TECHNIQUES FOR FOSTERING
ETHICAL THOUGHT IN THE CLASSROOM
Edward F. Zukowski Jr., Ph.D.

Discussions about teaching ethics in the classroom usually evoke questions like "Whose values?" Teaching ethics also raises concern about the teacher imposing her or his personal values upon the students, especially in a society that claims to cherish pluralism and multiculturalism. Some teachers attempt to allay these concerns by insisting that one can simply help students clarify their own values without indoctrinating them in any particular set of values. This is especially true of the disciples of the late Lawrence Kohlberg.   Kohlberg, founder of the Harvard Center for Moral Education, whose theory about the stages of moral development has become classic (Kohlberg, 1981; Berk, 1997). The purported neutrality of such "values clarification" is justifiably disputed since Kohlberg's theory itself seems to implicitly recommend certain particular values as justice (Puka, 1994a). Furthermore, questions are raised by Carol Gilligan and others about whether Kohlberg's emphasis upon justice reflects a masculine gender bias that neglects feminine concern about caring (Puka, 1994b).

Whatever the outcomes of those debates, however, there can be no doubt that many of the general strategies and specific techniques described by Kohlberg, Sidney Simon, one of the doyens of the values clarification movement (1995), and others have proven to be extremely effective. Teachers, who think that they ought to remain personally neutral and for those committed to promoting a particular secular or religious moral viewpoint, will find the strategies and techniques described in this essay useful for fostering ethical thought in the classroom.

Effective Strategies and Techniques:

This section will describe some of the general strategies with examples of specific techniques that research and experience has shown to be effective in moral education. The list does not claim to be exhaustive and the order of appearance does not necessarily indicate any relative importance. All techniques mentioned presuppose certain basic characteristics applicable to any type of effective education: appropriate to age, level of intellectual development, and circumstances of the students; clear; avoiding of obscure allusions; timely; well-prepared; varied; neither too short nor too long; etc. This material is drawn from the literature and "oral tradition" within the fields of moral philosophy, theology, and education as well as personal experience.

Making the Exercise Concretely Relevant:

There is a time and place for rather fanciful and highly imaginative exercises like Kohlberg's famous dilemma of Heinz for whom it appears that the only recourse is to steal an extremely expensive medicine for his wife if she is to live (Kohlberg, 1984). Sometimes, however, it is important at least initially to try to get the students to think about an ethical issue that is much more concretely relevant to their concerns.

One way to do this is to allow the management of the classroom itself to provide occasions for ethical discussion as section one described. The teacher does model ethics both in her or his own person and in the conduct of the classroom. Concrete manifestations of fairness, compassion, mercy, respect for the dignity and freedom of others within limits, responsibility and other moral qualities say volumes more to the students than mere teaching or preaching. They can also become occasions for discussion about these morally desirable qualities.

For instance, a teacher might ask the class to think about the justice of a certain disciplinary action. Students can be asked to reflect upon what they would do in such circumstances. The teacher should call attention to factors that students might not realize on their own, for example, "compassionately" not giving detention to one student because she or he was "only a minute" later than the previous student who was not disciplined. At the same time, the teacher should help students make some distinctions and not fall into a mindless tendency towards generalizations which neglects specific individual differences. For example, there is a big difference between a death in the family and a fight with one's girlfriend as grounds for allowing a student extra time to complete an assignment without a penalty, despite how "unfair" that may appear to the romantically inclined.

One high school teacher had a rather lengthy and detailed list of rules for the classroom. He would occasionally solicit the opinion of the students about "fairness" of the policies before painstakingly explaining the concrete events and reasons which prompted them. He also agreed to experiment with certain changes in the rules, as a result of discussions so that the students could concretely see that he valued their opinions and trusted their good will.

The teacher can also imaginatively create situations or exercises which tap into the concrete concerns of students. One example would be the "Bozo Statement." Two statements are written on a piece of paper. The first followed by a signature line reads: "I am a Bozo. I am absolutely stupid and never study! Please, Darling Teacher, give me five extra points on our next test." The second statement simply states, "No, Thank you!" The paper can be festooned with a cartoon of a clown.

The students are given three options: sign and hand in the Bozo statement for the five points, sign and hand in the statement declining the offer of five points as a personal favor to the teacher, or simply do nothing if they wish - for whatever reason. The teacher emphasizes that any student who signs the Bozo statement will indeed get the five points - no strings attached. No questions are to be answered, apart from clarifications about the instructions (This includes not answering questions about what they would get if they refuse to sign.).

After the papers are handed in, the teacher polls the class as to what they did as a whole. Individual students are then asked what they did and asked to explain their reason or answer. Those who refused to sign the Bozo statement usually put their fingers on what in fact are the issues that this exercise is intended to focus upon: honesty, integrity, concern for truth for the sake of truth rather than mere expedience.

In order to derive the greatest possible benefit from this exercise, however, it is absolutely crucial that the teacher bait the students to dialogue with each other. For example, when students say that they wouldn't sign the Bozo Statement because that would be selling out, the teacher should ask whether the student thinks that those who signed sold themselves out. Some will insist that they are only speaking about themselves but here the teacher should ask the student to speculate as to what they would advise their future children to do in such a situation. On the other hand, the teacher should also ask those who signed what they think about those who refused an easy five points.

One can ratchet up the discussion, by asking the students who refused to sign the Bozo Statement for five points to speculate as to whether would they sign it for twenty-five...then fifty...then one hundred points...and finally an A for the course (after carefully making it clear that these are not actual offers). If any student confesses that she or he would do it for more points, the question naturally arises as to how much - if any real - difference there is between him or her and any student who signed for only five points.

Almost invariably there is at least one student who insists that she or he would not do it, even for the grade of A in the course. This is usually greeted by incredulity and ridicule by those who signed. But the teacher can then point out that there have been people throughout history, who have sacrificed much more for the sake of honesty, truth, or integrity. An example that could be adduced for evidence and for further discussion is Thomas More who was eventually executed for refusing to sign the Act of Supremacy condoning the divorce of Henry VIII, as dramatized in the film "Man for All Seasons."

Toward the end of the discussion, the teacher can announce that all who signed the second statement will receive four points. The teacher emphasizes that anyone who signed the Bozo statement will not lose any points. They have simply been put into the position of having "sold their souls" for one measly point and should realize that they should not be surprised by anything done by a mentality that would offer such a Faustian bargain to begin with. Those who handed in nothing are told that they will get the appropriate wage - nothing. The "fairness" of this can itself become an object discussion if time permits, with the teacher in the end graciously granting four points to these students as well. Alternatively, the teacher may decide that neither of these two groups will be given any points in order to emphasize the hard reality that sometimes integrity entails at least foregoing benefit, if not experiencing hardship and pain.

The teacher can conclude by suggesting that it is not necessarily true that someone who sells out in small matters will sell out in large ones. On the other hand, the students can also be asked how likely it is that someone will stand up in great matters if she or he cannot in small ones.

This one exercise can be used to illustrate even more ethical concepts than honesty: truth for the sake of truth, integrity, and responsibility. In higher grades it can be used to illustrate the hoary distinction between a deontological ("acting on principle") (Spinelllo, 1994) and a teleological ("weighing the relative consequences"-pragmatic) approach to morality (Morelli, 1994). Whatever the concept, however, the key to the success of this particular exercise is that it "goes there" from a starting point of practical and concrete relevance to the student.

Ethical Issues Suggested by the Subject Matter

Sidney Simon, Howard Kirschenbaum and others have written extensively about ways to allow ethical discussion to flow directly out of the course material in a variety of different subject areas (Simon, 1965; Kirschenbaum, 1973; Dodsen, 1993; Elkins, 1977; Steele, Shirley, 1983). Thus, a history teacher's lessons about wars caused by the U.S. government's breaking of treaties with Native Americans could be the occasion of a discussion about the importance of keeping one's word on both personal and political levels. After examining the mechanics of cloning, a biology teacher might not only raise the obvious question about the morality of cloning humans but also discuss the meaning of being an individual. Even a math teacher might prompt a discussion about respect for the property of others by formulating a problem as "How many of his eight apples did Johnny have left after Billy took three when he wasn't looking?"

Provocatively Outrageous Positions to Foster Understanding Through Contrast

Sometimes it can be helpful to present students with a position that will in all likelihood be so diametrically opposed to their own that it will force them to refine their thinking by way of contrast. This is a variation on "perspective taking" which both Piaget and Kohlberg saw as important for cognitive, and therefore moral development (Berk, 1997, p. 473). For example, in talking about issues of sexual morality with more mature students, the teacher could bring in an article describing the organization known as, "North American Man Boy Love Association" (NAMBLA), which lobbies for lowering the legal age of consent to eleven (Leo, 1993). Discussion of this case can allow the teacher to touch upon a whole host of sexually related issues ranging from the general meaning of sexuality to the notion of consent.

The teacher could also present the student with the proposal of "legal birth" by Nobel Laureate Francis Crick, whereby, infants would not be considered human until three days after their birth so that any infant found to possess birth defects could be legally " terminated" (Omni, 1982). Or students could read an article by controversial ethicist Peter Singer of Princeton University who proposes "compassionate termination" of infants with certain diseases and defects just as we have for animals (Singer, 1999). These men raise issues of the meaning and beginnings of human life, euthanasia, the differences between humans and animals, etc. A side discussion could ensue as to whether these gentlemen should be hired to teach in any school or university.

A variation on this would be to bring people into the class who either believe in some of these ideas or who can play the role of people who do. The closer the guest speaker is to the age of the students, the better. One might even get students to role-play. On the other hand, students might feel more secure being involved in a debate on the topic with several opponents on each side. Although some may find this type of technique too adversarial, with good preparation and management, it can serve to show that intelligent people can have a disagreement without it becoming a screaming match.

In connection with this and other techniques, experience has shown that "props" can be important. To adduce an article, picture or object associated with the topic is to engage more of the senses and better guarantee student interest. Thus, actually having an article about Crick can be much more evocative than simply telling the students about it. Showing a picture of a starving baby or a concentration camp can communicate much more than the most poignant oral description by the teacher. Producing a Satanic Bible with its gospel of selfishness makes students reflect much more forcefully upon the virtue of altruism than simply talking about it.

Allowing students to "Reinvent the Wheel" for Appreciation of the Wisdom of Certain Traditional Values

It is said that "we stand on a giant's shoulders." Progress is certainly wonderful but not everything old is bad, and not everything new is good. Teaching and preaching about values found by experience to be good often falls on deaf ears. Thus it is sometimes good to allow students to have an experience in which they themselves must labor to see the wisdom of past experience and certain traditional values.

One example of this would be the "Marooned" exercise. Students are asked to imagine the entire school going on a cruise that ends tragically when a typhoon sinks the ship off a remote South Sea island with only 200 survivors: 125 females and 75 males. The one square mile island has some peculiar characteristics: there is only one source of fresh water on the island which produces exactly only 200 pints per day; only about one quarter of a mile of the coast is a beach suitable for landing of ships or bathing; approximately three quarters of the island is desert that is too hot in the day and too cold at night for prolonged habitation; and the rest of the island is wooded land containing fruit trees and wild boars. Finally the survivors know that neither they nor their possible descendents will ever be rescued.

There are two clusters of questions to be answered: 1) Do you think that the group ought to have any rules; why or why not; and how do you go about making them? 2) What specific rules would you have; would you have any kind of sanctions and why; and what specific kinds of sanctions would you have? Discussion of these questions can be done in either small or large groups. If it is done in small groups, it is important that the teacher monitor what's going on and prompt the students to areas that they might not have thought about. For example, what will be the result if they don't take strict measures against people taking even minute amounts of extra water? What will happen to the water supply if people start having babies? Should there be rules about where to perform certain bathroom functions, given the limited inhabitable land?

There are a number of obvious issues that this exercise raises: the responsibility of individuals to the community, the purpose of law, the best kind of government, responsible parenthood, etc. Although one might object that this is all too fanciful, the skillful teacher can also use it to raise profound questions about the ultimate meaning of sex in general, he morality of particular sexual practices, and other ethically relevant issues such as whether human beings are basically good or bad and how that influences the kind of rules or law that we have. Experience has shown that students find this exercise both enjoyable and thought provoking.

"Sneaking in the Back Door"

Sometimes the techniques that a teacher uses might be a little too heavy-handed. For example, the purpose of the Bozo statement mentioned above is rather obvious. Sometimes it is more effective to allow the student an experience where the main point comes as something of a surprise. The "Money Auction" is a good example of this.

The teacher divides the class into two physically separated groups. Each group is asked to determine a spokesperson and a treasurer. The treasurer stands at the board. The teacher announces that ten nickels are to be auctioned off, one at a time for whatever price the groups are willing to bid on them. The teacher will take the bid only from the spokesperson. This means that each person should make sure that his or her view is made known, since the group actually will have to pay whatever is bid if it is the highest. Spokespersons should therefore also listen to their constituents. Bids must be in actually negotiable terms, i.e., at least a penny. After each nickel is auctioned off, the treasurer of the group will write down on the blackboard what the group owes the teacher for the nickel it just bought. No questions are to be answered about the point of this exercise; the students may construe it as they wish.

As each nickel is auctioned, the teacher – like any good auctioneer – should goad the sides to bid higher – by either asking, "Are you going to let them get away with getting those nickels?" or by saying, "This is your golden opportunity to get a nickel." The teacher finally ends with the traditional: "Going once…going twice…" The teacher gives the nickel to the appropriate treasurer who writes down on the board how much the group paid for it. For the last nickel, the teacher announces that the rules will be changed slightly. Bids will be accepted from anyone on behalf of the group, provided that a person agrees to pay for it.

Experience has shown that almost invariably one group at some point will eventually bid more than five cents for a nickel. One group engaging in the exercise ended up bidding $15.00 for one nickel while another bid a total of $55.00 for eight nickels.

When all nickels are auctioned off, the teacher asks the treasurers to add up what is owed to the teacher and pay up, although in the end the teacher will simply ask for the original ten nickels back. The teacher then begins the discussion by asking whom they thought won. Some think simply that whatever group got more nickels did, while others think that the group who got more for less won. This, of course, raises the question of what they thought the point of the exercise was. The students usually have no idea.

Still not telling the students the point, the teacher asks why they didn't do the following: since the teacher said that he or she would give them a nickel for whatever is bid, why didn't the spokesperson of the one group suggest to his or her counterpart that he or she would not bid on the first nickel so that the other group could get it for a penny. The second group could then reciprocate on the second nickel and so on and so forth through all ten nickels. At the end of that strategy, each group would have ten nickels for an investment of five cents or 500% profit. What ultimately was the purpose in bidding more than five cents for a nickel? Is it greed…wanting to be Number One?

Usually the students protest that it was the teacher who separated them into two groups. But why should that have ruled out the possibility of cooperating? The teacher then points out that one might see in this exercise, an analogy for the distribution of resources in the world. Is it possible that there are enough resources in the world for all to equitably share? Is it possible that we do not now share because of the way that humans have chosen to allocate resources, sometimes out of selfishness?

This exercise provides, in effect, a way of entering into a discussion of social justice. It can also be used to illustrate other issues: how should representatives be chosen, how representative should a representative be, is majority rule the best policy, etc.?   Whatever the issue, experience has shown that students find this an emotionally-charged and thought-provoking exercise.

Emotionally Evocative

Modern moral pedagogy has come to recognize the role that emotion and affect play in morality. Most of the exercises discussed so far tend to operate on the analytical level that is certainly a priority in academic context. Literature and film are well suited for provoking an approach to ethics and morality that involve powerful emotions. A teacher could use any number of excepts from novels or essays read or distributed to the class that could foster such discussion, for example, an essay on the villagers of Chambon, France who chose to save Jews from the Nazis at tremendous risk to themselves. Indeed, contemporary literary criticism, philosophy, and theology has come to emphasize the importance of "narrative" – "story-telling" – in communicating the deeper truths of existence. William Bennett (1996, 1997) has assembled several volumes that can be very useful in this regard .

But literature in itself is a bit too cerebral for some students. This is where the judicious use of film can come in. There are a number of short powerful films that can fit this bill. One of the most powerful is Joseph Schultz (1981), a true story of a German soldier on a firing squad who refuses to shoot civilians being executed in retaliation for the death of a German soldier in Yugoslavia. He is ordered to either shoot them or join them; he chooses the latter. The issues that this real life incident raises are obvious, and the use of this film has encouraged intense discussion among students. One could also show a film on the decision of the priest Maximillian Kolbe who volunteered to take the place of a married man who was chosen to die in retaliation for an escape at Auschwitz.

There are innumerable commercial films containing scenes that could prompt such fruitful discussion. The poignant scene from Man for All Seasons where Thomas More insists upon the importance of integrity in response to his family's pleas for him to sign the Act of Supremacy since everyone knows that he really doesn't believe in it is just one of many possibilities. Clips of television shows can also prove extremely useful, especially those which might be very popular among the student population and that includes soap operas.

In some cases it is necessary for the teacher to provide an adequate context for the film. At other times particular scenes might have to be judiciously edited to eliminate extraneous elements that might serve to confuse and unduly complicate the issue. We live in an age where most people have VCRs and now dual deck editing units are becoming less expensive. Also more schools have audio-visual departments that can easily do whatever editing is necessary.

Real Life is Sometimes Better than Fiction

Lawrence Kohlberg is famous for his use of dilemmas as a vehicle for having students clarify values. As previously mentioned, these dilemmas are obviously contrived and sometimes appear a bit too fantastic for the students to take seriously. But experience shows that students are often impressed with albeit extraordinary situations if they turn out to have actually happened. Thus, for example, most students are entranced by the following true story told by eminent Jewish scholar David Daube in his classes.

The mayor of a small village in Belgium during World War II was summoned to the Nazi commandant. The resistance had killed a German soldier and the Germans were going to execute 15 civilians in retaliation. Among the 15 people rounded up were the mayor's own two sons, aged 15 and 17. The commandant, who was somewhat sadistic, told the mayor to select one son to take home in consideration for his cooperation with the occupying forces. What would you do if you were the mayor? [The mayor in the story, after first begging to take his son's place, refused to choose one, a position later criticized by his wife.]

Another idea is for the teacher to ask the class to respond to the case of Cassie Bernall who is said to have been shot by one of the killers of Columbine High School after being asked if she believed in God (Bernall, 1999). There are also the great cases taken from history, e.g., President Truman's decision to drop the bomb on Japan, a decision that to this day still has vocal critics.

Such real life cases are often reported on the television news or in the print media and the provident teacher will tape or cut them when viewed. The teacher can also ask the students if they are aware of similar real life episodes that have impressed them. Use of these items culled from the day's news obviously can satisfy the criterion of timeliness that can promote or enhance effectiveness. One could even make it a standing assignment that students will report relevant items that they have seen or read to the class.

You Can also be imaginative – Make up your own or Modify and Adapt the techniques of others

Even a new teacher should consider constructing his or her own dilemmas or other types of situations that can evoke ethical discussion specifically tailored to his or her own students. Moral philosophers and ethicists have been doing this for many years. Graduate school courses in ethics and morality are rife with such famous dilemmas and conundrums passed on through an oral tradition whose ultimate sources are obscure or unknown. Here are a few samples:

The deathbed-promise: You are stranded on an island with your best friend who is dying. The friend asks you to promise that when you get back to civilization that you will tell her daughter where she stashed away a million dollars that no one knows about. You promise. When you get back to civilization, you discover that in your absence the daughter won millions of dollars in a lottery so that she really doesn't need any more money. You also discover that there is a terrible earthquake in Mexico that has an urgent plea for aid. It occurs to you that many could be helped without harm to your friend's daughter who doesn't even know about the money. Should you keep your promise to your friend? Why or why not?

The frame-up: A white woman is raped and killed in an extremely racist town of long ago. The white population assumes that a black man did it and they are ready to burn down the black neighborhood and hang a few black men. You are the sheriff who happens upon a young black man drunk out of his mind. The thought occurs to you that you could grab this young man, drag him in front of the rioters, claim he was the culprit, and hang him on the spot to cool down the rioters, thus saving the lives and property of innocent people. Would you do it? Why or why not?

Ho Chi Minh's Proposal: You are captured by the forces of Ho Chi Minh who tells you that Ho Chi Minh will immediately stop the Viet Nam War, thus saving the lives of 57,000 American soldiers and countless North Vietnamese soldiers as well, if you will agree to kill a six-month old baby. Would you do it? Why or why not? If you wouldn't, is the life of one baby worth more than the lives of 57,000 adult men, many of whom have families?

Your Child or Spouse: You are on the bank of a lake as you watch in horror as a rowboat with your spouse and small child sinks. You know you can only save one of them. Who will you save and why?

The teacher might also consider making an assignment that the students create some type of ethical dilemma. Such a task in itself forces the student to think in ethical terms. The teacher might then choose to use the best ones for future discussion.

Fostering Logical and Critical Thinking as an Important Element in Morality

Lawrence Kohlberg, most philosophers, and most religious insist that correct ethical thinking pre-supposes proper functioning of the thinking process. Although particular teachers may balk at the idea of promoting particular values, there should be no hesitation on the part of anyone in academia that discussions about ethics and morality should be done rationally, logically, and critically.

Accordingly, teachers who are interested in ethical thinking ought to take special care in their discussions that they call attention to errors in thinking and arguing. This is especially true of such common logical fallacies as begging the question (circular argument), equivocation, ad hominems, factual error, and unwarranted assumptions that are defined clearly for students in a number of fine sources that discuss them in relation to ethical thinking (Chesbrough, 1981). Having the students see the logical weaknesses of their position is part of the "cognitive disequilibrium" that Piaget and Kohlberg thought necessary for cognitive and therefore also moral development. (Berk, 1997, p. 473)

Challenging such erroneous thinking can be done within the context of ethical discussions themselves or it can be the subject of separate exercises. Jeffry Schrank (1972) has composed a marvelously entertaining but serious test to show how easily unwarranted assumptions enter into our thinking. An example is, "Standing all by myself in my bedroom at a lamp that is located 12 feet away from my bed, using no kind of strings or contraptions, how can I turn the light out on that lamp and hop back into bed before the room is dark?" Answer: You do it during the daytime. Most people ASSUME that it is nighttime. Such a test could be used as an introduction to the teacher's announcement of his or her attempt to foster good thinking throughout the term. After this test the teacher could review the various fallacies in thinking mentioned above. In this way, the students will have a point of reference if such errors come up in subsequent discussions.

An emphasis upon logical and critical thinking is especially important with respect to the teacher's reaction to moral relativism that some students will probably champion since it has become so prevalent in modern society. Many students think it is eminently tolerant to refuse to moral judgments on the actions of others – "for them it is right." The teacher ought to be willing to show that this position itself is a moral position that must be justified and that, at the very least, implicitly makes a negative judgment upon anyone who makes a moral judgment upon others. In effect, such relativism appears to be a self-contradiction.

RULES OF ENGAGEMENT

Even techniques that most inherently effective can fail if they are not executed properly. Most of what can be said about this in moral education applies equally to other types of discussion and group work and need not be rehearsed here, e.g. not allowing certain students to monopolize the conversation, keeping the discussion on target, etc. There are, however, a few other considerations that are peculiar to exercises in moral education.

The teacher must take special care not to ridicule, disparage, or in any way appear to "punish" students who hold positions that might even radically diverge from either the commonly accepted moral communal standards and/or the teacher's. This does not mean that the opinions cannot be challenged, but it does mean that the teacher ought to create an atmosphere in which all students will feel as free as possible to voice their opinions. If students do not feel free to voice, albeit questionable opinions, there will be little chance that anything can be done to change them. That a student could feel free to voice an opinion that might prove to be unpopular would, in itself, be further evidence of the teacher's commitment to freedom and respect for people.

Especially in situations where there is no official moral position of the institution, the teacher should make clear to the student to the student his or her personal views. One teacher does this by stepping away from the podium with fan-fare, to indicate his personal position.

1. The teacher should feel comfortable admitting his or her ignorance or confusion about some of the issues if that is the case.

2. The teacher should, as age allows, push the students to provide whatever rationale for their arguments they can produce. All too often students try to short-circuit a discussion by simply saying that is the way they "feel" and/or invoking relativism as making such rationale superfluous. The teacher should continually ask "why" and be willing to help students think critically about what they hear. At the same time, the teacher should recognize that there are often times when, as Blaise Pascal reminds us, "The heart has reasons that head knows not."

3. The teacher must be able to think on his or her feet in a variety or respects: for example, the teacher must be able to make connections between classroom exercises and events and issues in the real world. At times, the teacher must be able to allow the discussion to follow a natural progression to consideration of other related or contingent issues without obscuring the main point under discussion. At other times, the teacher must be able to improvise new situations to clarify the situation as it evolves. Thus, for example, if a particular student doesn't seem personally interested in the issue at hand, the teacher may ask him or her to consider what he or she would say to his or her own younger brother or sister who asks for advice.

4. It is absolutely crucial for the teacher to keep emphasizing that criticism of an opinion is not necessarily disrespect for the person who holds that opinion or is not a manifestation of intolerance. This can be an uphill battle in light of the prevailing relativism and overly simplistic notions of what respect for diversity means in today's society.

Conclusion

This paper has described some general strategies and specific techniques that research and experience has shown to be effective in fostering ethical thought in the classroom. Like all teaching methods, they must be tailored to meet the specific students in terms of their age, level of development, interest, etc. The effective teacher will feel free to improvise and adapt whatever is necessary to reach his or her students. An ongoing process of careful evaluation and assessment will be needed to preserve, refine, and enhance what works, and to modify or eliminate what doesn't.

This task can be difficult, often resulting in frustrating dead ends and blind alleys. The teacher, interested in moral education, therefore, needs to be patient with himself and herself as well as with the students. But when all is said and done, the teacher will no doubt find satisfaction in having helped students learn about those larger values that give ultimate meaning and direction to the pursuit of those other subjects that they teach like math and science. And perhaps other may say of such a teacher what a sage wrote long ago: "those who instruct the people in goodness will shine like the stars for all eternity." (Liturgy, 1975, p. 1783)

References

Bennett, W., (Ed), (1975). <u>Moral compass: Stories for a life's journey</u>. New York: Simon & Schuster.

Bennett, W., (Ed), (1996). <u>The book of virtues: A treasury of great moral stories.</u> New York: Touchstone.

Bennett, W., (Ed), (1997). <u>The book of virtues for young people: A treasury of great moral stories.</u> New York: Simon & Schuster.

Berk, L.E. (1997). Chapter 12: Moral development. Child Development. Boston, MA: Allyn and Bacon, 460-499.

Bernall, M. (1999). She said yes: The unlikely martyrdom of Cassie Bernall. Nashville: Plough Publishing.

Chesbrough, L. & Sachs, D. (1981). <u>Ethical issues in decision making.</u> Scarsdsdale, NY: Scarsdale Union Free School District Board of Education.

Codding, J., Sachs, D. et al. (1980). <u>Ethical issues in decision making: A teacher's handbook.</u> Scarsdsdale, NY: Scarsdale Union Free School District Board of Education.

Dodson, M. (1993). <u>Teaching values through teaching literature.</u> Bloomington,IN: Eric Clearinghous-Reading & Communication Skills.

Elkins, D.P. (1977). <u>Clarifying Jewish values: Clarification strategies for Jewish groups.</u> Rochester, NY: Growth Associates.

Interview. <u>Omni </u>(1982, March) 75-78.

Joseph Schultz (1981). Zastava Films.

Kirschenbaum, H. (1973). <u>Clarifying values through subject matter: Applications for the classroom.</u> Minneapolis: Winston Press.

Kohlberg, L. (1981). <u>Essays on moral development: Volume I: The philosophy of moral development.</u> Cambridge, MA: Harper & Row.

Leo, J. (1993, October 11). Pedophiles in schools. <u>U.S. News & World Report.</u> 37.

The Liturgy of the Hours. Volume IV. (1975). New York: Catholic World Publishing Company, 1783.

Morelli, M. (1994). Telogical ethics. Ethics, Volume I. Pasadena, CA: Salem Press, 860-861.

Puka, B. (ed.) (1994). <u>Kohlberg criticism: Volume 4: The great justice debate.</u> New York: Garland Publishing, Inc.

Puka, B. (ed.) 1994). <u>Kohlberg criticism: Volume 6: Caring voices and women's moral frames-Gilligan's view.</u> New York: Garland Publishing, Inc.

Schrank, J. (1972). Teaching human beings: One hundred one subversive activities for the classroom. Boston: Beacon Press.

Simon, S., Howe, L. & Kirshenbaum, H. (1995). Values clarification: A practical, action-directed workbook. New York: Warner Books.

Singer, P. (1999, October 7). A new ethic for living and dying. <u>New York Daily News</u>, 57.

Spinello, R. (1994). Deontological ethics. Ethics. Volume I. Pasedena, CA: Salem Press, 219-220.

Steele, S. & Harmon, V. (1983). <u>Values clarification in nursing.</u> Norwalk CT: Appleton—Century-Crofts.

Appendix A

A-1:   Sample Instructional Plan for Pre-school

1   **Name of teacher/presenter**:   U. Nique
2   **Subject/Topic:** Preschool / I am special
3   **Analyzing the Target Audience:** Grade level/ Age/ Characteristics of Group
         Grade Pre-K, 3-4 yrs., Average ability
4   **Behavioral Objective:**
         The children will be able to:
  •   demonstrate an awareness of their own unique qualities
  •   freely express what makes them special
5   **Addressing Learning Standards**:
  •   Demonstrates competence in speaking and listening as tools for learning.
  •   Displays effective interpersonal communication skills.
6   **Prior Knowledge:**
         The children have been in school for two months. They already know the names of the
         other children in class. They have been speaking openly about themselves during class
         news period.
7   **Rationale for Lesson/Presentation**:
         Describing ways in which they are special will allow the children to develop confidence
         and self-esteem. This lesson also allows the children to practice their oral language skills.
8   **Materials:**
  •   mirror
  •   construction paper
  •   name tags
  •   crayons
9   **Procedures:**
         Motivational Activity:
  •   Ask the children if anyone ever told them that they looked like someone
          else. Parents? brother or sister?
  •   Ask children how they feel about it?
         Developmental Activity:
  •   Provide a large mirror for the children to view themselves.
  •   Ask questions concerning hair color, eye color, height, etc.
  •   Encourage other children to join in the discussion.
  •   Ask the children to identify something special about themselves.

- The teacher will write that special trait on the name tag and place the tag on each child.

Summary Activity:
- Each student will be asked to share with others why they are special
- Each student will be asked what does the name tag say about them.

10   Procedural Adaptation:

Younger children will need more time to discuss and explore the idea of how everyone is special, work with only four students at a time in the language art's center.

11   Determining Follow-up Activities/ Homework:

Review: Ask each child to draw a picture of themselves and their special trait.
Ask children how they are special, before leaving class for the day.

Application: Ask children to describe something special about a classmate.

12   Evaluation:

Teacher/Presenter Strengths:

Teacher encouraged all the children to participate in the discussion of special traits.

Teacher /Presenter Weaknesses:

The mirror suggested that children focus on physical traits. Ask the children if there is anything special about them that cannot be seen immediately. For example, Gregory is funny, Matthew is strong, or Samantha shares.

Student Learning:

The children enjoyed the lesson and were eager to share their special traits. The children shared their special traits with parents and siblings when leaving school for the day as family members inquired about the writing on the name tags.

A-2: Sample Instructional Plan for Elementary Reading

1   **Name of teacher/presenter:** U.R.A. Reader
2   **Subject/Topic:**   Reading/Phonics, Letter Sound Recognition - "b"
3   **Analyze the Target Audience:** Grade level/ Age/ Characteristics of Group or Audience
            Grade 1, 5-6 yrs., Average ability
4   **Behavioral Objective**:
            When examining magazines, the students will be able to:
            •   identify words that begin with the letter "b".
            •   cut out pictures of objects which begin with the letter '"b".
5   **Addressing Learning Standards:**
            •   Students will read a wide range of print and non-print texts to build an
                    understanding of texts.
            •   Students will apply knowledge of language structure and language conventions to
                    discuss print and non-print texts.
6   **Prior Knowledge**:
            The children have already learned the alphabet and are aware that there are many words
            that begin with the letter "b".   The children are familiar with books and understand
            concepts related to print.
7   **Rationale for Lesson/Presentation:**
            Learning letter sounds will enhance students' ability to identify unfamiliar words in their
            readings. This knowledge will also improve their journal writing.
8   **Materials**:
            •   Chalk
            •   Chalk board
            •   Teacher's Surprise Bag - A shopping bag decorated with "?"
            •   Objects which begin with the letter "b", ball, book, boat, bear, bird, bus, bib, etc.
            •   Poster board
            •   Martin, B. (1967). Brown Bear, Brown Bear What Do You See? New York:
                    Henry Holt Publishers.
9   **Procedures**:
            Motivational Activity:
                    •   Introduce students to the "Teacher's Surprise Bag"
                    •   Draw a large letter "b" on the board and announce that today is "B" day.
                    •   Tell students that in the bag are objects which begin with the letter "b" and
                            have the "b" sound
                    •   Ask students to guess what objects might be in the bag
                    •   As students respond, list words on the board which begin with the letter
                            "b" (ball, boot, bird, bed, book, and bus).
            Developmental Activity:
                    •   Read the story Brown Bear, Brown Bear What Do You See?
                    •   Indicate and emphasize words which begin with the letter "b"
                    •   Ask students to brainstorm additional words which begin with the letter
                            b.
                    •   List additional "b" words on the board
                    •   Review the word list. Pronounce each word and have the children read the
                            words chorally. (Emphasize the initial consonant sound.)
                    •   Invite individual students to come up and lead the group in choral reading
                    •   Quiz the students by selecting the words in a random manner.

Summary Activity:
- Arrange the class in groups of four.
- Give each group magazines.
- Ask students to find pictures of "b" words.
- Have students glue pictures on poster board to form a collage.
- Post collages on bulletin board for review.
- Add to the list of "b" words throughout the day.

10   Procedural Adaptation:

For slower learners, tape a large index card on their desk. Print the letter "b" on the card. Pair slower learners with faster learners for group work.

11   Determining Appropriate Follow-up Activities/Homework:

Review: Ask children to write the letter "b" (2 lines on a worksheet). Provide space for them to draw a picture of a "b" word. Example: ball, boat, bed, bus, etc.

Application: Ask children to collect two objects from home that begin with the letter "b."

Bring them in to school for show and tell.

12   Evaluation:

Teacher/Presenter Strengths:

Teacher motivated students effectively. Students were excited to guess the items included in the surprise bag. Teacher encouraged active participation. The children enjoyed the book <u>Brown Bear</u> and read chorally along with the teacher.

Teacher /Presenter Weaknesses:

Students should see the concrete objects throughout the week to review the concept of the letter "b." Place "b" objects in the learning center immediately following the lesson and prepare an appropriate activity to provide additional practice.

Student Learning:

John had some trouble paying attention during the lesson. Next time, have John sit in front of the room. The children were successful in finding many "b" pictures in the magazines. Small group discussions indicated that the children had grasped the concept.

A-3:   **Sample Instructional Plan for Elementary Social Studies**

1   **Name of teacher/presenter:** Susan Smart
2   **Subject/Topic:** Social studies /Prejudice
3   **Analyzing the Target Audience:** Grade level/ Age/ Characteristics of Group
         Grade 3, 8 years, Average ability
4   **Behavioral Objective:**
         The students will be able to:
         •   define prejudice
         •   identify and describe examples of prejudice
         •   discuss ways to prevent prejudice
5   **Addressing Learning Standards:**
         •   Understands that culture and experience influence people's perceptions of places
               and regions.
         •   Understands conflict, cooperation, and interdependence among individuals, groups
               and institutions.
6   **Prior Knowledge:**
         The children have some exposure to the topic, but they have not had a formal lesson on
         prejudice.
7   **Rationale for Lesson/Presentation:**
         Our society is plagued by conflicts that grow out of a wide variety of prejudices that are
         often learned early in life and that is hard to reverse. This lesson is meant to help children
         begin to understand prejudice so that, ultimately, they can control it in themselves and be a
         positive influence on others.
8   **Materials:**
         •   Geisel, T.S. & Geisel, A.S. (1960). <u>Green eggs and ham.</u> New York: Beginner
               Books.
9   **Procedures:**
         Motivational Activity:
               •   Read Green Eggs and Ham
               •   Discuss the main character's attitude towards green eggs and ham at the
                     beginning and at the end of the story.
               •   Ask why the character's attitude changed.
         Developmental Activity:
               •   Tell students that the main character in the book was prejudiced against
                     green eggs and ham.
               •   Ask if anyone can explain what the term "prejudice" means.
               •   Write the definition of the board. Prejudice is having an opinion about
                     something or someone without really knowing anything about it.
               •   Ask the children if they were ever like the character in the book.
               •   Ask the children the following questions? Record responses on the board.
               •   How many children like to eat snails?
               •   How many of you would like to live in Alaska?
               •   How many like pizza?

               Ask these follow-up questions:
               •   How many of you ever at snails?
               •   How many of you have visited Alaska?
               •   How many have eaten pizza?

- Compare student responses to the situation in <u>Green Eggs and Ham.</u>
- Focus on how experience was the key to a changed attitude.

Summary Activity:

- Direct children to draw a picture or write a story about on prejudice they have and how they could change it.

10   **Procedural Adaptation:**

For tactile/kinesthetic learners, invite the children to choose between two packages, one poorly wrapped but containing a treat and the other nicely wrapped but containing dirt. Discuss the reasons for their choice.

11   **Determining Follow-up Activities/Homework:**

Application: Look for one example of prejudice on television. Write it down and bring it in to school tomorrow.

Preparation: Think about whether prejudice can ever be good. Ask someone at home. Write down your ideas. Be ready to talk about them in class tomorrow.

12   **Evaluation:**

Teacher/Presenter Strengths:

This was a very important topic, very real and meaningful to the children. Using Dr. Seuss kept the topic age-appropriate and adequately impersonal to allow for safe and comfortable discussion.

Teacher/Presenter Weaknesses:

There was too much teacher-talk; give more voice to the students.
Using a book that familiar to so many students created various problems; provide and explanation of why and how we are going to use this book in the lesson.

Student Learning:

The students did meet the objectives of this lesson. They were able to relate to the book and to write or draw their own impressive stories. The children showed much sensitivity and wisdom in their ideas about how to change their prejudices.

Submitted by Dr. Rosemarie Pace

A-4:   Sample Instructional Plan for Elementary Mathematics

1   **Name of teacher/presenter:** U.R. Bright
2   **Subject/Topic:** Mathematics/Picture Graphs
3   **Analyze the Target Audience:** Grade Level/Age/Characteristics of Group
         Grade 4/ 9 years old/Mixed Ability
4   **Behavioral Objective:**
         The students will be able to:
         • 	gather, record, and interpret data on picture graphs.
5   **Addressing Learning Standards:**
         • 	Uses a variety of strategies in the problem solving process.
         • 	Understands and applies basic and advance concepts of statistics and data
             analysis.
         • 	Understands the general nature and uses of mathematics.
6   **Prior Knowledge:**
         The children have already seen and made picture graphs in previous grades.
7   **Rationale for the Lesson:**
         In this lesson, students will review and expand their knowledge, using a scale for the first
         time. This will develop their skills in collecting and representing data in a way that is
         efficient and meaningful. It will nurture the abilities to plan and decide, and it will provide
         a practical application for their multiplication facts.
8   **Materials:**
         • 	graph paper
         • 	crayons
9   **Procedures:**
         Motivational Activity:
             Present a real problem to the class. For example: The school coach is trying to
             plan the sports schedule for the year. He sent home letters to parents to find out
             how many children want to be involved in team sports (basketball, softball,
             soccer) and received hundreds of replies. Now, he wants your help in organizing
             the information. What can we do? Share the data below and brainstorm ways to
             organize them. Guide the class in the direction of developing a picture graph.
             Create a simple sample that includes a scale.
                 Children interested in playing basketball------225
                 Children interested in playing softball---------175
                 Children interested in playing soccer----------200
         Developmental Activity:
             • 	Invite the students to identify their own questions that they will be able to
                 answer by gathering data and representing them on picture graphs, using
                 scale.
             • 	Organize responsibilities among several small groups. Allow time and
                 provide materials for them to solve their problems.
         Summary Activity:
             • 	Have each group present its graph to the rest of the class. They may
                 explain their problem, accept questions from their classmates, and ask
                 questions as well.
             • 	Discuss the advantages and disadvantages of depicting information this
                 way. Post the completed graphs around the room.

10   **Procedural Adaptation:**
         For slower learners, invite just one question on which the whole class can work together under teacher direction.

11   **Determining Appropriate Follow-up Activities/Homework:**
         Application: Look through newspapers, magazines, almanacs, atlases, or other resources provided by the teacher to find examples of picture graphs that use scale. Share what you found with the class, naming the topic of the graph, explaining the scale used, and summarizing the information the graph presents.
         Preparation: Count the number of T-shirts, pants, and sneakers you own. Write down the numbers and bring them in tomorrow.

12   **Evaluation:**
         Teacher/Presenter Strengths:
             The sports topic aroused the students' interest in the lesson.
             The lesson was very participatory, with students very active throughout.
         Teacher/Presenter Weaknesses:
             The specific problem of helping the coach, to organize sports teams, was a bit vague and difficult for the students to grasp.
             This lesson required more time than was anticipated or available.
         Student Learning:
             The students did achieve the objectives, due to the hands-on nature of the lesson.

Submitted by Dr. Rosemarie Pace

A-5:   Sample Instructional Plan for Elementary Science

1   **Name of teacher/presenter:** Bea A. Scholar
2   **Subject/Topic:** Science / Conductors and Insulators
3   **Analyze the Target Audience:** Grade level/ Age/ Characteristics of Group
4   **Behavioral Objective:**
     The students will be able to:
     - define conductors
     - define insulators
     - analyze ten familiar articles to determine if they are conductors or insulators
5   **Addressing Learning Standards:**
     - Understands energy types, sources, and conversions, and their relationship to heat and temperature.
6   **Prior Knowledge:**
     The children have already studied the general principles of energy and static electricity.
7   **Rationale for Lesson/Presentation:**
     This lesson is part of a complete unit on current electricity. Current electricity is one of our most common forms of energy. It is also a source of some controversy as we face concerns about limited resources, environmental impacts, and conservation options. The entire unit attempts to inform students about how current electricity is produced and converted into other forms of energy, so as to nurture appreciation and respect for its responsible use. Understanding conduction and insulation is critical to an understanding of current electricity.
8   **Materials:**

• dry cell	• lightbulb	• paper
• wires	• aluminum foil	• door key
• rubber band	• a nickel	• plastic ruler
• other items selected by the students.		

9   **Procedures:**
     Motivational Activity:
     - Play a prediction game of conductors and insulators.
     - Ask students to guess which items (among many listed above) will conduct electricity.
     - Record student guesses on the chalkboard.

     Developmental Activity:
     - Assign students to work in groups of three or four.
     - Refer to chart and review the following directions for the lab experiment:

Experiment: Conductors or Insulators
Materials:

• dry cell	• aluminum foil	• rubber band
• light bulb	• paper	• a nickel
• 3 wires	• door key	• plastic ruler

Procedure:
     - Connect the one wire to each pole on the dry cell.
     - Connect one of the dry cell wires directly to the light bulb. Connect the third wire to other side of the light bulb. (You should have a circuit with two unattached wires.
     - Hold the covered part of the loose wires. Touch the uncovered ends of the wires and notice that the light goes on.

- Next, touch the uncovered ends to the aluminum foil. Record your results.
- Repeat step 4 with each of the other materials listed above.

Observation:

Notice what happens to the light bulb each time that the ends of the wires touch different types of material.

Conclusion:

Decide which materials are conductors and which are insulators. Record your conclusions on a chart.

Summary Activity:

- Review students' initial predictions.
- Discuss how students discovered which items are conductors and which are insulators.
- Ask the children to formulate a definition for each term, conductor and insulator. Write definitions on the board for students to copy into their notebooks.

10   Procedural Adaptation:

Hyperactive student can assist the teacher in handing out and setting up materials for the experiment.

11   Determining Appropriate Follow-up Activities/Homework:

Application: Write a funny story or draw a cartoon where the main character misapplies the concept of conductors and insulators.

Create a list of at least five conductors and insulators found among common items at home. Explain how each functions as either an insulator or conductor.

Review: Have students create a word puzzle that uses words that describe insulators and conductors.

12   Evaluation:

Teacher/Presenter Strengths:

The teacher was enthusiastic and the activity was fun.

The materials were well organized for smooth lesson implementation.

Teacher /Presenter Weaknesses:

Not all the light bulbs worked; check all equipment before the lesson and replace equipment as needed.

Student Learning:

The students did meet the objectives as evidence by their responses in their summary activity and their homework.

Submitted by Dr. Rosemarie Pace

A-6:   Sample Instructional Plan for Elementary Physical Education

1   **Name of teacher/presenter: Drib L. D. Ball**
2   **Subject/Topic:** Basketball/ Ball handling skills
3   **Analyzing the Target Audience:** Grade level/ Age/ Characteristics of Group
           Grade 4-5, 9-10 years, Average ability
4   **Behavioral Objective:**
           When playing basketball, students will be able to:
           •   dribble the ball with right and left hand
           •   correctly execute a chest pass
5   **Addressing Learning Standards:**
           •   Uses a variety of basic and advanced movement forms.
           •   Uses movement concept and principles in the development of motor skills.
           •   Understand the social and personal responsibility associated with participation of physical activity.
6   **Prior Knowledge:**
           The children are familiar with the game of basketball. In lower grades they have played games requiring dibble and pass strategies.
7   **Rationale for Lesson/Presentation:**
           Learning how to dribble and pass well will allow the children to effectively play the game of basketball as a team. These skills will enable the children to enjoy the game experience. Basketball is an excellent form of exercise that can be played with as few as two players. Individuals can also exercise independently by practicing shooting skills.
8   **Materials:**
           •   One basketball for every 10 students in class.
9   **Procedures:**
           Motivational Activity:
           •   Provide time for warm up activities (practice shooting, jumping jacks, stretching exercises)
           Developmental Activity:
           •   Introduce the basketball dribble. Allow students to practice with both right and left hand.
           •   Demonstrate the cross over from right to left and left to right. Have students practice and pass to partners.
           •   Demonstrate the bounce pass. Allow time for students to practice the bounce pass with students in their group.
           •   Set up students on opposite sides of the gym. Require students to dribble down the court, change hands while dribbling. When they get about 8 feet from their teammate, students should use the bounce pass to pass the ball. Student will go back to the end of the line to repeat the drill.
           Summary Activity:
           •   Arrange students into groups of ten at each basket in the gym.
           •   Students will play a game of basketball.
           •   Teacher will give extra credit to students who dribble with either hand and/or bounce pass.

10   **Procedural Adaptation:**

For less coordinated learners, the teacher will work with them individually during the practice session.   After school there are open gym sessions for all students.

11   **Determining Appropriate Follow-up Activities /Homework:**

Review: Next class begin the session with students practicing dribble and bounce pass.

Long range: Make arrangements for fourth graders to have an intramural tournament with another school in the district.

12   **Evaluation:**

Teacher/Presenter Strengths:

Teacher encouraged students who were less enthusiastic about basketball to enjoy the activity.

Teacher encouraged active participation by carefully planning and executing drills.

Teacher /Presenter Weaknesses:

Teacher chose the best athletes to help demonstrate the dribble and bounce pass. The bounce pass is relatively simple to execute and even the poorer athletes could have been selected.

Student Learning:

John had some trouble sitting still during the instructional phase of the lesson. Next time I should select John to demonstrate the skill.

The children were successful in executing the skills in the drills, but many could not transfer learning to the game situation. Adapt the rules to require students to dribble and bounce pass twice before taking a shot at the basket.

A-7:   **Sample Instructional Plan for Secondary English**

1   **Name of teacher/presenter:**   U.R.A. Learner
2   **Subject/Topic:**   Reading/Vocabulary Development
              Text: <u>My Brother Sam is Dead</u>
3   **Grade level/ Age/ Characteristics of Group:** Grade 7, 12-13 yrs, Average ability,
4   **Behavioral Objective:**
         The students will be able to:
-   define new vocabulary words which appear in the text, <u>My Brother Sam is Dead</u>.
-   apply new vocabulary words by writing new sentences.

5   **Addressing Learning Standards:**
-   Demonstrates competence in the general skills and strategies for reading a variety of literary texts.
-   Uses grammatical and mechanical conventions in written composition.
-   Understands the impact of the American Revolution on politics, economy and society.

6   **Prior Knowledge:**
         The students are familiar with the Revolutionary War from their social studies curriculum. Students are experienced with historical fiction as a form of literature.

7   **Rationale for Lesson/Presentation:**
         The purpose of this lesson is to teach new vocabulary words which students will encounter in their reading. This lesson will reinforce the use of context clues.

8   **Materials:**
-   Collier, J.L. and Collier, C. (1962). <u>My Brother Sam is Dead.</u> New York: Macmillan.
-   Chalkboard
-   Chalk

9   **Procedures:**
        Motivational Activity:
-   Ask students to close their eyes and imagine traveling back in time to colonial America.
-   Imagine you (a young teen) are sitting in an old colonial inn? What do you see? What are you wearing?
-   Imagine there are patriots in town and you hear that the British are in the vicinity. You have not chosen sides. How do you feel? What might you be thinking?
-   Ask students to share reactions. Explain that in the text to be read we meet a young man who finds himself in a similar situation.

        Developmental Activity:
-   Read aloud from chapter 1/ Discuss significant events.
-   Write the new vocabulary words that students encounter on the board.
-   Ask students to identify word meanings based on context.
-   Discuss word meanings as these relate to the reading.

        Summary Activity:
-   Have students copy new vocabulary words into their notebooks.
-   Ask students to work with a partner and write a sentence for each new vocabulary word.

10   Procedural Adaptation:

For slower learners, provide students with definitions in the form of a review sheet. Pair slower learners with faster learners for group work.

11   Determining Follow-up Activities /Homework:

Preparation: Ask students to read the next chapter and record new vocabulary words in their notebooks.

Review: Study the vocabulary words for a quiz on Friday.

Application: Imagine you are a young adult during the Revolutionary War. Decide whether you will be a Patriot or a Loyalist. Write a paragraph using ten words from the vocabulary list.

12   Evaluation:

Teacher/Presenter Strengths:

Interest in reading the text was stimulated by the imaginary journey back in time. Teacher's oral reading was expressive and served as a model for students' oral reading.

Teacher/Presenter Weaknesses:

Students should see concrete objects related to the Revolutionary War in order to stimulate their imagination. Bring in pictures of an old colonial inn. The library has picture books on Williamsburg that may be helpful.

Student Learning:

Mary had some trouble paying attention during the lesson. Next time I should ask her to read aloud.

Students were successful in identifying word meanings from context clues. Writing new sentences with self-selected partners was effective.

A-8:   Sample Instructional Plan for Secondary Social Studies: An Integrated Technology Approach

1   **Name of teacher/presenter**.   Dr. Tech Nology

2   **Subject/Topic:** Social Studies /Global Studies/ Culture/ Geography/

3   **Analyzing the Target Audience:** Grade level/ Age/ Characteristics of Group

Grade 9, 13-14 year olds, heterogeneously mixed groupings

4   **Behavioral Objectives:**

The students will be able to:

- identify characteristics of land, people, culture, and lifestyles in Nigeria, Ghana, Egypt, Morocco and South Africa through presentation of an oral report.
- demonstrate how to use the Internet as a tool to research five African countries and their culture.

5   **Addressing Learning Standards:**

- Understands the characteristics and uses of maps, globes, and other geographic tools and technologies.
- Knows the locations of place, geographic features, and patterns of the environment.
- Understands the physical and human characteristics of place.
- Understands that culture and experience influence people's perceptions of places and regions.
- Knows the characteristics and uses of computer hardware and operating systems.
- Gathers and uses information for research purposes.

6   **Prior Knowledge:**

Students have learned about the continent of Africa but have not researched individual countries. Students have used the Internet to research topics in science and literature.

7   **Rationale for Lesson/Presentation:**

The social studies curriculum requires that students acquire an in depth understanding of different cultures. This is just one of several research projects that requires students to explore world cultures. The use of the Internet as a research tool will serve students well in future academic research and study. Students will also address learning standards for technology.

8   **Materials:**

- Notebooks to keep track of websites that may be of interest at a later date.
- Handout: Teacher prepared worksheet that outlines topics to be explored by students.

Technology Resources.

Hardware requirements: Five networked computers, Netscape browser and MS OFFICE software.

Teacher Resources:

University of Pennsylvania website: follow the "K-12" links to "K-12 African Studies. Includes lesson plans, e-mail accounts for students to communicate with schools in Capetown.
http://www.sas.upenn.edu/African_Studies/AS.html

Egypt WWW Index has links to cultural, political, historical, religious, and business sites. Maps of the area can also be found here. http://pharos.bu.edu/Egypt/

Student Resources:
Africa OnLine has a special "kids' corner" for students to explore.
Scriptorium's Odyssey in Egypt. Students can follow the excavations of an archeological dig site.
http://www.scriptorium.org/odyssey/

9   **Procedures:** *(Computer technology should be an integral part of the instructional sequence)*

Motivational Activity:
- Inform students that we will be visiting various countries in Africa. List countries on the board. Ask students what they know about these five countries.
- Display a map of the area (http://pharos.bu.edu/Egypt/) using the computer and the projection panel. Show students the location of each country.

Developmental Activity:
- Assign four students to each group. Assign each group to research each country on the Internet. Provide worksheet to guide student research.
- Direct students to the following web site:
  http://www.sas.upenn.edu/African_Studies/AS.html
- In today's lesson, students will find:
  Size of country in miles
  Major geographical features (find a picture and paste into Word)
  Major languages
  Major religions
  Type of government
  Major ethnic groups
  Name of country leader
  Major cities and populations
- Students will bookmark web site addresses that may be helpful in subsequent research.
- Web site addresses will be also be noted in students' notebooks.

Summary Activity:
- Each student group will assign a spokesperson to share the result with the larger class.
- Students will also share websites of interest that they may have found.

10   **Procedural Adaptation**:
Slower learners will be paired with faster learners for group work.
Visually impaired students will use larger fonts when preparing written reports. The teacher worksheets for the visually impaired students will also have larger fonts.

11   **Determining Follow-up Activities / Homework**
Review: Students will record information in a document and send as an attachment to other four groups in the classroom. Each group will read and comment on report and send back to the original group. Students must pose two questions concerning what else they would like to know about the country.

Long Range: Students will use the data collected in today's lesson as part of a larger project, composed and presented via PowerPoint. The district Media Center for presentation on the district cable TV station will record PowerPoint presentations.

12   **Evaluation:**

Teacher strengths:

Lesson was well prepared and teacher directions were clear. Teacher suggestions for internet research were excellent and students immediately located the materials needed for class project.

Teacher weaknesses:

More class time needed to adequately explore the topic. Meet with technology instructor who may be able to schedule double class periods for this type of lesson.

Student Learning:

Students were very motivated and actively involved in the learning process.

A-9:   Sample Instructional Plan for Secondary Business

1   **Name of Teacher:**   Dr. Hy Yield
2   **Subject/topic:**   Business/Finance: Understanding the Organized
                        Financial Markets: The New York and The American Stock Exchanges.
3   **Analyze the Target Audience:** Grade Level/ Age/ Characteristics of Group
            Grade 12   (17-18 years of age with mixed abilities.)
4   **Behavioral Objective:**
            The students will be able to:
            •   discuss the dynamics of the organized financial markets by participating
                    in a simulation activity.
5   **Addressing Learning Standards:**
            •   understands basic features of Market structures and exchanges
            •   understands characteristics of different economic systems, economic institutions
                    and economic incentives
6   **Prior Knowledge:**
            Students have studied how corporations operate and the factors that can influence stock
            prices; they have a general knowledge of stocks and bonds.
7   **Rationale for Lesson/presentation:**
            To educate students in the operations of the New York and the American Stock Exchanges
            in order for them to be better-educated consumers, investors, and business people.
8   **Materials:**
            •   Newspaper and magazine articles dealing with current events affecting businesses
                    and the stock market.
            •   Newspaper "financials," i.e. from *The Wall Street Journal.*

9   **Procedures**:
            Motivational Activity:
                    •   Set up an investing competition.
                    •   Have students work in groups to select stocks and bonds to include in
                            their investment portfolios.
                    •   Have students monitor and analyze the changing values of their
                            investment portfolios.
                    •   Have students compare the beginning and ending values of their
                            investment portfolios.
                    •   Reward the group whose investments were the most profitable.
            Developmental Activity:
            Have students:
                    •   explain how they chose their particular stocks and bonds.
                    •   determine if their selections were influenced by a current event affecting
                            a company or by the product or marketing (reputation) of the firm.
                    •   analyze why some stocks were good investments while others were not.
            Summary Activity:
            Have students:
                    •   explain their stock selections to the other groups of students.
                    •   explain what they learned about the forces which affect stock prices.
                    •   determine how they would invest differently in the future.

10   **Procedural Adaptation:**
Arrange students in balanced groups of faster and slower learners.

11   **Follow-up Homework:**

Application:
Have students:
- interview adults about their considerations when making investments.
- determine if their investments were too risky or too conservative, and why.
- prepare a typed report regarding the outcome of the competition.

Preparation:
- Find newspaper articles dealing with corporate activities and a force which might have influenced corporate stock prices.

12   **Evaluation:**

Teacher/Presenter Strengths:
- Students were motivated to learn because the competition added a game component to the lesson.
- Students were motivated to research for their own investments.
- Teachers can determine the appropriate "reward" to motivate students.

Submitted by Dr. Tracey J. Niemotko, J.D., C.P.A.

A-10:   Sample Instructional Plan for College Health Education

1   **Name of teacher/presenter:** I.M. Fit
2   **Subject/topic:** Health & Fitness 101/ Nutrition
3   **Analyzing the Target Audience:** Grade level/Age/Characteristic of Group
        College/18+, Average ability
4   **Behavioral Objectives:**
        After today's presentation, the learner will be able to:
- Identify the essential nutrients and their primary sources and functions.
- Assess whether he/she needs to change his/her eating patterns to better adhere to recommended U.S. dietary goals and guidelines
- Plan nutritionally balanced menus that include foods from the daily food guide (food pyramid)
- Plan well-balanced meals that meet his/her calorie intake goals
- Change his/her attitude towards a more healthy eating pattern

5   **Addressing Learning Standards**
- Understands essential concepts about nutrition and diet.
- Know how to maintain and promote personal health.

6   **Prior Knowledge:**
        The students have learned in a previous lesson the importance of the roles of both diet and exercise in order to achieve and maintain a desirable body composition.

7   **Rationale for Lesson/Presentation:**
        Learning about "Eating Right" will hopefully help students make informed decisions about foods that are essential to good health and fitness.

8   **Materials:**

Overhead projector	Overhead transparencies
#66 - Essential Nutrients	#67 - Dietary Guidelines
#68 - Dietary Goals	#69 - Food Guide Pyramid
#80 - Sample Menu Planner	#81 - Portions and Calories

- Kusinitz, I. & Fine, M. (1995). Your guide to getting fit. 3rd Ed., CA: Mayfield Publishing Co.
- Teacher made overheads
- #1 - Six Categories of Essential Nutrients
- Handouts - Homework
- Schmalz, K. (1995). Nutrition for the college student. College conference manual. School Guide Publications.
- #6 - Evaluating Your Eating Habits
- #7 - Improving Your Diet
- Source: Glencoe Publishing Co. (1989). Glencoe health: A guide to wellness. Glencoe Publishing Co.

9   **Procedures:**
        Motivational Activity:
- State: "Today we will be discussing Chapter 8 in your book. The title is Eating Right."
- Review any questions not answered last week from the "One minute paper." Ask students if there are any questions.

Developmental Activity:
- Show OH #66 - Essential Nutrients
- Discuss how the six categories of essential nutrients fulfill three primary functions in the body
- Show OH #67 - Dietary Guidelines
- Explain the U.S. dietary goals
- Show OH #68 - Dietary Goals
- Discuss current diet versus dietary goals
- Show OH #69 - Food Guide Pyramid
- Discuss the food guide pyramid
- Show OH #80 - Sample Menu Planner
- State, "As you may recall from last week's lesson, I showed you plastic food models and spoke about food portions."
- Show OH #81 - Portions and Calories
- Explain calorie plan
- Ask for volunteers to share what calorie plan they will follow. (1000 - 2100 calories)
- Refer learners to Appendix C - Food Exchange Plan (page 296)

Summary Activity:
- Review
- Ask the following questions.
  - "Without looking at your notes, can someone tell me the six categories of essential nutrients?"
  (Ans. Protein, carbohydrates, fats, vitamins, minerals and water)
  - "Can someone tell me three major food sources where you get protein from?"
  (Ans. Meat, poultry, fish, eggs, milk and milk products, dry beans, peas and nuts)
  - "Can someone tell me in what major food source, can vitamins be found?"
  (Ans. Abundant in fruits, vegetables and grains; also found in meat and dairy products)
- Closure:
  Today we discussed Chapter 8 - "Eating Right" which provides basic information to help you make informed decisions about foods essential to good health and fitness. It is up to you what you do with this information. There is a saying, "You are what you eat."

Instruct students to proceed to the Fitness Center

10   Procedural Adaptation:

For visually impaired students, enlarge photocopies of student handouts.

11   Determining Follow-up Activities/Homework:

Review:	Read "Nutrition for the college student"
	Ask learners to complete "One Minute Paper."
Application:	Complete handouts #6 - Evaluating Your Eating Habits and #7 - Improving Your Diet
Preparation:	Be prepared to discuss in next class.

12   **Evaluation:**

Teacher/Presenter Strengths:

Discussion of Food Pyramid was clear and visuals enhanced student understanding. Teacher provides examples that students could easily relate to personal experiences.

Teacher/Presenter Weaknesses:

There are many teacher notes and overheads used in this lesson. Remember to organize the materials before beginning the class, so that the teacher does not have to search during the lesson for the next handout or overhead.

Student Learning:

Students were very interested in the topic and motivated to improve their personal wellness. Students were active participants in the class discussion.

Appendix B

Guidelines for American Psychological Association Referencing (APA 1994)

The American Psychological Association (APA) has published a set of guidelines for producing written reports and manuscripts. In the fields of Education and Psychology, professional journals require that you adhere to the guidelines adopted by the APA. It is a good idea for classroom teachers to adhere to these guidelines in all written work.

This section briefly summarizes some of the major requirements when using APA style. A more comprehensive discussion of the style can be found in the Publication Manual of the American Psychological Association. You can also find information at their web site http://www.apa.org/journals/faq.html.

For term papers, journal articles, and other written work, writers should follow these guidelines:

- Type all papers using a word processor. Use 8.5" X 11" bond paper. Each page should have 1" margins on all sides. Do not write corrections in pen or pencil.
- All typing must be double-spaced. Skip two spaces after each sentence.
- Other than the title page, number all pages in the upper right-hand corner.
- All written work must conform to Standard English usage. Good writing is reflected in its organization, grammar, spelling, and punctuation.
- All terms used should be clearly defined.
- You must reference or identify any source that is not your original work. You must provide the author's last name and publication year.
- Always keep the author's last name and the year of publication together, for example (Banks, 1991). See example (paraphrase).
- The Reference List at the end of your paper consists of references in alphabetical order (by author's last name). The Reference List begins on a new page. The references are not to be numbered.
- All references should appear in the text wherever appropriate (see example). Do not use footnotes or endnotes.
- Do not include in the reference list any items not in the text of your paper.

In order to illustrate the use of APA style in your writing, consider that in your research, you found the following paragraph in a text entitled Teaching Strategies for Ethnic Studies, (5th ed.) written by James A. Banks (1991).

Ethnic studies courses in the elementary and high schools have not fared as well as those on university campuses. Most school districts have tried to incorporate the history and culture of ethnic groups, as well as those of women, into the mainstream curriculum rather than to establish separate courses on ethnic groups and women. The rationale for this approach is intellectually defensible and laudable. It has, however, had mixed results. In most schools, the textbook is the curriculum. In the early 1970's, when the civil rights movement was at its apex and publishers were being pressured to integrate textbooks, large bits and pieces of ethnic content were inserted into textbooks. Because the civil rights movement has lost much of its momentum and national influence, however, the pressure on textbook publishers has lessened. Consequently, the ethnic presence in elementary and high school textbooks today is less visible than it was during the late 1970's. (p. 22)

When writing your research paper you can cite the work of James A. Banks by paraphrase, short direct quotation or long direct quotation.

Paraphrase: If you rephrase the ideas of another author, you must acknowledge the source of these ideas in your written work. In APA Style, you must indicate the author's name and the year of publication.

Let's examine how this is done with the above selection.

According to Banks (1991), the introduction of ethnic studies courses in the public schools has developed more slowly than those at the college level. Many public school districts have attempted to integrate ethnic studies and women's studies into the curriculum with varied results.

Textbooks often reflect political movements, as evidenced by the increase of ethnic content in textbooks during the 1970's; however, changes in the political climate can cause textbook publishers to modify materials when political movements lose momentum.

Short direct quotations are used when directly quoting from another source. For short direct quotations you must indicate the author, year of publication, and page number. Short quotations (fewer than 40 words) are incorporated into the text and enclosed by double quotation marks.

Using the above selection, the following sample illustrates how to incorporate a short direct quotation into the text.

Much discussion has focused on how best to incorporate multicultural issues into the curriculum. "Most school districts have tried to incorporate the history and culture of ethnic groups, as well as those of women, into the mainstream curriculum rather than to establish separate courses on ethnic groups and women" (Banks, 1991, p.22).

or

Banks (1991) observed, "Most school districts have tried to incorporate the history and culture of ethnic groups, as well as those of women, into the mainstream curriculum rather than to establish separate courses on ethnic groups and women." (p.22) Thus, much discussion has focused on how best to incorporate multicultural issues into the curriculum.

Long direct quotations: Quotations that are forty or more words in length are considered long quotations. They should be displayed in a block, indented, and double-spaced. The following example illustrates how to cite a long direct quotation.

> Ethnic studies courses in the elementary and high schools have not fared as well as those on university campuses. Most school districts have tried to incorporate the history and culture of ethnic groups, as well as those of women, into the mainstream curriculum rather than to establish separate courses on ethnic groups and women. The rationale for this approach is intellectually defensible and laudable.
>
> It has, however, had mixed results. In most schools, the textbook is the curriculum. In the early 1970's, when the civil rights movement was at its apex and publishers were being pressured to integrate textbooks, large bits and pieces of ethnic content were inserted into textbooks.
>
> Because the civil rights movement has lost much of its momentum and national influence, however, the pressure on textbook publishers has lessened. Consequently, the ethnic presence in elementary and high school textbooks today is less visible than it was during the late 1970's. (Banks, 1991, p. 22)

REFERENCE FORMAT:

Writers must correctly list all resources in the reference list that appears at the end of the research paper. The correct format depends upon the type of material (book, journal article, computer software, film, etc.) and the author. Note that the first line of each reference is indented, titles are underlined and each entry is double-spaced.

A book with one author:

Banks, J. A. (1991). Teaching strategies for ethnic studies (5th ed.). Needham Heights, MA: Allyn and Bacon.

Becker, H. (1993). Outsiders. New York: The Free Press.

A book with two or more authors:
        Cone, J. D., & Foster, S. L. (1993). Dissertations and theses from start to finish:
Psychology and related fields. Washington, DC: American Psychological Association.

A book with an editor:
        Gibbs, J. T., & Huang, L. N. (Eds.). (1991). Children of color: Psychological interventions with
minority youth. San Francisco: Jossey-Bass.

A book with a corporate author:
        American Psychiatric Association. (1985). Diagnostic and statistical manual of mental disorder -
revised. Washington, D. C.: American Psychiatric Association.

An article in a journal:
        Klimoski, R., & Palmer, S. (1993). The ADA and the hiring process in organizations. Consulting
Psychology Journal: Practice and Research, 45(2), 10-36.

An article in a book:
        Bjork, R. A. (1989). Retrieval inhibition as an adaptive mechanism in human memory. In H. L.
Roediger II & F. I. M. Craik (Eds.), Varieties of memory and consciousness (pp. 309-330). Hillsdale, NJ:
Erlbaum.

An article in a newspaper:
        O'Neill, G. W. (1982, January 5). In support of DSM-III [Letter to the editor]. APA Monitor, p.
4.

An article in a magazine:
        Posner, M. I. (1993, October 29). Seeing the mind. Science, 262, 673-674.

Film:
        Mass, J. B. (Producer), & Gluck, D. H. (Director). (1979). Deeper into hypnosis [Film].
Englewood Cliffs, NJ:Prentice-Hall.

How to Cite Information from the World Wide Web
        As the Internet has increased in value as a research tool, the need to properly cite that information
has also increased. The 4th edition of the APA Publication Manual does not take into account information
retrieved from the World Wide Web. The current style for citing this information as prescribed by the
APA is found at their web page (http://www.apa.org).
        All references begin with the same information that would be provided for a printed source (or as
much of that information as possible). The Web information is then placed at the end of the reference. It is
important to use "Retrieved from" and the date because documents on the Web may change in content,
move, or be removed from a site all together.

An article posted on a Web site:
        Ciampa, L. (1999, October 5). Fruits and vegetables may reduce risk of stroke. CNN.com.
Retrieved October 7, 1999 from the World Wide Web:
http://cnn.com/HEALTH/9910/05/stroke.fruit/index.html.
        Jacobson, J. W., Mulick, J. A., & Schwartz, A. A. (1995). A history of facilitated communication:
Science, pseudoscience, and antiscience: Science working group on facilitated communication. American

Psychologist, 50, 750-765. Retrieved January 25, 1996 from the World Wide Web:
http://www.apa.org/journals/jacobson.html

An article from a database accessed via the Web:

Schneiderman, R.A. (1997). Librarians can make sense of the Net. San Antonio Business Journal, 11(31), pp. 58+. Retrieved January 27, 1999 from EBSCO database (Masterfile) on the World Wide Web: http://www.ebsco.com

An abstract:

Rosenthal, R. (1995). State of New Jersey v. Margaret Kelly Michaels: An overview [Abstract]. Psychology, Public Policy, and Law, 1, 247=96271. Retrieved January 25, 1996 from the World Wide Web: http://www.apa.org/journals/ab1.html

Within the text of your paper, you should cite the author and year of publication, even if the material was retrieved from the Internet. Note that in the above examples, the authors and year are known.

To cite a web site in text (but not a specific document), it is sufficient to give the address (e.g., http://www.apa.org) there. No reference entry is needed.

Appendix C

Professional Subject-Area Organizations

The Arts
Music Educators National Conference
1902 Association Drive
Reston, VA 22091
703-860-4000
http://www.menc.org/

Civics and Government
The Center for Civic Education
5146 Douglas Fir Road
Calabasas, CA 91203
818-591-9321
http://www.civiced.org/

Economics
The National Council on Economic Education
1140 Avenue of the Americas
New York, NY 10036
212-730-7007
http://www.nationalcouncil.org/

Foreign Language
American Council on the Teaching of Foreign
Languages
Six Executive Plaza
Yonkers, NY 10801-6801
914-963-8830
http://www.actfl.org/

Geography
National Council for Geographic Education
1600 M Street, NW, Suite 2500
Washington, DC 20036
202-775-7832
http://multimedia2.freac.fsu.edu/ncge/

Language Arts
National Standards for the English Language Arts
Project, The International Reading Association,
Division of Research
800 Barksdale Road
P.O. Box 8139
Newark, DE 19714-8139
302-731-1600, ext. 226
http://www.reading.org/

Mathematics
National Council of Teachers of Mathematics
1906 Association Drive
Reston, VA 22091
703-620-9840
http://www.nctm.org/

Physical Education
National Association for Sport and Physical
Education
1900 Association Drive
Reston, VA 22091
703-476-3410
http://www.aahperd.org/cgi-
bin/counter.pl/naspe/naspe.html

Science
National Science Education Standards
2101 Constitution Ave., NW
HA 486
Washington, DC 20418
202-334-1399
http://www.nap.edu/readingroom/books/nses/

Social Studies
National Council for the Social Studies
3501 Newark St., NW
Washington, DC 20016
202-966-7840
http://www.ncss.org/

Health Education
Association for the Advancement of Health
Education
1900 Association Drive
Reston, VA 22091
703-476-3437
http://www.aahperd.org/cgi-
bin/counter.pl/aahe/aahe.html

History
National Center for History in the Schools
UCLA, 231 Noore Hall
Los Angeles, CA 90024
310-825-4702
http://www.sscnet.ucla.edu/nchs/

Technology Education
International Technology Education Association
1914 Association Drive
Reston, Virginia 20191-1539
703-860-2100
http://www.iteawww.org/

Vocational Education
National Center for Research in Vocational
Education
University of California, Berkeley
2150 Shattuck Avenue, Suite 1250
Berkeley, CA 94704
510-642-4004
http://vocserve.berkeley.edu/

INDEX

NOTES